Archaeology of Korea

An Outline with Emphasis on Prehistory

Sahoipyoungnon Academy Co., Inc.
56 World Cup buk-ro 6-gil, Mapo-gu, Seoul, 03993, Korea
http://www.sapyoung.com

ISBN 979-11-6707-044-9 93910

FRONT COVER Part of a whaling scene engraved at the Neolithic petrographic site of Ban-gu-dae in Ulsan. The original ink-rubbing is kept at the Seoul National University Museum (see Figure 3.23).

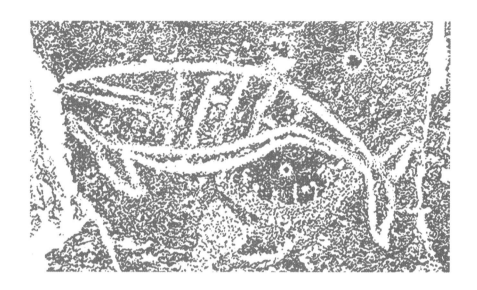

Archaeology of Korea

An Outline with Emphasis on Prehistory

Seonbok Yi

Sahoipyoungnon Academy

CONTENTS

LIST OF FIGURES

ACKNOWLEDGEMENTS

I have been indebted to many friends, colleagues and students throughout my career as an archaeologist. The current monograph was possible only with their help and camaraderie. To everybody who had to endure me, my sincere thanks and apologies. Especially, Yoo Yongwook, Kim Dongwan, Lee Jeongeun and Yang Si-eun had to bear with me for so many years. Some of the arguments and conclusions in Chapter 2 were possible only because of their hard work. My deepest thanks go to them for their loyalty and dedication as well as all the others toiling in the field to shed light on the forgotten past.

PREFACE

In the Republic of Korea, more commonly known as South Korea, archaeology is thriving today. In 1976, the Korean Archaeological Society was founded with 37 members, not everybody an archaeologist. Now, its homepage indicates 1,590 members as of January 1, 2020. Since the 1990s, adoption of a strict cultural resource management system has resulted in an explosive increase of archaeological activities. Throughout the country, hundreds of professional archaeologists are toiling in the field every day, surveying and excavating sites covering the periods all the way from the Pleistocene on up to the 20th century. They are supported by hundreds of staff members and technicians. There are mountains of published reports, proceedings, journals and books.

With such overwhelmingly rapid accumulation of data, the urgency of the publication of an up-to-date introduction of Korean archaeology has been raised by many for a long time since the only available one was published in 1986. The result was the publication of *Hanguk Gogohak Gangeui* (한국고고학강의) in 2007. It required a team of researchers and several years to complete, and the current author participated in the project as the chief editor and a contributor of three chapters. By the time it was on the shelves of bookstores, immediate revision was deemed necessary and the revised edition appeared in 2010. Time is long overdue for the third edition but hopefully it will be available in the near future.

At any rate, to prepare a monograph about the archaeology of Korea in western language is not an easy task. Nevertheless, there has been increasing demand for such a guidebook as *The Archaeology of Korea* (S. M. Nelson, 1993, Cambridge University Press, Cambridge) is the only available one, which was rather hastily prepared "to put Korea on the map" of the world of archaeology as the author says. I have felt increasing pressure from friends abroad and domestic to prepare one since 2007 after the publication of *Gangeui*. While reluctant at first, I decided to work on it, realizing that, if not now, perhaps I would never. That was December 2014. But I was hindered by administrative duties as the director of the university museum whilst serving as the president of several academic societies. It was only in late 2019 that I was able to organize myself.

A successful introduction to any regional archaeology is possible only when one has a thorough understanding of the data and can maintain a balanced judgement even in describing simple facts, but one always has one's limits in grasping new developments in the field. Moreover, discussion of historical periods would require a whole series of volumes even for describing many astounding discoveries alone. Thus, I considered to prepare a monograph as a guidebook to prehistoric archaeology of Korea but with short discussions about historical archaeology for interested readers as chapters under the headings of *Dawn of History* and *Three Kingdoms Period and After*.

As an introduction, the current volume must deal with evidence from North Korea. However, unfortunately, there is so little that one can talk about. There, archaeology as an academic discipline has ceased to exist since the late 1960s, and we have only extremely limited and antiquated information. The problem poses an immense hurdle, which is impossible to overcome by any means within the foreseeable future. Thus, readers are advised to remember that some of the 'interpretations' mentioned in the text, such as the southerly diffusion of various cultural traits are still mere hypothetical suggestions or conjectures, which need to be proved in the future. At the same time, while what can be termed as the Korean Culture Sphere had once existed from the Bronze Age well beyond the physical boundaries of the Korean Peninsula with fluctuating boundaries, much of this vast area north of Korea remains uninvestigated. As a result, many questions raised in Korean archaeology cannot but remain unanswered.

The situation makes it all the more important for the current monograph to be a fair summary of current understandings about the archaeological past of Korea. In preparing the manuscript, I tried to maintain a balanced judgement so that it can adequately introduce generally accepted opinions while avoiding those interesting but potentially problematic ones. One can only wish that personal biases had not crept into the final product so much as to distort the real picture.

I had considered the final publication would look something like an illustrated and enlarged version of a volume in the series *A Very Short Introduction* by the Oxford University Press. There is not an appended bibliography but only a list of recommended readings for each chapter. I also beg the indulgence of the readers of Korean archaeology and history who will find perhaps some delicate issues are dealt with rather crudely or even ignored. Such treatment was felt necessary in order to make the reading less confusing for the general readers, most of whom must not be fluent with the Korean language. Finding suitable visual images was the most difficult part of the work, which had not been possible without help from many former and present students as well as staffs of various institutions across the country. Especially, Hong Seungyeon, who was finishing her master's degree by the time of publication, was instrumental in improving the quality of some of the images, and Figure 1.4 is entirely her own work. I also thank Matthew Conte, a doctoral student, for going over the manuscript to polish the writing. After all, English remains a difficult foreign language with such strange rules as tense agreements, subject-verb concordance, subjunctive mood, articles, passive voice, etc. But, of course, any shortcomings, errors and mistakes that crept into the writing are the author's sole responsibility.

Finally, transliteration of proper nouns and personal names followed the National Institute of the Korean Language(NIKL) Romanization system, which is the official system adopted in Korea. As it avoids symbols other than Roman characters as much as possible, readers familiar with the McCune-Reischauer system may find some transliteration unfamiliar, especially for some diphthongs. Although English speakers may find the latter more useful for practical purposes, once understanding the basic rules of the transliteration, the NIKL system may help to have a better approximation of the original Korean wording regardless of the reader's linguistic background. For pronunciation and transliteration, interested readers may refer to the NIKL homepage at https://www.korean.go.kr/.

December 2021

CHAPTER 1

INTRODUCTION

Archaeology of Korea – A Brief History

Korea is a peninsula lying at the eastern edge of the Eurasian continent. The country was divided into two at the end of the World War II as the American and the Soviet army occupied the peninsula along the 38th parallel. Soon the bloody Korean War erupted in 1950, and the Military Demarcation Line set up in 1953 has become the *de facto* border between the Republic of Korea in the south and the Democratic People's Republic of Korea in the north [**Figure 1.1**]. The division and the war have brought about so much trauma and tragedy to all Koreans, and communications between the two Koreas have effectively stopped at all levels ever since the war. As a matter of fact, there has hardly been any conversation or cooperation between the archaeologists of the south and the north except a couple of politically arranged showy fieldworks conducted on the northern side of the DMZ. As a result, any monograph about the archaeology of Korea cannot but be imperfect and lopsided. It is more so as archaeology as a scientific discipline vanished in the north as shall be discussed.

In both Koreas, archaeology is a young discipline. It is best demonstrated by the fact that archaeology was included in the college curriculum in South Korea only in the 1960s. In the intellectual history of Korea before the encounter with Western civilization in the late 19th century, there had been no real interest in material remains of the past, thus, no attempt of archaeological survey or systematic collection of artifacts. It was as late as 1890 when interests in the archaeological past of Korea appeared in writing for the first time. Such interest was shown not by a Korean but an unusual visitor who came to Korea with a specific purpose in mind to conduct a reconnaissance survey of the archaeological potential of this hermit kingdom. The first archaeological field research, however, was not conducted by him or any other visitor from the West. Archaeology as a modern academic discipline was transplanted by the Japanese imperial power at the beginning of the 20th century.

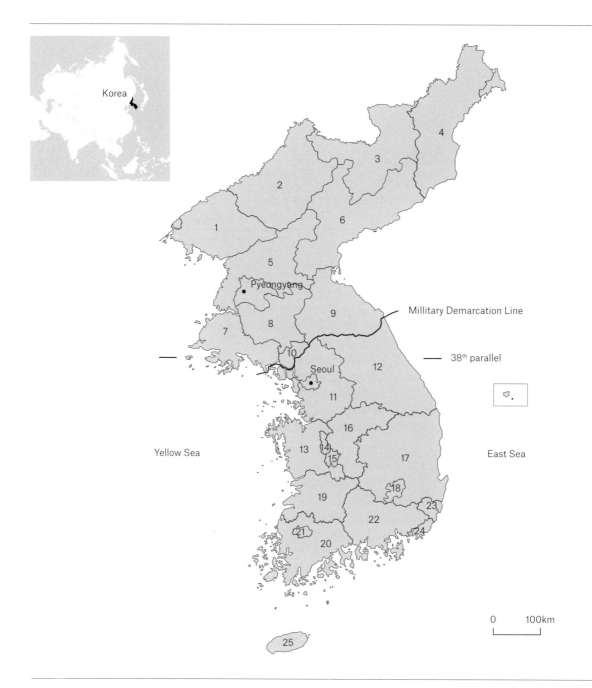

Figure 1.1 Location of Korea and the primary administrative units. After the World War II, Korea was divided into the Republic of Korea in the south and the Democratic People's Republic of Korea in the north along the 38th parallel. With the end of the Korean War in 1953, the Military Demarcation Line has become the *de facto* border between the two Koreas. Today, South Korea has 15 primary administrative units in addition to its capital, Seoul. There are 10 of them plus the capital Pyeongyang in North Korea. In the map, units 1 to 10 indicate those of the north. 1: Pyeonganbuk-do; 2: Jagang-do; 3: Yanggang-do; 4: Hamgyeongbuk-do; 5: Pyeongannam-do; 6: Hamgyeong-nam-do; 7: Hwanghaenam-do; 8: Hwanghaebuk-do; 9: Gangwon-do; 10: Gyeonggi-do; 11. Gyeonggi-do; 12: Gang-won-do; 13: Chungcheongnam-do; 14: Sejong; 15: Daejeon; 16: Chungcheongbuk-do; 17: Gyeongsangbuk-do; 18: Daegu; 19: Jeollabuk-do; 20: Jellanam-do; 21: Gwangju; 22: Gyeong-sangnam-do; 23: Ulsan; 24: Busan; 25: Jeju-do. For Jeju-do, it is translated as Jejudo to indicate the name of the island *per se*.

Of course, the lack of interest in the archaeological past among intellectuals does not mean that they did not know about the existence of the ruins and monuments of the past. For example, a famous scholar bureaucrat of the early 13th century named Yi Gyubo left a short phrase about a dolmen he had encountered while touring the southwestern province as a young man. Nevertheless, his is an exceptional case. Although Korea is proud of its long tradition of literacy and history of documentation, curiosity about the relics of the past is hard to find.

Counting from Yi Gyubo's time all the way up to c. 1900, merely a couple of dozen short writings related to the so-called "thunder axe" can be found, which is a term that first appeared in 8th-century China to indicate stone axes found in nature. The term itself reflects the popular belief that it was the axe of the Thunder God who used it to make thunder and lightning. Because it is a divine material that fell from the heaven, people believed that it had special healing power. In Korea, most of the writings about the thunder axe are found in the annals of the Joseon dynasty, the earliest one dating to the mid-15th century. They are about incidents of discovery or speculations about its origin and efficacy, i.e., its practical value as medicine. The earliest record is in the form of a suggestion to the king by medical doctors who recommended to seek it in consideration of its presumed medicinal values. The king took this advice and issued an order to search. Three years later, those who found the stone tools were well rewarded. What were found are stone daggers and arrowheads which were also regarded as variant forms of the thunder axe.

Regardless of such popular belief, the mainstream intellectuals laughed at the thought that the stone tools were heavenly things and dismissed them as natural objects. This attitude reflects the teachings on their origin by the masters of Neo-Confucianism, which was introduced to Korea in the 13th century shortly after it was established in China. Korea has been deeply immersed in its teachings since it was taken as the governing philosophy of the Joseon dynasty in the late 14th century. Even today, its teachings exert a lot of influence in the social life and culture of Korea. What the masters of this new learning had said about nature had enabled Korean intellectuals to easily explain away the origin of any material object and natural phenomenon, whether extreme weather conditions, unexpected blooming of flowers or the occurrence of stone tools. That is, to explain why the things are so, they simply referred to the circulation and interaction of five different natural forces, i.e., the qi, of fire, earth, metal, water and wood. About the thunder axe, the founding fathers of the Neo-Confucianism had already prepared an explanation in the 12th century in order to persuade the superstitious populace not to waste away their fortunes serving the fictitious Thunder God. What these masters taught is that they were formed in nature when the qi of fire in the form of lightning strike hits the ground to consolidate the qi of earth so that it transforms and hardens the soft earth to stone. As such, there was no question in the minds of the intellectuals that it had to be a product of nature.

If there was any exception which questioned the two thoughts, one can merely find a short essay of the 15th century. After observing the thunder axes, the writer wondered whether they might not be artifacts left by some deft and experienced hands because it was difficult for him to accept that the flow of qi could make such specific shapes looking just like common axes. However, he could not tell what the truth really is so the writing finishes by stating merely that one could only wait for help from a knowledgeable person in future. Of course, the help never came during his life, nor for another four hundred years.

In such an intellectual environment, it had to be impossible for any person to try to think about the location of the lost burial of a king who lived more than a thousand years ago unless one was as knowledgeable as Kim Jeonghui (1786-1856), a 19th century scholar who was famous even in China. In a short but brilliant essay entitled <On King Jinheung's Tomb of Silla>, he succinctly summarized the historical geography of the 6th and 7th century Gyeongju, the capital of Silla(신라), and identified the location of the king's burial. He began the essay with an assertion that many of the mounds in Gyeongju could not be 'artificial mountains' as people said but burial mounds, and continued to explain why. He reviewed the historical records related to the location of various royal burials and important places, and pinpointed the location of the tomb. In addition to this essay, he also deciphered various ancient inscriptions, and concluded that the stone projectiles he accidentally discovered during his exile in a northern province were the remains of the Suksin (Sushen) people. Given his activities, he might have been able to sow the seeds of archaeology before western contact. However, his knowledge and academic endeavors had failed to find a successor with his political demise.

Twenty years after his death, Korea was forced to open its ports to foreign powers under threats from Japanese iron gunships. Soon, Japanese merchants settled in southern port cities and began to collect archaeological relics, mostly looted burial goods. In 1883, a visitor named Pierre Louis Jouy, a curator of the U.S. National Museum, was able to observe such collections in Osaka, Japan, before he crossed the Korean Straight with a desire "to form similar collections in Korea" to what were made with Japanese relics by Edward S. Morse whose excavation of a shell-midden in Tokyo Bay in 1877 marks the first archaeological excavation in Japan. Travelling across Korea diagonally from Busan to Seoul, he noticed that the country is "one vast graveyard" which is "abounded in monuments of great antiquity and evidences[sic] of long occupation of the soil". It seems that his writing represents the first observation by a trained eye.[1]

In 1895, an article appeared in London which discusses dolmens in Korea.[2] While residing in Japan, the author visited Korea in 1894 which he believed "likely to be the original home...of the Japanese race". In the articke, he evaluated observations on dolmens recorded by the British diplomats in Seoul and suggested his own opinion about their origin. Another noteworthy account was made by a Frenchman who travelled to Korea in 1903 as a self-appointed "Ingénieur de la Maison Impériale de Corée". To a journal published by the Anthropological Society of Lyon, France, he contributed a short piece and photographs of dolmens he took, commenting that they looked just like those in his hometown and should be

......

1 Jouyi, Pierre Louis. 1890. The collection of Korean mortuary pottery in the United States National Museum. *Report of the National Museum, 1887-'88.* pp.589-596, plates 82-86. Washington, Smithsonian Institution.

2 Gowland, W. 1895. Notes on the Dolmens and Other Antiquities of Korea. *The Journal of the Anthropological Institute of Great Britain and Ireland* 24:316-331.

prehistoric ruins.[3]

In 1905, a mere 28 years after the first archaeological excavation in Japan was made by Morse, an archaeological survey of Korea was conducted for the first time by a Japanese researcher. In that year, Korea involuntarily had become a protectorate of Japan and her fate was doomed to be annexed in five years. The dying dynasty commissioned a professor at the Laboratory of Architecture, Tokyo Imperial College, now the University of Tokyo, to compile a list of valuable cultural properties worthy of protection and preservation. While examining architectural and other extant relics in many corners of Korea, he also surveyed archaeological sites, both prehistoric and historic, and conducted testing occasionally.

During the occupation by Japan which ended in 1945, the colonial government realized the usefulness of the archaeological information in controlling the populace, thus, conducted research in its own systematic way to obtain evidence to 'educate' Koreans that their past was merely 'passive, submissive and inconsequential', thus, bound for the ultimate subjugation to and the forced enlightenment by the superior Japan. Archaeological findings in general were treated as valuable only when they were found useful to satisfy the political agenda of justifying the Japanese occupation. In practice, that meant that archaeological investigation focused upon burial sites in expectation of obtaining material evidence that Korea was colonized by Japan and China already in ancient times. Meanwhile, after an accidental discovery in 1921 of a Silla royal burial, Geumgwanchong, the Tomb of Golden Crown, attention had been given to similar burials in Gyeongju to recover more of those dazzling artifacts which would help to promote the recognition of Japan as a cultured nation in international society. For example, when the Crown Prince Gustav of Sweden was visiting East Asia in 1926, he was invited to join the excavation of a nearby burial and to scoop up a golden crown. The smiling photograph of Gustav with the golden crown in hand was a PR bonanza for the Japanese government, and the tomb was given the name of Seobongchong, the Tomb of Swedish Phoenix.

Of course, it would not be fair to deny categorically that all the works done by the Japanese are prejudiced and poor in quality. Nevertheless, it is true that the generally poor scholarship can be easily noticed from the fieldwork reports of the most important sites. Likewise, discussions about the archaeological past of Korea by the respected scholars of the time are not completely free from prejudice, whether intentional or incidental. Moreover, it cannot be denied that so many relics had been looted *en masse* directly by the hands of Japanese or instigated by them with the connivance of the colonial power. In some cases, even Japanese officials were shocked by the scale of looting, and lamented at the horrible and appalling scene. At the same time, archaeological activity had been monopolized by the Japanese, and no Korean was invited to participate in any fieldwork or management of collections.

Following the end of World War II, Korea was occupied by the U.S. and the Soviet military, and divided into two countries. With subsequent social and political turmoil that culminated in the Korean War, systematic research and education were

......

3 Bourdaret, Emmile. 1904. I. Note sur les dolmens de la Corée. II. Les monuments préhistoriques de l'île Kang-Hoa. *Société d'anthropologie de Lyon*. Séance du 4 juillet 1903, pp.3-7. Lyon, A. Rey & C.

difficult, if not impossible entirely, for many years in South Korea. On the other hand, however, North Korea was far more ready to start archaeological research with its own hands as many qualified intellectuals crossed the 38th parallel to the north after the division. Notably, there were two figures who earned their doctoral degrees in archaeology at University of Vienna. Therefore, North Korea was able to organize systematic fieldwork already in 1946. Having had a head start over South Korea, new and exciting evidence was reported one after another. Including the discovery of evidence of the Palaeolithic and the Bronze Age, whose existence had been denied by the Japanese researchers, the apex of archaeological research in North Korea was reached with the publication of *Prehistoric Archaeology of Korea* (조선원시고고학) in 1960.

However, happy days were short-lived and archaeology in the north began to lose its luster rapidly from the late 1960s as the country was turning into an extremely harsh authoritarian regime. As the personal worship of the dictator had been firmly established, even archaeological publications began to repeat the doctrinal interpretations. Any deviation from the official interpretation was not permitted and met with dire results. Soon, the director of the Institute of Archaeology was persecuted and publication had stopped. When the publication of the official journal of archaeology reappeared in 1986 under a new title, issues were filled with only a few short writings with little factual information. Then, in the 1990s, the whole chronological table had changed overnight with new "interpretations" of the old data as the regime tried to promote its "historical legitimacy", about which more will be mentioned in Chapter 4.

Indeed, the situation in the north has been so bizarre that it is difficult to understand for an outsider. In the early 1990s, through a series of journal articles, it was declared that an advanced civilization had flourished in Pyeongyang[4] and its vicinities. As more shall be told later, it is sufficient here just to mention that, according to the claim, metallurgy was invented here at least 1,000 years earlier than any other place in the world, for example. However, no convincing evidence was given to support the claim. As such, discussion of archaeological evidence in the northern parts of the Korean Peninsula cannot but rely on writings published decades ago. Although those published in the 1960s were already tainted with the political dogma, it was not as severe as the later publications so that one may glean at least bits of facts from them. These problems and the lack of communication effectively prevent us from having a full picture of the archaeological past of the whole Korea.

Compared to North Korea, the first generation archaeologists of the south were in their early 20s when World War II ended, about to complete their college education. With the lack of trained personnel, little could be done. For example, the first excavation in South Korea conducted in 1946 was possible under the guidance of a Japanese researcher, a former colonial museum staff member who was asked to remain in Korea to teach the Koreans basics of excavation and museum management. The Korean War and subsequent social turmoil had denied any hope to conduct field research during the 1950s. It was only in 1961 that archaeology was recognized as an independent discipline and the first academic unit was estab-

......

4   The name of the North Korean capital is more often spelled as Pyongyang in the media.

lished at Seoul National University by the late Prof. Kim Won-yong.

During the 1960s, slowly archaeological research began to gain public support. A huge momentum was provided in 1971 when the Tomb of King Muryeong (reign: 501-523) of Baekje was discovered in a fully preserved state (cf. Chapter 7). Public excitement was more heightened when another spectacular finding was made in 1973. A gold crown and other treasures were retrieved from a rather plain-looking mound lying close to Geumgwanchong. The burial was later named as Cheonma-chong, the Tomb of the Heavenly Horse, to denote the discovery of the pictures of a flying horse drawn on mudguards. As a better approximation of the archae-ological past was possible by this time, the first edition of *Introduction to Korean Archaeology*(한국고고학개설) was published in 1973. In this book, the late Prof. Kim introduced a coherent chronological framework of the archaeological past for the first time. Over the years, it has been modified but the basic idea has remained unchanged.

From the 1970s, with a booming economy, demand for rescue excavation increased explosively in South Korea, which resulted in sudden and uncontrollable quantitative growth of archaeological activities. By the beginning of the 1990s, it reached a level that could not be dealt with solely by governmental and academic sectors, and news of tension and conflict surrounding emergency excavation filled the media. To cope with exponential increase in demand [**Figure 1.2**], there was a major overhaul in the cultural resource management system in the late 1990s, which allowed the involvement of private institutions for archaeological research. It turned out to be a mixed blessing, however.

The good news is that the new measure has enabled institutions to meet the demand for rescue works efficiently, thus, helped to prevent rampant destruction. As issuance of excavation permits has increased, there have appeared so many

Figure 1.2 Growth of archaeology in South Korea in terms of excavation permits granted. They are shown as the cumulative chart with 5-year intervals from the 1950s (left) and the number of permissions per annum since 1991 (right). Raw data can be found at http://www.cha.go.kr/. Governmental permission is mandatory for archaeological excavation regardless of its nature, size and duration as well as the ownership of the land. Therefore, it provides a proxy to figure out the general state of archaeological activities. The actual number of excavations is greater than the numbers shown because multiple excavations may be carried out separately under one permit.

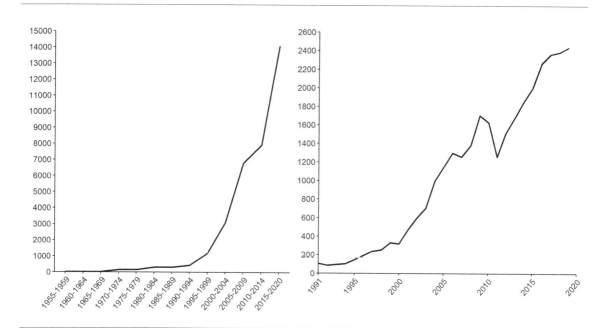

reports every year. When traveling, one can see casually through the window some excavation going on by the roadside or far in the field, covering all periods from the Pleistocene all the way up to the 20th century. As archaeologists deal with extremely diverse fieldwork situations, technical expertise of fieldwork and reporting also has been improved markedly across the board. In general, sophistication in conducting archaeological fieldwork in South Korea nowadays does not fall behind any industrialized nation. At the same time, Korean archaeologists are working in less industrialized nations to help to build the infrastructure for research. What we see today is truly remarkable considering what the situation was like in the 1960s.

Yet, the enormous increase of salvage excavations is casting unforeseen shadows over the discipline. To begin with, the adoption of the 'excavate-everything-while-developer-pays-all' policy has raised the thorny issue of conservation versus development to a totally different level. At the same time, the sudden explosion of data has demanded quick answers for new questions while adding new problems to the old ones. Some of the standard answers turned out to be obsolete and wrong but alternatives are hard to come by. The problem is exacerbated by the poor reporting of the data and the failure to disseminate information in a timely manner.

It is widely felt that the time has been long overdue to reshape the overall program of education and training. It is also necessary to reprogram the administrative procedures for excavation and protection of the archaeological heritage. Unfortunately, there remains the question where and how to start the change. Clearly, archaeology in South Korea is facing a huge challenge. The voice asking <Whither Korean Archaeology?> has been raised for some time. A harmonious answer is yet to be heard.

Scope of the Monograph

Ever since the 1970s, archaeology in South Korea has relied upon the chronological scheme proposed by the late Prof. Kim Won-yong as mentioned above. It adopts the familiar terms of Palaeolithic, Neolithic and Bronze Age for prehistory. They are continued by the Early Iron Age and the Proto-Three Kingdoms Period, followed by the historical period names such as the Three Kingdoms Period. In this scheme, perhaps it must be explained what the Early Iron Age and the Proto-Three Kingdoms Period mean.

In the history of Korea, the generally accepted earliest state is Gojoseon(고조선). Many think it appeared during the Bronze Age, not within the Korean Peninsula but somewhere to the north of Korea what is today the Chinese northeast region. However, written accounts about Gojoseon are not available until around 300 BCE. They are only fragmentary in nature so that there is no information even about the location of its center. In other words, information is vague until when the Samguk-sagi(삼국사기), the oldest historical record, describes the beginning of the Three Kingdoms Period.

The title of the book is translated as the Chronicles of the Three States, and it is basically a record about the rise and fall of the three kingdoms of Silla, Baekje(백

제) and Goguryeo(고구려). According to the chronicle, they were established in 54, 18 and 37 BCE, respectively. Thus, it is commonly said that the Three Kingdoms Period began in the 1st century BCE. However, historians and archaeologists alike agree that these dates do not correctly represent the historical reality.

As shall be repeated in Chapter 7, archaeological evidence strongly suggests Goguryeo had almost reached the state level at least a couple of centuries earlier than the mentioned date. On the other hand, Silla and Baekje had remained for a long time as mere plain polities among dozens of cohorts distributed across the southern parts of the Korean Peninsula. Thus, historians tend to separate the first three hundred years of the Three Kingdoms Period as defined in the chronicle, and designate it the Early Three Kingdoms Period, the Tribal Nation Period or the Samhan(삼한) Period. In short, it is widely said that the Three Kingdoms Period began in earnest from around 300 CE when statehood was established in Silla and Baekje. In consideration of such understanding, the term Proto-Three Kingdoms Period was coined for archaeology by the late Prof. Kim to designate the period roughly between 0 and 300 CE. He also defined the ending of the Bronze Age at around 300 BCE because he saw that iron was introduced at this time. The 300-year period before the Christian Era preceding the Proto-Three Kingdoms Period was named the Bronze Age II, which was soon renamed as the Early Iron Age to emphasize the use of iron. Thus, the chronological framework as we know today appeared in the 1970s.

Although his scheme has been accepted as the standard in South Korea, a growing number of researchers began to voice their dissatisfaction. There are two key reasons. One is that the timing of the appearance of bronze and iron metallurgy in archaeological records is equivocal and they appeared at different times at different places. The second problem is that the Proto-Three Kingdoms Period can be accepted only for the southern parts of Korea. This means that the scheme is unsatisfactory because a clear-cut definition for the boundaries between the Bronze Age, the Early Iron Age and the Proto-Three Kingdoms Period cannot be made. Such weakness arises from the fact that the scheme was proposed when information was limited. It was based on what was known mainly in the southeastern corner of Korea. At the same time, the scheme did not really take into consideration the problem of defining the Korean Culture Sphere but rather evaded the issue.

Including Goguryeo, many ancient Korean states had risen outside of the Korean Peninsula, which covers much of the three Chinese provinces of Liaoning, Jilin and Heilongjiang. Especially, the eastern part of the Liaoning province east of the Liaohe, the Liao River, demonstrates strong cultural affinities with Korea from the prehistoric times on. And it is here that many believe that Gojoseon had appeared. With movements of people and fluctuations in political and ethnic boundaries, distribution of different groups of people and their culture had changed a lot. That is, the stage for Korean culture and history had not always been confined to the Korean Peninsula. Quite the contrary, there once had existed diverse groups and political entities ancestral or closely related to modern Koreans across the large area abutting Korea. It is only from the early 10th century that the Korean Culture Sphere had been more or less confined to the peninsula. Borders with China and Russia were not clearly defined even in the 17th century.

As far as it relies on information from a small corner of Korea, Kim's chronological frame cannot cover adequately the whole Korean Culture Sphere. Some even question nowadays whether it can adequately describe the data found within South Korea. Nevertheless, it is still used despite the deficiencies because it provides a convenient, if not an accurate, frame of reference to organize the data. Therefore, as far as the current monograph attempts to provide an outline of the archaeological past of Korea, there would be little harm to be done if it is organized according to the scheme for the sake of convenience. In doing so, it will focus on findings made in South Korea. At the same time, there will be efforts to incorporate different opinions as much as possible. One must admit that satisfactory answers are yet to be obtained for many important questions while discussions among the South Korean archaeologists are mainly about culture history and related technical issues. Readers may find that much of the summary presented in this outline may sound speculative and lack substantive details. Nevertheless, an improved picture will soon emerge, considering what has been achieved over the last few decades.

Korean Peninsula – Physical Geography

Many Korean archaeologists think that the Korean Culture Sphere with a meaningful spatial boundary had appeared in the late 2nd or the early 1st millennium BCE with the beginning of the Bronze Age. It is also believed that its formation would somehow be related to the appearance of the Gojoseon state. At this time, bronze daggers and other artifacts of shared characteristics appeared across Korea and northeast China. It is here that those ancient Korean states of Buyeo(부여), Goguryeo and Balhae(발해) appeared later along with other minor entities such as Okjeo(옥저) and Eumnu(읍루). Also, as the late Bronze Age farmers emigrated from southern Korea to western Japan in large numbers, the northern Kyushu region could be included in the sphere for that period.

It took a long time for the Korean Culture Sphere to be formed. Long before its formation, there had appeared some shared features in material culture across Northeast Asia, which is best seen in pottery. From the early Holocene times, pottery made in Korea and the neighboring regions of Northeast Asia appear simple in form and decoration, thus, clearly different from the ornate Jomon pottery in Japan or diverse Painted Pottery of the Chinese Neolithic. Slowly, diversification and consolidation had occurred over millennia in the composition of the material culture. By the late 2nd millennium BCE, material culture in and around the Korean Peninsula had shared characteristics which are distinctive enough to define the Korean Culture Sphere.

Then, for a proper understanding of the archaeological past of Korea, it is important to include in the discussion information from northeastern China as well as the Russian Far East. However, as a quick guidebook to Korean archaeology, only archaeological findings made in Korea will be dealt with, mainly in South Korea. The review would better begin with the explanation of the physical environment of Korea which had helped to shape the characteristics of its culture.

Protruding in N-S direction, the Korean Peninsula lies roughly between 34°

and 43° N latitude and 124° and 131° E longitude, bordering China and Russia on land and separated from the Japanese Archipelago by a narrow strait about 50km wide.[5] The largest island of Jejudo, Jeju Island, is twice distant from the mainland. The longest axis of the peninsula runs roughly in NE-SW direction so that the distance from the Russo-Korean border to the southwestern corner is about 1,000km. When measured along the latitude, its width is about 350km at the widest and about 170km at the narrowest with an average of about 250km at most of the points. The size of the whole peninsula is modest, slightly larger than 220,000km² which is about 90% of Great Britain and as large as Idaho or Kansas.

Today, some 75 million ethnic Koreans live in the peninsula in two completely different societies, roughly two thirds of them residing below the DMZ. The size of South Korea is about 100,000km², comparable to Iceland, Hungary, Kentucky or Tennessee. Seoul has been the capital since 1394 when the Joseon Dynasty chose to locate its royal residences and the government offices here. In the middle of the city of 10 million lies Hangang, the Han River, one of the major channels in Korea. Its counterpart in the north, Pyeongyang, has been the center of northwestern Korea throughout history, and had been the capital of Goguryeo from 427. Daedonggang, the Daedong River, flows through this city of about 3 million people. Before the division, the whole of Korea had one special district of Seoul and 13 provinces as the primary administrative units. Now, there are a lot more of them in both Koreas [Figure 1.1].

Despite its relatively small size, its physical environment is anything but simple and monotonous. Most notable is its rugged topography. It is often said that more than 70% of the surface consists of mountains and hills, reflecting prolonged orogenic events and erosional processes [Figures 1.3, 1.4]. Along with its complex geology, more than a dozen unique physiographic zones can be recognized for South Korea alone [Figure 1.5]. The landform would give a newly arrived an impression of staggering succession of narrow and semi-independent intermontane valleys winding in between steep hillsides. Hills and mountains are often covered with deeply weathered reddish residual soils. With channel systems developed along narrow and sinuous valleys, deposition has been less important than erosion for forming the geomorphology. No loess deposits are seen as in North China, nor development of wide coastal plains as in Japan. Distribution of volcanic landscape is also limited. Except a few volcanic mountains and islands, there are developed Quaternary basalt plains at a couple of places but in limited scale. One of these lying in the center of the peninsula turned out to produce many important palaeolithic localities as shall be seen in the following chapter.

Coastal geomorphology is highly contrasting between the east coast and the other two sides. As the East Sea had been formed by a series of fault movements, the seabed plunges into the abyss steeply from the coastline and there are only a handful of islands as well. Spinal mountains run parallel with the coastline within a short distance from the sea, making it difficult to move across the range and resulting in markedly different climatic conditions between the opposite sides. In

......

5   More information about the physiography, cartography and visual images of Korea are provided by the National Geographic Information Institute at https://www.ngii.go.kr.

Figure 1.3 Annual mean temperature, precipitation and vegetation of Korea (modified after Yi, Seonbok, 1989, Figure 6; Yi, Sangheon, 2011, Figure 2). A: Subalpine Conifers; B: Deciduous Broadleaved Forest (Northeastern temperate zone); C: Deciduous Broadleaved Forest (northwestern temperate type); D: Deciduous Broadleaved forest (central temperate zone); E: Deciduous Broadleaved Forest (southern temperate zone); F: Evergreen Broadleaved Forest (subtropical-warm temperate zone).

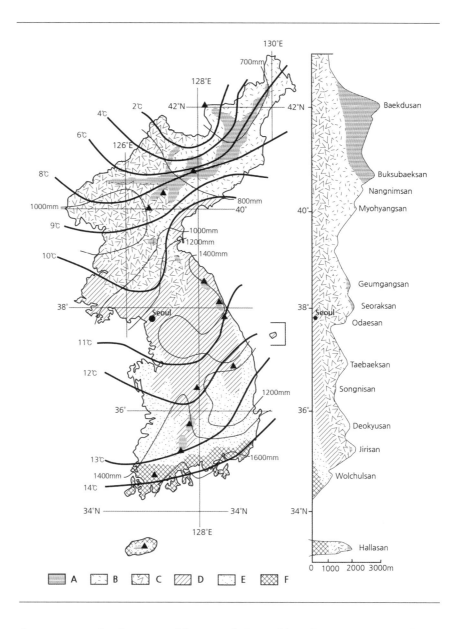

the meantime, development of the coastal plain, although narrow at most places, has provided a N-S passage along the coast from prehistoric times on, allowing diffusion and movement of culture and people with relative ease.

On the other hand, coastlines are heavily indented on the west and the south, forming the typical submerged rias coast. At the same time, tidal flats are well developed at many places, and extreme degrees of tidal difference are observed at many places. Off these coasts are more than 3,200 islands, 95% of which fall within the territory of South Korea. Although about 500 of them are inhabited, most islands are small to tiny so that only seven of them are larger than 100km² in size. Archaeological sites are found on these and other relatively large islands. The largest one, Jejudo, is a volcanic island of about 1,800km². As the Yellow Sea on the

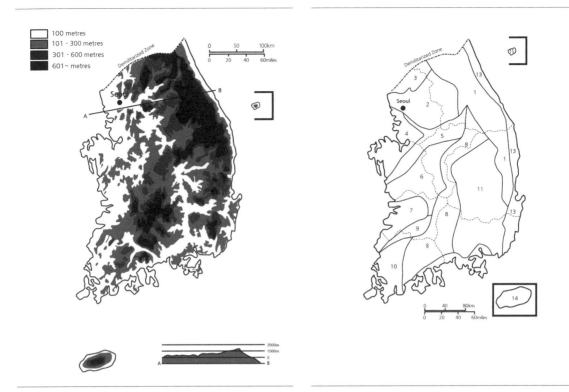

Figure 1.4 Topography of South Korea (modified after Bartz 1972, Map 4).

Figure 1.5 Physiographic regions of South Korea. (modified after Bartz 1972, Map 6). 1: Taebaek mountains; 2: Han river lowlands; 3: Imjin river basin; 4: Pyeongtaek coastal plain; 5: Charyeong ranges; 6: Geum river basin; 7: Honam plain; 8: Sobaek mountains; 9: Noryeong mountains; 10: Yeongsan plain; 11: Nakdong river basin; 12: South coast; 13: East coast; 14: Jejudo; 15: Ulleungdo.

west and the South Sea are shallow, especially the former which is barely deeper than 100m at the deepest point, much of the sea bed had been often exposed as dry land under glacial conditions, connecting Korea with China and Japan, not to mention Jejudo and other islands.

The general climatic condition is continental with pronounced seasonality in temperature and precipitation. Monsoonal circulations from the Pacific provide hot and humid summer conditions while winter is bitterly cold and dry with arctic air mass swooping down over the peninsula. Nevertheless, local conditions are highly different according to the latitude and altitude. For example, between the south coast and the northeastern inland region, there is a difference of about 12°C in mean annual temperature and 800mm in mean annual precipitation. In addition to such longitudinal differentiation, weather pattern is markedly localized at the same latitude, thanks to the generally rugged landscape. For example, on a given mid-summer day, Seoul may be simmering with 35°C temperature and 95% humidity but Gangneung on the east coast at the same latitude may be chilly with 25°C temperature under the howling wind while the town of Munsan 30km north of Seoul may be inundated by a flash flood caused by sudden torrential rain.

Such climatic conditions brought about the zonal distribution of vegetation along the longitude but with marked localization within a given zone. Thus, the northernmost part of the peninsula is covered by the sub-Alpine forest, especially in the northern highlands. But sub-tropical *Magnolia-Camellia* belt has developed along the south coast and in Jejudo [**Figure 1.3**]. Moving from south to north

between these two extremes, vegetation changes gradually from temperate deciduous *Quercus-Alnus* (oak-alder) forest to coniferous *Pinus-Abies* (pine-fir) forest.
At the same latitude, vegetation tends to include warmer species in the coastal
areas *vis-à-vis* the inland. However, actual vegetation composition within a given
zone may demonstrate difference from place to place because of localized climatic
conditions just mentioned. Variations in climate and vegetation should have been
responsible for bringing about differences in the composition of archaeological
remains from the prehistoric times on.

It goes without saying that the natural conditions of Korea today as summarized above should have changed a lot throughout its archaeological past as the
Quaternary climatic conditions had fluctuated, oscillating between warm and cold
episodes. Such change should have influenced not only the palaeolithic inhabitants but those after them as climatic amelioration during the Holocene resulted in
shrinking of the dry land. Vast changes had occurred in the coastal geomorphology
especially for the western coastal region facing the shallow Yellow Sea. In general,
these climatic fluctuations should have occurred following the global pattern as
revealed by the deep-sea and ice-core studies but with minor local adjustments.
Accordingly, the landform has been reshaped and the flora and fauna redistrib-
uted many times ever since the earliest hominin occupation. The inhabitants had to
adjust their way of life to cope with the changing environment. The pace and scale
of such adaptive responses should have been different from time to time depending on the magnitude of change in natural conditions as well as sociocultural and
technological means available at a given time.

CHAPTER 2

THE EARLIEST INHABITANTS

Pleistocene Environment

The Palaeolithic period refers to the prolonged time from the appearance of tool-making till the end of the Pleistocene epoch about 12,000 years ago. Traditionally, the Pleistocene is divided into three stages of the Lower, the Middle and the Upper Pleistocene. Its beginning is now set up at 2.58 MA (million years ago). Boundaries between the stages and with the Holocene are defined at 0.774, 0.129 and 0.0117 MA. It is generally believed that the first hominin reached East Asia sometime during the Lower Pleistocene although details are murky. This means that during the Middle and the Upper Pleistocene much of East Asia had been occupied by *Homo erectus* and other hominins such as the so-called Denisovans and, possibly, the Neanderthals. Although it is not unreasonable to expect the discovery of remains pertaining to the Lower or Middle Pleistocene in Korea, almost all of the evidence is known from the Upper Pleistocene context. Among them, only a handful of sites may be older than 100 ka (thousand years ago).

Like anywhere else, the palaeolithic inhabitants of Korea had to cope with fluctuating environmental conditions of the Pleistocene. During the glacial episodes, the natural environment was totally different from what we know today. On the other hand, the interglacial environment was somewhat similar to or even warmer than today. Climatic oscillation had occurred frequently, each episode lasting for hundreds to tens of thousands of years and punctuated by abrupt reversals lasting a few thousand or hundred years.

With each episode of climatic oscillation, the landform had been reshaped due to changes in the fluvial regimen. During the period of marine regression, flowing water had to travel longer distances to reach estuaries. Around Korea, the Yellow Sea had been exposed completely whenever the sea-level dropped more than 100m. Therefore, during the Last Glacial Maximum (LGM), rivers flowing into the Yellow Sea from Korea and China had merged and the waters had flowed hundreds of kilometers farther to the sea to debouch into the Pacific [**Figure**

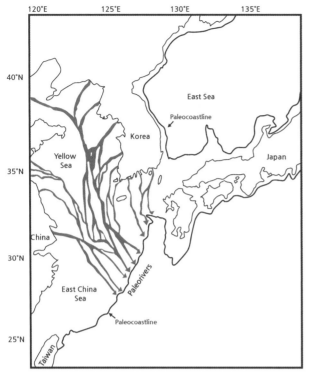

Figure 2.1 Palaeogeography of East Asia during the LGM (modified after Park *et al.* 2006, Figure 12-2)

Figure 2.2 Cave bear fossil from Durubong Cave in central South Korea. © Chungbuk National University Museum

2.1]. With climatic amelioration and rising sea-level, changes had occurred in the opposite direction. As the channel length and the positon of the estuary had changed, inevitably the longitudinal gradient of the channel had to change, causing changes in fluvio-geo-morphological processes. In this way, the palaeolithic landscape had never remained the same throughout the Pleistocene. Quite the contrary, the landform had become vastly different from one episode to another.

It is not easy to grasp the magnitude of such change in the landscape. If one drives a car on the riverine highway around Seoul, one may occasionally notice the gravels exposed high above on the profile revealed by road-cut. They were left by an ancient channel flowing at that altitude, and stone tools may be found within the associated sediment layer. The landscape that the makers of these stone tools saw cannot be the same as today. Paleolithic artifacts found in Jejudo demonstrates that the Pleistocene hunter-gatherers had roamed across the exposed sea bed during the glacial episode.

With fluctuating climatic conditions, distribution of flora and fauna also had to change a lot. A comprehensive understanding about such change is hampered by the poor preservation of remains. For faunal evidence, only a handful of discoveries are known. For example, a mammoth tooth was discovered in 1961 in North Korea at around 41° N latitude while clearing a peat deposit. In 1996, another tooth was found with other skeletal parts in South Korea at a reclamation site on the west coast, which is kept at the Natural Heritage Center (www.nhc.go.kr). The location of the discovery lies slightly below the 36° N latitude, suggesting that the tundra step condition had once developed on the exposed bed of the Yellow Sea far to the south. The habitat might have been shared with other grazers like woolly rhinoceros, horse and bison. It might be that the remains left by the hunters of these animals are lying at the bottom of the shallow sea. For other species adapted to the cold climatic conditions, remains of cave bear (*Ursus spelaeus*) were found in an inland cave at around 37° N [**Figure 2.2**], indicating the harsh environment. On the other hand, there are also known remains of warm-climate adapted species such as Macaque monkey (*Macaca* sp.) and rhinoceros (*Diceros* sp.), demonstrating that sometimes conditions were sub-tropical to tropical and much warmer than today.

For the flora, available Quaternary pollen profiles usually cover only a few thousand years on both sides of the Pleistocene-Holocene boundary. Not surprisingly, they show changing vegetation in response to climatic amelioration. For ear-

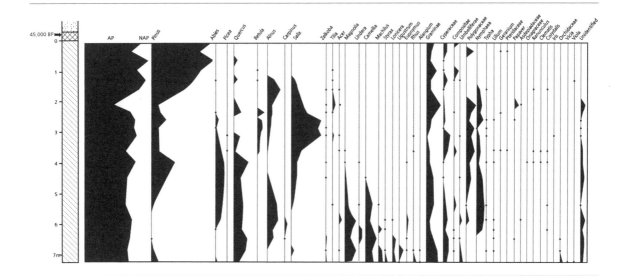

Figure 2.3 A late Pleistocene pollen profile obtained in central Korea (modified after Yi 1989, Figure 17). Notice the presence of the warm climate adapted species of *Camellia* and *Magnolia* at the bottom of the profile and the sudden dominance of coniferous species of *Pinus* and *Abies* above.

lier times, there is only a single case study made in the Imjin Basin at 38° 00′ N and 127° 13′ E. Here, samples were taken from a lacustrine deposit formed by the damming of a channel by lava flow [**Figure 2.3**]. At the bottom of the profile, the presence of *Camellia* and *Magnolia* indicates that there once prevailed much warmer conditions than today in central Korea. They were replaced by species of the temperate deciduous forest, implying that the climate had become similar to today. Then, the broadleaved species were rather swiftly replaced by *Pinus*, suggesting the development of the coniferous woodland condition [cf. **Figure 1.3**]. If we can take a single TL date at its face value, climatic conditions had deteriorated rapidly soon after 45 ka.

Although meager, what the evidence seems to tell us is that climatic conditions of this part of the world also had fluctuated a lot as confirmed by the deep-sea and the ice-core studies. These researches revealed that, during the Upper Pleistocene to which most of the palaeolithic evidence in Korea belongs, climatic reversals had occurred often and unpredictably. The early inhabitants of the Korean Peninsula had to adapt to the capricious nature.

Foundation and Development

In the Korean Peninsula, the first palaeolithic site was discovered in North Korea in 1962 at Gulpo-ri on the east coast close to the Russian border. Here, while excavating a shell-mound, researchers realized the presence of flaked stone tools in the deposit below the Neolithic layers. It was followed by the discovery of Seokjang-ri in South Korea in 1964, where stone tools were found imbedded within a fluvial terrace deposit. More discoveries had followed in both sides but only sparsely so that there had been known only about ten sites until the 1970s even including the dubious ones [**Figure 2.4**].

In North Korea, the discovery came at an opportune time for the regime as it was

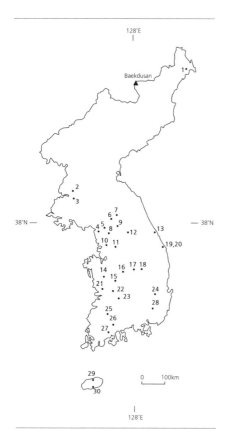

about to strengthen the authoritarian grip over the whole society as mentioned earlier. Soon, there began an intensive search for palaeolithic evidence at limestone caves in and around Pyeongyang. It was a part of a politically motivated and concerted endeavor to propagate the legitimacy of the regime and the historical importance of its capital. Within a few years, reports had appeared of cave localities where alleged early hominin and animal fossils and/or stone tools were retrieved. Their number does not seem to exceed 10 as far as the published accounts are concerned, but the reports are plagued with ambiguities in describing the stratigraphy and the materials found. From a few photographs provided, many of the claimed stone tools look more like geofacts. Likewise, the so-called bone tools may turn out to be naturally fractured pieces than artificially worked ones.

This is exactly the case for Geomeunmoru, the site claimed to be the oldest in the Korean Peninsula. When it was first reported in 1967, its age was estimated 500 ka in consideration of its faunal content, and now it is said to be one million years old. Since the 1990s, the site has become the key evidence for the political efforts of propagating the notion of the 'pure-bloodedness of Koreans over one million years'. However, the cave at best may be accepted as a Pleistocene faunal locality. From the published accounts, the only reliable locality in North Korea after Gulpo-ri is the Mandal-ri cave in Pyeongyang. If there is any other one, it is not well reported. Here, a *Homo sapiens* calvarium was discovered in association with microlithic industry, which suggests its age should belong to the final few thousand years of the Pleistocene.

Figure 2.4 Paeleolithic localities mentioned in the text and other major sites. Gawol-ri: 5; Geomeunmoru: 3; Geumgul: 18; Gigok: 20; Gorye-ri: 28; Gulpo-ri: 1; Haga: 22; Hajin-ri: 17; Hopyeong-dong: 8; Hwadae-ri: 9; Jangheung-ri: 7; Jangsan-ri: 4; Jeongok-ri: 6; Jin-geuneul: 23; Mandal-ri: 16; Mansu-ri: 9; Oji-ri: 25; Pyeongchang-ri: 10; Sam-ri: 11; Sangmuryong-ri: 12; Saengsugwe: 30; Seodu-ri: 21; Seokjang-ri: 14; Simgok-ri: 13; Sinbuk: 27; Suyanggae:17; Wolso: 19; Wolpyeong: 26; Wolpyeong-dong: 15; Wolseong-dong: 24; Yongdam-dong: 29

In South Korea, Seokjang-ri had represented the palaeolithic occupation for many years. From rounds of testing conducted there, the deposit had been claimed to have a number of well-stratified cultural layers of the Middle and the Upper Pleistocene. Similar claims had been made by the same team for some other discoveries in the early 1970s. But, including Seokjang-ri, reports made in the 1960s and 70s lacked reliable stratigraphic and chronometric information to validate such assessments. Also, many of the stone tools looked rather dubious than genuine. Therefore, it was difficult to discuss the meaning of these discoveries. The claims associated with them are generally discounted nowadays. For Seokjang-ri, the presence of the layers predating the late Pleistocene is not appreciated by and large.

Then, in 1978, the 'Acheulian-like' handaxes and cleavers were discovered at Jeongok-ri (Jeon-gok-ri)[1]. The site lies on the Hantangang, a tributary of the Imjingang, the Imjin River, and only a few kilometers away from the DMZ [**Figures 2.5**]. Because of its proximity to North Korea, the whole Imjin Basin is heavily militarized and civilian activities are strictly restricted even today at many places, which explains why it was discovered by a U.S. soldier stationed nearby [**Figure 2.6**].

......

1 According to the McCune-Reischauer system, the name is spelled as Chŏn'gok-ri or Chon'gok-ri. Over the years, there have appeared slightly different versions of the transliteration in the literature.

Figure 2.5 Aerial view of Jeongok-ri and the Hantan River. The photo was taken in 2010 when the Jeongok Prehistoric Museum was under construction, which is seen in the middle. The site covers a large area behind it. The DMZ lies along the ridge running across the photo in the background. The old rail bridge made the border between South and North Korea before the Korean War.

Figure 2.6 Handaxes from the Imjin Basin. Two specimens on the left were discovered at Jeongok-ri in 1978 by Greg Bowen, then, a U.S. Air Force sergeant stationed at a base nearby (© Seoul National University Museum). Photos and line drawings are not to scale. The actual size can be read in the chart by referring to the grid, each measuring 20 by 20cm (after Lee 2010). The length/width ratio and the amount of flaked surface for each specimen can be read from the horizontal and the vertical axis of the chart.

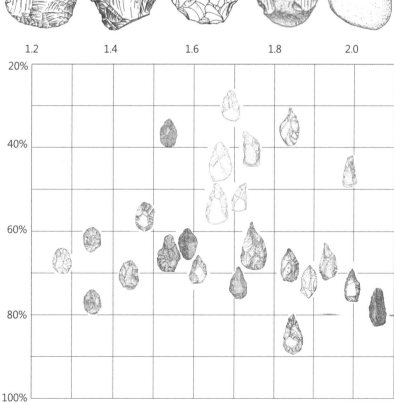

Flowing south from their headwaters in the north, both rivers meet nearby Jeongok-ri, after which the Imjin flows west along the DMZ to debouch into the Yellow Sea. In the basin, thanks to the late Quaternary volcanic activities, basalt flows had filled the river valley to form the lava plain, providing a stratigraphic key to interpret the Quaternary history of the basin. The basalt bedrock is covered by thick fluvial sediments within which artifacts are found. As channels later cut deep into the basalt, erosion has revealed the presence of artifacts at many places. Now, there have been reported some 60 palaeolithic localities on top of the basalt including Jeongok-ri, and there must be more within and on the other side of the DMZ.

A few of these Imjin Basin localities belong to the terminal Pleistocene and produced microblade technology and various small tools. However, most of them are older sites with handaxes and other crude, archaic-looking stone tools made of quartzite cobbles. In the west, these tools are usually found as remains of the Lower and/or the Middle Palaeolithic. Now, they and related stone tools are found frequently [**Figure 2.7**], representing the palaeolithic of Korea until the appearance of the Upper Palaeolithic industry. Related to the age of these artifacts, Jeongok-ri has been quoted in many secondary writings as a site of 300 ka. However, as discussed

Figure 2.7 Handaxe and related artifacts are found frequently in Korea, if in limited amount. Their occurrence is well demonstrated by an exhibition at the National Museum of Korea. They are found with other large tools such as cleavers, choppers and polyhedrals. Also, there are found various small tools such as scrapers and a variety of utilized pieces. Typically, these tools are made of quartz or quartzite. The poor quality of raw material had forced their makers to take opportunistic approach in tool-making, and formal typology may be difficult to apply to describe many of these pieces. © Seoul National University Musem (cleaver, choppers)

below, it is a gross misrepresentation of known facts.

The discovery of Jeongok-ri certainly has stimulated palaeolithic research so that the number of palaeolithic sites has soared since then. While there were known only about 20 localities until 1985, it was estimated by 2010 that there would be about 1,000 of them. The number might have been doubled by now. Despite such an explosive increase, well-preserved sites are rare and the absolute majority are mere secondary deposits made within limited space or loose accumulations of a few roughly shaped pieces. It appears that many Pleistocene deposits have survived under highly fortuitous circumstances. Deposits at open-air sites usually turn out to be a loose mixture of sediments and stone tools which had undergone repeated geo- and bioturbations. For caves and rock-shelters, the ground water activity has effectively worked against the preservation of the deposit. The problem is exacerbated because of dating problems. C-14 dating for Upper Palaeolithic evidence is possible only in rare cases due to the lack of suitable samples and an alternative is hard to come by for older sites. Although OSL (Optically Stimulated Luminescence) dating has been widely applied in recent years, the method has its limitations as samples cannot but be taken blindly and the problem of incomplete leaching of sediment grains is beyond our control. As such, we are limited in our capability to discuss the nature of evidence in many cases.

Of course, circumstances have been improving for the Upper Palaeolithic so that its beginning is dated to 43~42 ka or earlier. With accumulation of discoveries, a sequential change in the assemblage composition has been slowly revealed. Thus, we may now define several stages for the Upper Palaeolithic industry. Even so, accurate dating of assemblages is a huge problem, and there is plenty of room for improvement.

The Imjin Basin Handaxes

The problematic claims of very early dates for some evidence continued in the 1980s and after as discoveries were reported with exaggerated or unsubstantiated arguments. The cave locality of Geumgul in central South Korea is an example. Here, there were recovered stone tools from the lower part of the washed-in fluvial deposit in the early 1980s. Since then, it has been known as a Middle Pleistocene locality of 700 ka. In this case, the cave lies barely above the lowermost fluvial terrace of probable terminal Pleistocene or early Holocene age so that its occupation was not possible before this time. For another example, when a piece of handaxe was recovered at the open-air locality of Mansu-ri, it was claimed to be 800,000 years old on the basis of a single Be^{10} date from a gravel within the deposit. But, the problem lies with the context of the sample so that it is questionable whether the date can correctly represent the timing of the deposition of the sediments and artifacts.

The claim of Jeongok-ri as a 300 ka site is no exception. Such age estimate had first appeared almost immediately after its discovery, which is solely based on the impression provided by the archaic morphology of the stone tools [**Figure 2.6**]. Some twenty years later, a few OSL dates from the deposit and K-Ar and fission-track dates of the basalt were sewn together with a set of shaky assumptions and hypotheses about the site formation process, from which the lowermost part of the deposit was claimed to be 300 ka. In secondary literatures, the date was quoted as the age of the site and the industry. In addition to problems in interpreting various dates and the depositional process, unfortunately, a single point in time cannot represent the "true age" of the artifacts scattered throughout the thick deposit which should have been formed over many years. The proponents of such arguments knew only too well the presence of a late Upper Pleistocene volcanic ash within the deposit but chose to ignore it to emphasize the Middle Pleistocene age of the artifacts.

For Jeongok-ri and other post-lava flow localities in the Imjin Basin, important evidence was found in 1995 which defines the upper limit of the age of the deposit. As just mentioned, the uppermost part of the deposit at Jeongok-ri and nearby Gawol-ri produced grains of the volcanic ash originated from a massive eruption of the Aira caldera in southern Kyushu, Japan, about 30,000 years ago. Commonly known as the Aira-Tanzawa tephra, or AT in short, its grains are found widely across Northeast Asia, serving as the most valuable region-wide stratigraphic marker. In the Imjin Basin, handaxes and other crude stone tools occur throughout the deposit up to the level slightly below the AT. Thus, betraying their archaic appearance, they had been manufactured continuously almost up to 30 ka. Its discovery provided an answer to the question why there are so many 'young' dates at handaxe localities within and outside of the basin [e.g., **Figure 2.8**].

The lower chronological limit of the site is of course determined by the basalt bedrock lying below the deposit. It is generally regarded that the lava plain of the Imjin Basin is made of two lava flows of about 0.52 and 0.17 MA, respectively. The older flow is observable as far as nearby the town of Jeongok-ri while the second flow above the former had travelled farther downstream. Thus, localities like Jeon-

Figure 2.8 A stratigraphic profile revealed at Jeongok-ri in 2004 (drawing modified after Yi *et al.* 2006, Figure 5).

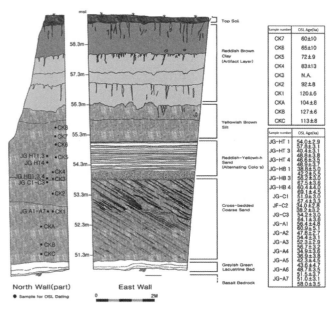

Sample number	OSL Age(ka)
CK7	60±10
CK6	65±10
CK5	72±9
CK4	83±13
CK3	N.A.
CK2	92±8
CK1	120±6
CKA	104±8
CKB	127±6
CKC	113±8

Sample number	OSL Age(ka)
JG-HT 1	54.0±2.9
JG-HT 3	57.8±3.1
JG-HT 4	40.4±3.1
JG-HB 1	46.6±3.0
JG-HB 3	42.5±2.5
JG-HB 4	60.4±4.0
JG-C1	51.0±3.0
JF-C2	38.2±3.2
JG-C3	54.2±3.0
JG-A1	64.1±3.9
JG-A2	47.8±2.7
JG-A3	52.3±2.9
JG-A4	34.9±1.6
JG-A5	39.9±4.4
JG-A6	51.5±2.7
JG-A7	58.0±3.5

North Wall(part)   East Wall
● Sample for OSL Dating   0   2M

gok-ri lying on top of the lava bed should have been formed only after 0.17 MA.

Recently, a more surprising discovery was made at Jeongok-ri. That is, C-14 dates ranging between 50 to 40 ka were obtained from a carbonized tree trunk captured by a lava flow. Similar dates were also obtained from sediment samples taken below the lava bed, hinting at the possibility of another eruption much later in time. If further study verifies the date and the late volcanic activity, the 7+ meter-thick deposit should have been formed within less than 20,000 years between c. 50 and 30 ka.

So far, it looks like the site of Jangsan-ri is the only reliable Middle Pleistocene evidence known in Korea. The site is located in the downstream area of the Imjin River, about 50km away from Jeongok-ri along the channel. Here, two pieces of crude handaxes were retrieved with other smaller tools from a limited testing. Its Middle Pleistocene status is easy to recognize because the artifact-bearing deposit forms a part of the fluvial terrace lying more than 20m above the lava flow of 0.17 MA [**Figure 2.9**]. However, its exact age needs to be determined as only inconclusive luminescence dates have been obtained.

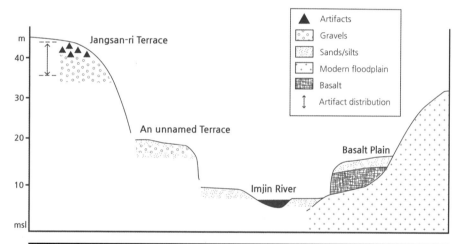

Figure 2.9 Artifacts and the schematic stratigraphic cross-section of Jangsan-ri in relation to major Quaternary features in the Imjin Basin (modified after Yi *et al.* 2004, Figure 2).

An Early Palaeolithic?

Including those known from the Imjin Basin, the palaeolithic industry of Korea until the appearance of the Upper Palaeolithic is dominated by crude-looking artifacts made of coarse-grained quartzite and quartz cobbles. While some of them are made of large flakes, the dichotomy of core versus flake tool is not a useful concept as some heavy tools are made from flakes. They include choppers, large scrapers and spheroids as well as handaxes and close relatives like cleavers and picks. Individual assemblages may lack some of them but their presence/absence does not mean much. For small tools, there are scrapers, notched pieces and denticulates in addition to a number of utilized flakes whose edges show secondary retouches or scars from utilization. In general, one cannot but receive an impression that these assemblages are full of crude stone tools, comparable to the Lower Palaeolithic industry of the west.

Despite the presence of some well-shaped artifacts, it takes only a cursory look to appreciate that they are dominated by amorphous and 'atypical' pieces so that formal typological classification is difficult to apply. They appear to have been made by opportunistic exploitation of the raw material. Indeed, even for those well-shaped handaxes, their makers had shaped the edge by efficiently taking advantage of the original form of the raw material. While these stone tools had been made over a long period of time, little difference is seen in the assemblage composition and the shape of individual artifacts so that they all appear to be of the same age. If there had occurred any change in time, it is hard to recognize.

Therefore, although researchers may refer to the threefold division of the whole Palaeolithic into the Lower, the Middle and the Upper Palaeolithic in their discussion of the Korean palaeolithic, there is little real basis to differentiate the Lower and the Middle Palaeolithic on the basis of the morphology of stone tools alone. Assemblages assigned to the Middle Palaeolithic are hardly different from those of the alleged Lower Palaeoltihic in the shape of the tools and the technology of manufacture as well as raw material. Given this problem, it is conceivable to adopt the term Early Palaeolithic to indicate all of the pre-Upper Palaeolithic evidence.

However, the archaic-looking assemblage had existed side by side with the Upper Palaeolithic industry during the Marine Isotope Stage 3 [MIS 3 (57~29 ka)] as seen at Jeongok-ri. Outside of the Imjin Basin, many localities are also known with 'Acheulian-like' handaxes and dates pertaining to the MIS 3. Therefore, it is a tricky business to designate these archaic-looking stone tools of the MIS 3. It is difficult to find or devise an appropriate term for them. As such, they will be called below merely as the Pre-Upper Palaeolithic for the sake of convenience.

While the age of individual Pre-Upper Palaeolithic assemblages is difficult to tell from the artifact morphology, dominance of those crude-looking, amorphous pieces makes the handaxes and their cousins highly conspicuous despite their small number. While we cannot answer the question when and how they appeared, their discovery is not surprising any more in East Asia. Handaxes remarkably similar to those known in Korea have been reported at many places in China. Recently, they have been found in the Philippines and Vietnam. Their occurrence across East Asia from the tropical to the temperate zone indicates that they were an integral element of the regional palaeolithic for a long time, perhaps beginning from the late Lower Pleistocene on. As a matter of fact, their morphological traits fall numerically within the range of variation shown among the Acheulian handaxes [cf. **Figure 2.6**]. The rarity of those aesthetically pleasing specimens with thin, lenticular cross-sections in East Asia is probably related to the lack of suitable crypto-crystalline raw materials.

If so, we may ask whether the term Acheulian can be adopted for the handaxe industry of East Asia. In other words, this is the question whether or not these handaxes represent the Old World-wide distribution of the Acheulian industry somehow associated with the early hominin radiation. If so, their presence in East Asia may be attributable to technological diffusion or population migration. But if they represent an independent development in the region, thus, a case of cultural convergence, more questions may be asked in relation to their appearance, such as ecological and technological background for their manufacture, identity of their makers, etc.

Palaeolithic researchers of the region are not yet ready to answer this and other related questions. Nevertheless, making a handaxe does not require highly sophisticated skills and techniques. Its manufacture might have been imbedded in the mind of the early hominins once the tool was struck out for the first time, which could have been easily pulled out of the imaginary technological reservoir whenever and wherever necessary. In this sense, its presence would mean merely that its manufacture was required by the environs. Rather than merely asking when and how handaxes appeared in the region, what seems to be more important is to pay attention to the context of their manufacture and use as well as the formation process for individual sites if we are interested in asking why these East Asiatic handaxes tend to be cruder in appearance and fewer in number and continued to exist much longer than their Acheulian counterparts.

Upper Palaeolithic Sequence

During the MIS 3, the Upper Palaeolithic had appeared abruptly as a full-blown blade industry a few thousand years before 40,000 BP. The new industry is different from the old one in every respect, changing the scene completely. More than anything else, it is impossible to miss the presence of qualitatively different artifacts such as projectile points [**Figure 2.10**]. At the same time, those heavy, chunky pieces made on quartzite and quartz cobbles are not seen anymore. Exploiting finer cryptocrystalline rocks, these new artifacts were produced by retouching blades produced by systematic reduction strategy. Interestingly, the presence of the so-called Initial Upper Palaeolithic is not confirmed, which seems to be the case for Japan and most of China although the Upper Palaeolithic in China is poorly known.

The appearance of the Upper Palaeolithic means that two completely different industries had existed side by side at least for about 10,000 years. It could be that the new industry had appeared as a result of the arrival of *Homo sapiens* to this

Figure 2.10 Upper Palaeolithic industry of Hajin-ri, also known as the Suyanggae Locality 6. Here, three artifact-bearing layers are separated by sterile layers in between them. Blade industry of the lowermost layer continues to appear in the middle layer and microblades are added. The top layer is dominated by the microblade. Edge-ground axes are also present. An elongated cobble from the middle layer shows a number of short parallel lines incised along the side. Details are shown separately. © Institute of Korean Prehistory

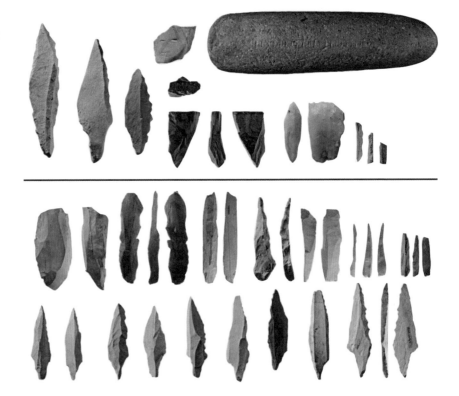

far eastern edge of Eurasia. Given their contrasting nature, it is hard to imagine that the new industry was suddenly invented by the handaxe makers. Handaxes had been made already long before the appearance of the anatomically modern hominins in East Asia which is so far dated between 120 and 80 ka. Given the 'young' age of the handaxes from the Imjin Basin and other places in Korea, it seems that the archaic population had managed to survive for a substantial period after the arrival of *Homo sapiens*.

In the neighboring regions, there is no known assemblage of similar age and composition to the Upper Palaeolithic in Korea. It is not reported in China, and the

Korean evidence predates the earliest evidence in Japan at least by several thousand years. If we look really hard, there may be some resemblance in the blade industry of the Altai region of southern Siberia and northern Mongolia with which one may hypothesize diffusion of the technology perhaps closely related to population migration from inner Asia. Yet, there lies a huge chunk of space stretching thousands of kilometers between Korea and these locales, which is empty of evidence to build up the hypothesis. As such, we cannot tell for now by what course, when and how the anatomically modern population first entered Korea. Given the palaeogeography [**Figure 2.1**], perhaps the answer may lie at the bottom of the Yellow Sea or the East China Sea, if not found in the northeastern provinces of China.

As the period is relatively close to the present, there are sometimes preserved features related to the production of stone tools *in situ*. However, convincing evidence of dwelling structures has not been uncovered, although there may be some camps or limited activity sites which might have been visited repeatedly. For artifacts, evidence is almost completely limited to stone tools and residues of their production. Changes in the composition of the lithic assemblage and technology of manufacture can be recognized. Thus, three stages or phases for the 30+ thousand years of the Upper Palaeolithic may be suggested.

In defining these stages, the appearance of blade and microblade technology is important. As mentioned, the beginning of the Upper Palaeolithic is marked by the production of the stemmed projectile points made on blades before 40 ka. The second phase following the first is set for the period between c. 25 and 18 ka, during which microblade technology had appeared and spread. There are several

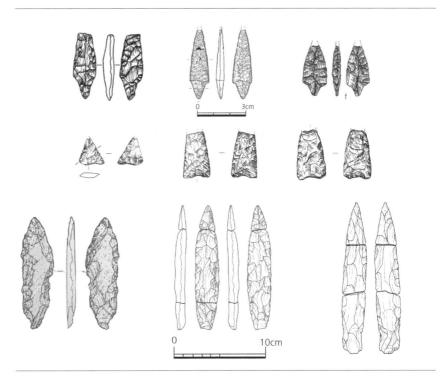

Figure 2.11 Projectile points of the terminal Pleistocene from various localities (modified after Seong 2018, Figures 1-3; Yi *et al.* 2018, Figures 244-245).

different microblade removal techniques. Finally, the last phase began around 18 ka when the stemmed points made on blades had disappeared. Lithic assemblages of this final phase are dominated by microblades and other artifacts. The most interesting ones among them are several types of thin, bifacially retouched projectile points [**Figure 2.11**]. Application of grinding techniques for tool-making had appeared during the second phase, if not earlier, and had been spread during the final phase [**Figure 2.12**]. It may be that the appearance of ground axes might reflect the changed mode of subsistence required by the changes in environmental condi-

Figure 2.12 Ground stone tools of the late Upper Palaeolithic retrieved in 2021 at Jaegyeongdeul in Jeonju. The location of the site is not shown in Figure 2.1 but roughly lies to the west of <23> in the map. As seen in the photo, one of them looks almost like a Neolithic tool. They were found with a number of microblade cores and small tools. In addition to the abundance of high quality raw material, a cache of microblade core preforms and the presence of unexploited cores suggests that the place was visited frequently for raw material procurement and stone tool manufacture.

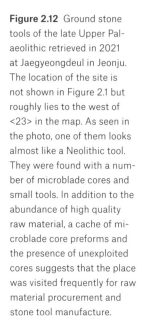

tions. The earliest dates obtained range between c. 25.5 and 18.5 ka.

These phases may further be subdivided by considering some important 'events' that occurred in the assemblage composition especially for the late Upper Palaeolithic. Among them, the most commonly mentioned are the exploitation of obsidian as raw material and the production of new types of projectile points. Yet, fine-tuning the three phases is not easy as data are insufficient although obsidian artifacts and the grinding technology had appeared apparently before the end of the second phase. Also, appearance of new types of points similar to those of western Japan might suggest interaction between southern Korea and western Japan during the last phase [**Figure 2.13**], which is also indicated by the introduction of imported obsidian.

This threefold scheme of the Upper Palaeolithic sequence may be refined with new evidence from the site of Hajin-ri, which is also known as Locality 6 of the Suyanggae site. Here, the earliest dates for the Upper Palaeolithic were obtained. More importantly, for the first time a sequential change in assemblage composition was revealed as the deposit is unusually well stratified for an open-air site formed in fluviatile context. Palaeolithic artifacts were identified from three layers which appear fairly stable, and many conjoinable pieces were found [**Figure 2.10**].

About the origin of the microblade technology in East Asia, it had been said that it first appeared in Siberia during the LGM or so as a technology of the big-game hunters and dispersed into more southerly locales such as Korea and Japan as they followed the large grazing animals moving south as the arctic steppe expanded under glacial conditions. In this way, occurrence of the same artifacts and removal techniques on both sides of the East Sea was explained. According to this scenario, microblade technology in Korea could not have appeared before c. 25 ka, and indeed C-14 dates for the microblade technology in Korea lied between 25 and 22 ka. However, much older dates from Hajin-ri challenge this view.

Here, radiocarbon dates suggest that the Upper Palaeolithic evidence had been accumulated over a period of more than 20,000 years. Dates from the top layer are fairly well concentrated around 18 ka. For the middle layer, there are 15 dates which fall roughly between 40 and 33 ka with two outliers of about 44 and 30 ka. In this layer, microblades were found, hinting that this new technology had been in use long before 25 ka. For the lowermost layer, C-14 dates suggest that the initial occupation had begun by 42 ka and as early as 46 ka, and many prefer to see the mid-point, 44 ka, for its timing. If so, it suggests that the Upper Palaeolithic with a full-blown blade industry had appeared several thousand years before 40 ka.

The assemblage from the lowermost layer consists of raw materials such as shale, tuff and hornfels. It is a complete departure from the archaic-looking assemblages known at such places as the Imjin Basin, which consist of much cruder raw materials. Blades made out of the new materials were further retouched into stemmed (or tanged) projectile points. For other types, there are many side- and end-scrapers, points, borers, axes and other small tools all of which demonstrate a high degree of standardization in shape and size.

Given the date, it is tempting to imagine whether the newly arrived Upper Palaeolithic people had ever encountered the handaxe-makers and there had occurred any gene flow between the two. It is now known that it did occur between *Homo sapiens* and the Denisovans in East Asia during the MIS 3 or before. To amplify the imagination, at the site of Pyeongchang-ri in Yongin, a crude assemblage made of quartzite and quartz was retrieved along with a few pieces classifiable as point and trapezoid. What is interesting is that these Upper Palaeolithic-like specimens are made of vein quartz, which is a material extremely difficult to handle to produce such tools. As they are from below the AT level, thus, older than 30 ka, it might be that these pieces represent an attempt of technological mimicking by a non-*sapiens* group who did not have knowledge about new raw material.

At any rate, the second layer of Hajin-ri demonstrates that microblade technology had appeared before 25 ka, which should represent one of the oldest, if not the oldest, microblade industry in Asia, posing an interesting question about its origin as mentioned. Also, in this layer a piece of elongated cobble was found measuring about 20cm long. Its surface is engraved with a number of short lines. Especially, one longitudinal edge shows more than 20 short lines of about 4mm in length [**Figure 2.10**]. This curious object reminds of those markings left on bones and stone slabs of the European Upper Palaeolithic, which are sometimes interpreted as prehistoric calendars.

Dates from the third layer are separated from those of the middle layer at least by 15,000 years, and the assemblage is dominated by microblade technology. Presence of edge-ground axes seems to confirm that the grinding technique had been spread by this time under the ameliorating climatic conditions.

Obsidian was exploited to produce microblades in the third layer. It is a rare material in Korea, and perhaps was sought after mainly to produce small tools and microblades. While Hajin-ri obsidian is neither the first nor the oldest discovery, its occurrence is important because it is associated with multiple and less problematic dates. Dates known at such sites as Hopyeong-dong, Sinbuk and Jangheung-ri are around 25 to 24 ka. But they are mixed with dates as young as c. 15 ka.

While obsidian is reported across South Korea, geochemical and mineralogical analyses indicate that it came from two different sources, one Korean, the other Japanese. Despite the claims of multiple obsidian sources within Korea, microlite analysis demonstrates that there is only one source, which is the volcanic mountain of Baekdusan, the highest peak in Korea lying at the Sino-Korean border [**Figure 2.4**]. Obsidian artifacts are also frequently found on the Chinese side of the mountain.

On the map, the distance from Baekdusan to Hajin-ri measures more than 500km, and it is over 800km for some other sites such as Sinbuk. The distance is quite substantial even without counting the topography. It is hard to imagine that obsidian was procured directly by those who left these sites even when taking into consideration the seasonal movement of the hunter-gatherers. Also, it seems unrealistic to assume that people actually had visited obsidian sources in Kyushu and brought back the material. As the amount of obsidian found at various sites is fairly limited, it seems that there had existed some kind of social network which allowed the movement of raw material over long distance by trade or exchange. Exploitation of obsidian from both sources of Baekdusan and Kyushu continued into the early Holocene.

Long-distance movement of obsidian is not surprising considering the distribution of exactly the same microblade removal techniques in Northeast Asia. Especially, sharing of technology between Korea and Japan is well shown by the occurrence of identical stone tools [**Figure 2.13**]. Whether by diffusion or movement of people, spread of technological expertise should have included the transmission of information and knowledge about the raw material and its procurement. Such region-wide sharing of technology in and around Korea might have been possible as the inhabitants of Northeast Asia during the last glacial episode had relied on big-game hunting for subsistence.

Despite such technological sharing in the circum-East Sea region during the MIS 2 (29~14 ka), the last phase of the Upper Palaeolithic in Korea between c. 18 and 12 ka has its own characteristics as exemplified by such artifacts as awl-shaped points, leaf-shaped points, stemmed bifacial points, triangular points and edge-ground axes [**Figures 2.11, 2.12**]. Some of them are reported with C-14 dates pertaining to the Holocene, implying that the Korean Peninsula had been continuously occupied after the Pleistocene by the same group of hunter-gatherers. Of course, information is yet too scanty for the period between 15 to 10 ka to discuss the transition from the Pleistocene to Holocene. Nevertheless, there is at least one site where stone tools similar to those of the terminal Pleistocene are found with pottery as shall be discussed in the following chapter. Appearance of new tools, especially projectile points, during the terminal Pleistocene and their continuation into the Holocene seem to indicate that the late Palaeolithic hunter-gatherers had been adapting to the changing environment, responding to new conditions caused by the rising temperature and sea-level.

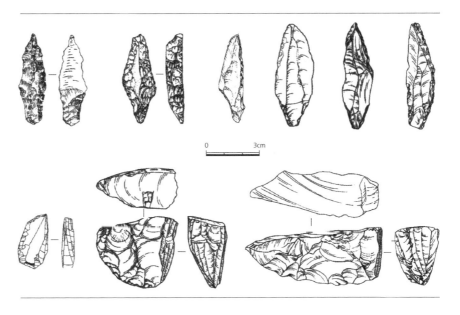

Figure 2.13 Awl-like points, backed scrapers and microcores from various localities which are also found among the Japanese Upper Palaeolithic (modified after Yi, Gigil, 2018. Figure 10). For microcores, from left to right, they represent three different removal strategies known in Japan as Hirosato, Yubetsu and Horokka Technique.

CHAPTER 3

FROM FORAGERS TO FARMERS

Neolithic in the Northeast Asian Context

In Korea, the period coming after the Palaeolithic is called the Neolithic. By the time this new period began, the natural environment had changed a lot from the glacial conditions. Sea-level during the terminal Pleistocene at around 15 ka was still low enough to expose the whole Yellow Sea and to connect Jejudo and the Japanese archipelago to the continent. However, continuous marine transgression separated these islands from the continent within a couple of thousand years [**Figure 3.1**]. The Yellow Sea was formed between Korea and China as we know today and the land-locked East Sea got connected to the Pacific Ocean. But it seems that the climatic conditions for the first several thousand years of the Holocene were somewhat cooler than today, and became warmer with the beginning of the mid-Holocene optimum around 7,500 BP [**Figure 3.2**]. By this time, many places of Korea were already occupied by people who were making pottery.

As people were adapting to the changed conditions, cultures different from the Palaeolithic appeared in Northeast Asia, comprising eastern Siberia and the Pacific Maritime Region of Russia, Mongolia, northeastern provinces of China, Japan and Korea. These cultures are customarily dubbed together as the Neolithic, except in Japan where it is called the Jomon. Of course, Neolithic is a term widely used around the world. Despite its familiarity, however, it is a poorly defined term. Its concept usually refers to the 'classic' definition put forward by V. Gordon Childe in the early 20th century. According to him, it is the period marked with technological innovations which ultimately led to the "Urban Revolution" and the rise of civilization. As the most notable innovations, he counted the appearance of pottery, ground stone tools, domestication of plants and animals and permanent villages. However, at no place in the world all of these traits had appeared simultaneously to start a "Neolithic Revolution".

His definition is especially difficult to apply in Northeast Asia as no two of the traits had appeared at the same time. Here, pottery and ground stone tools had

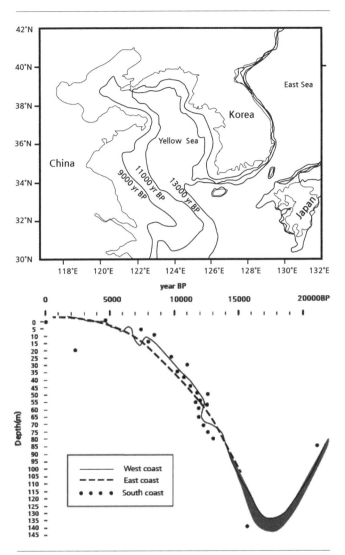

appeared before the end of the Pleistocene. Also, village life had no causal relationship with the increased food production supposedly brought by the practice of agriculture. Its best example may be seen in Japan. Under the circumstances, in continental Northeast Asia, beginning of the Neolithic tends to be equated with the appearance of pottery. The presence of pre-Holocene pottery is acknowledged in the discussion but regional Neolithic archaeology usually deals with the Holocene evidence and the question about the Palaeolithic-Neolithic transition and the early pottery tends to be put aside, quoting the scarcity of relevant data.

The ending of the Neolithic may be defined by the appearance of bronze artifacts. Nevertheless, it may not be always clear whether they were locally manufactured or introduced from the outside. The question may be more difficult to answer depending on who the neighbor was, in this case China. As a result, presence or absence of bronze artifacts may not be always useful to define the ending of the Neolithic in the region. As such, changes in the pottery assemblage is often accepted as the evidence of convenience for periodization instead.

Consequently, there is some confusion in the regional literatures about the beginning and the ending of the period. The lowest common denominator of different opinions is

Figure 3.1 Coastline and sea-level change around Korea during the terminal Pleistocene and the early Holocene (after Park *et al.* 2006, Figures 12-1, 4-10). Notice that Jejudo had been already separated from the mainland before Holocene.

that the Neolithic in Northeast Asia is the period between the Palaeolithic and the Bronze Age loosely marked by the appearance and change in the pottery assemblage. Then, it is not surprising to see that traditionally much effort has been paid to pottery typology and chronology, partially owing to the fact that there was little evidence available other than pottery. For Korea, the ending of the Neolithic is set around 1500 BCE because it is believed that new pottery appeared around this time. As shall be seen in the next chapter, this date is at least a few hundred years earlier than the earliest bronze artifact so far known within the Korean Peninsula.

Legacy of Colonialism

In relation to the beginning of the Neolithic in Korea, for a long time, there was no evidence from the early Holocene. Thus, a model appeared in the 1970s about

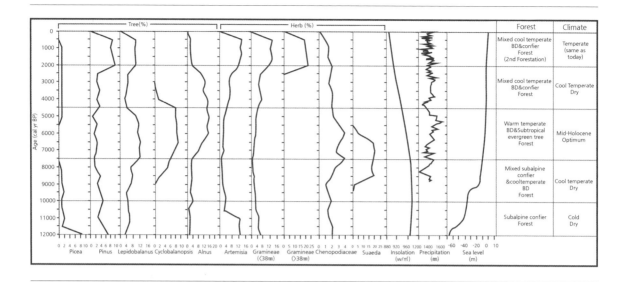

Figure 3.2 Vegetation and climate changes based on pollen indicators in South Korea during the Holocene (after Yi 2011, Figure 7). BD stands for Broadleaved Deciduous. Species of Lepidobalanus have been important throughout Holocene. Acorns from them had been exploited widely during the Neolithic (cf. Figure 3.25). Below is shown a leaf of *Quercus acutissima*, one of six indigenous acorn-producing oak trees in Korea, found at the Neolithic site of Hamori and on display at the Jeju National Museum.

the beginning of the Neolithic and the peopling of Korea which took it for granted that the Pleistocene hunters had left the peninsula following the retreating large game animals due to climatic amelioration. In other words, it assumed that the land was repopulated only when the "Palaeo-Asiatic" people with pottery had arrived around 3000 BCE from somewhere 'north', and that these Neolithic immigrants were replaced by or mixed with a group of "Tungus" people during the early part of the 1st millennium BCE, their arrival marking the beginning of the Bronze Age and the formation of the ethnic Koreans. This hypothesis of population replacement has exerted great influence in South Korea and beyond in explaining Korean origins. However, it began to lose its appeal with a realization that there is no real proof to support the hypothesis while much of the gap for the early Holocene has been gradually filled.

This outdated notion has its roots in the simplistic and diffusionistic perceptions held by the early 20th century Japanese researchers. As they launched fieldwork in the vicinities of Seoul, they soon recognized the existence of two contrasting prehistoric potteries, one pointed-bottomed in shape and decorated with geometric patterns, the other flat-bottomed and without decoration. They were accepted as remains left by two different contemporary groups of people who entered Korea from somewhere north of China sometime during the 1st millennium BCE, shortly before the beginning of historic times. The group with the decorated pottery was hypothesized to occupy the floodplain while the other chose to settle on hills and slopes.

This 'interpretation' proved wrong in time and the two potteries turned out to be of different periods, one Neolithic, the other Bronze Age. Anyhow, the early Japanese researchers decided that the decorated pottery represents a Northeast Asiatic version of the Kammkeramik of northern Europe because both have similar surface decorations. In other words, the pottery was regarded as evidence demon-

Figure 3.3 Examples of the Jeulmun Pottery. Two typical ones on the top left are from Amsa-dong in eastern Seoul. The others, which are younger, are from the coastal localities of Unbuk-dong and Jungsan-dong in Incheon (top). Below are from the Gado island in Gunsan, and inland localities of Galmeori in Jinan and Ojin-ri in Cheongdo. All of them are about 25 to 40cm tall with diameters around 25 to 30 cm. Decoration had become in time less articulated and/or covering less amount of surface with reduced pointedness in shape. Although the amount and the position of decoration is considered important in determining the relative age of the potteries, they are not always reliable indicator. © National Museum of Korea (Amsa-dong, Gado, Galmeo-ri and Ojin-ri); National Research Institute of Cultural Heritage (Unbuk-dong and Jungsan-dong)

strating the Eurasia-wide distribution of the same cultural tradition. Thus, they directly translated the term Kammkeramik into Japanese in naming the pottery. Later, from the Korean reading of the Chinese characters making up this Japanese vocabulary, the term Jeulmun Togi, i.e., Jeulmun Pottery was born. In English, it is known as Comb-Patterned Pottery or Comb-Decorated Pottery. In the 1980s, the first of the two Chinese characters which make up the term was translated into Korean so that nowadays both Jeulmun Pottery and Bitsalmun Pottery are officially used in South Korea to indicate this pottery with pointed bottom and surface decoration. The other pottery, through the same process, was named Mumun Pottery (Plain Coarse Ware), which is now also known as Minmuni Pottery.[1]

A typical Jeulmun Pottery is sometimes described as cannonball-shaped because of its round and pointed bottom and wide-open mouth [**Figure 3.3**]. Its surface is decorated with simple geometric motifs by several techniques, most often by incision [**Figure 3.4**]. It is now known that the distribution of typical Jeulmun pottery is limited both in time and space and centered in the central western part of Korea, especially in the Daedong and the Han River basins where they appeared at around 6,000 BP and spread to other places [**Figure 3.5**]. Not only is there pottery much older than Jeulmun, there are other contemporary pottery types, some of which are shown in **Figure 3.6**. Therefore, it is now generally regarded that Jeulmun Pottery

......

1   In the western literatures, Jeulmun has been transliterated as Chŭlmun or its simplified form, Chulmun. While Chinese characters are shared in East Asia, they are pronounced differently in different languages. Today in Korea, unlike Japan, Chinese characters are almost completely expelled in everyday life and the vocabularies made of them are being replaced by those based on Korean.

Figure 3.4 Examples of surface decoration of Neolithic pottery. Here are shown appliqué-decoration (upper left), incision (upper right), dotting or pressing (lower left) and stamping (lower right). © National Museum of Korea

does not and cannot represent the Neolithic and needs to be treated just as one of Neolithic potteries. Its conceived high visibility should have something to do with the popularity of geometric motifs for surface decoration throughout the period.

Before the diversity of the Neolithic pottery was appreciated in the 1990s, as Jeulmun Pottery was regarded as representing the Neolithic, a suggestion was made to call the period the Jeulmun Period instead of the Neolithic. By extension, the following period was suggested to be named as the Mumun Period in place of the Bronze Age. However, the opinion is not popular as Jeulmun Pottery is now considered as just one of many Neolithic potteries. For the Mumun Pottery, it had been made over a very long period of time even into historical times with a lot of variations in shape and size as shall be seen later.

In any case, the Kammkeramik hypothesis on the origin of Jeulmum Pottery had influenced a lot in determining the direction of research. In North Korea where research had been conducted according to the Marxist model of social evolution, by the early 1960s some evidence was presented supposedly demonstrating the presence of the 'universal' sequence of cultural evolution in Korea consisting of the Palaeolithic, Neolithic and Bronze Age. In South Korea, on the other hand, the basic framework of the hypothesis had not been critically re-examined until the 1980s and the diffusionistic perspective had prevailed which emphasized establishing a typology-based pottery chronology and culture history as the goal of archaeological research.

However, the legacy from the colonial past has been steadily chipped away, and new avenues of research are actively being sought after. New information from fieldwork and scientific analysis enables researchers to pursue such questions as subsistence pattern, spatial organization and population dynamics of the period. To summarize the current understanding about the period, the Neolithic inhabitants were basically foragers who had relied on various natural resources. The early Neolithic inhabitants had adapted to the coastal environment, and the exploitation of the inland niches had occurred later with the spread of incipient agriculture.

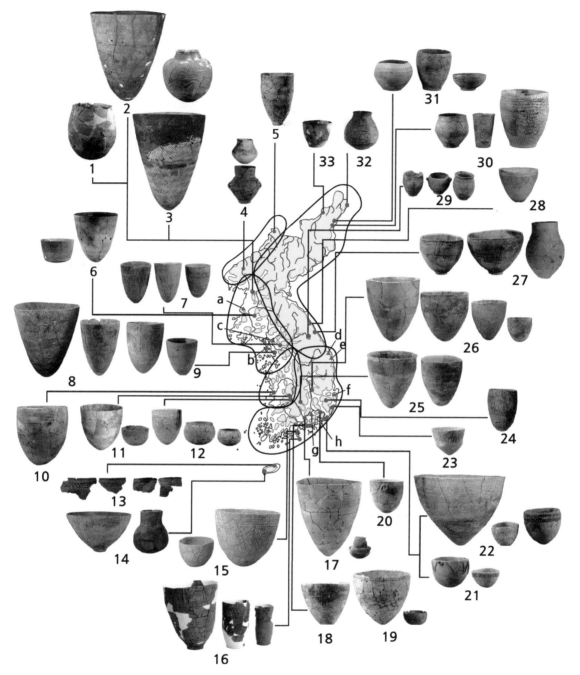

Figure 3.5 Major Neolithic sites and pottery types (modified after The Korean Archaeological Society 2010, Figure 19). Location of recent discoveries and those mentioned in the text are added and indicated as triangles and with alphabets. Encircled areas indicate generally recognized culture areas as defined by the distribution of characteristic pottery types.
1: Geumtan-ri; 2: Namgyeong; 3: Pyodae; 4: Sinam-ri (in Yongcheon); 5: Toseong-ri; 6: Jitap-ri; 7: Amsa-dong; 8: Neunggok; 9: Oido(O-i-do); 10: Gado; 11: Galmeori; 12: Jingeuneul (Jin-geu-neul); 13: Bukchon-ri; 14: Gosan-ri; 15: Songdo; 16: Ando; 17: Sangchon-ri; 18: Sangnodaedo; 19: Yeondaedo; 20: Suga-ri; 21: Yeongseon-dong; 22: Dongsam-dong; 23: Sinam-ri (in Ulsan); 24: Ojin-ri; 25: Imbul-ri; 26: Songjuk-ri; 27: Osan-ri; 28: Munam-ri; 29: Gyo-dong; 30: Wonsudae; 31: Nongpo-dong; 32: Seopohang; 33: Beomuiguseok (Beom-ui-gu-seok); a: Gungsan; b: Unseo-dong, Unbuk-dong, Yongyudo, Sammokdo, Dongmak, Samgeori; c: Daeneung-ri; d: Jukbyeon; e: Hupo; f: Sejuk, Hwangseong-dong; g: Bibong-ri; h: Gadeokdo.

A   B   C   D

Figure 3.6 Examples of non-Jeulmun pottery (not to scale). A: Thick-lined Incision Pottery from Dongsam-dong Shell-mound in Busan; B: Painted Pottery from Juk-byeon-ri in Uljin; C: Painted Pottery from Yeondaedo Shell-mound in Tongyeong; D: Double-Rimmed Pottery from Dongsam-dong. From the similarity to the classic Jeulmun Pottery, <A> is considered either a derived or the ancestral form of the latter, depending upon one's evaluation of its age. <D> is sometimes regarded as the transitional type from the Neolithic to the Bronze Age. ©National Museum of Korea

Apparently, cultivation played only a minor role in the subsistence economy even at the end of the period. Neolithic people in Korea were basically foragers rather than farmers.

Neolithic Sequence

When comparing the Neolithic evidence in Korea with contemporary cultures far and near, it appears that the whole period had been rather modest in its sociocultural complexity with limited population size. There is no hint of a religious or political center, nor any evidence of organized public activities and gatherings. Settlement sites are few in number and small in scale so that the number of pit-houses is usually less than ten to twenty. Little change is observed in spatial organization and settlement size through time. Individual pit-houses are likewise small and simple, and walls and roofs were supported with a few posts. These structures could have accommodated only a single nuclear family. Burials are also scanty, and the overall assemblage composition basically consists of a few clay vessels and stone tools, i.e., items essential to sustain life. Art objects or personal decorations are also rare, which are also rudimentary. If we can see any discernible stylistic differences among the artifacts, it is only from the pottery. Their shape and surface decoration demonstrate a certain amount of spatial and temporal variation.

The earliest Neolithic evidence is marked by the site of Gosan-ri in Jejudo, which had been formed over a long period of time [**Figures 3.5, 3.7**]. Although the site now sits on top of a coastal cliff, given the sea-level change [**Figure 3.1**], it should be that the site was not immediately adjacent to the coast at the time of occupation. Here, the basal layer of volcanic clasts had been laid by 14 to 13 ka and the whole process of deposition had ended around 1,500 BP. The stratigraphy consists of largely two occupation layers. The early occupation of the site is represented by a sandy clayey layer lying over a sterile bed. Nevertheless, because of the poor condition of deposition, artifacts of different ages had crept into the layer, causing some confusion in understanding the stratigraphy. In any case, the site has attracted a lot of attention because pottery and stone tools, mostly arrowheads, were found resembling those known at some pre-Holocene sites in the Russian Far East [**Figure 3.8**]. Interestingly enough, similar arrowheads are now known in the mainland at some terminal Pleistocene localities [cf. **Figure 2.11**].

Occupation of Gosan-ri had occurred after the island was cut off from the main-

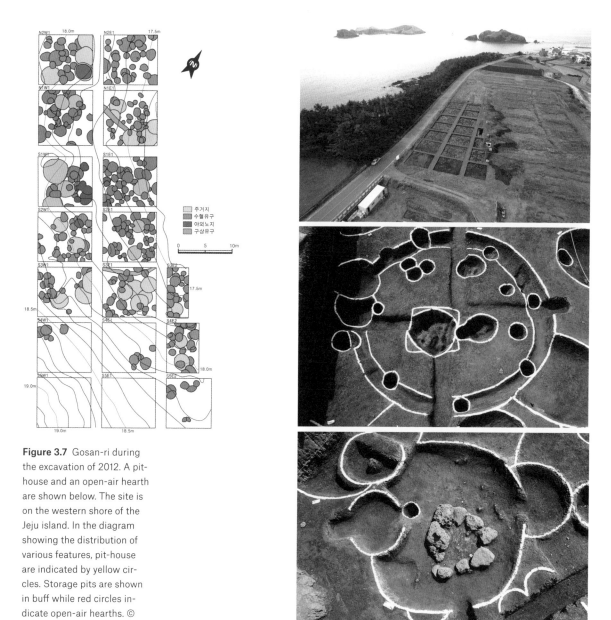

Figure 3.7 Gosan-ri during the excavation of 2012. A pit-house and an open-air hearth are shown below. The site is on the western shore of the Jeju island. In the diagram showing the distribution of various features, pit-house are indicated by yellow circles. Storage pits are shown in buff while red circles indicate open-air hearths. © National Research Institute of Cultural Heritage

land [**Figure 3.1**]. However, given the grand change in geography from the late Pleistocene on, similarities in stone tools and pottery between Gosan-ri and the continental sites in the far north might mean the widespread sharing of a similar mode of adaptation established at the end of the Pleistocene before the island was isolated due to marine transgression.

Pottery from the earliest layer are of two kinds. They did not appear at the same time and are presumed to be of different age as suggested by the dates directly obtained from the potsherds. The older one is known as Gosan-ri Type Pottery. It is yet to be determined when it was made for the first time. So far, the oldest date of c.

Figure 3.8 The Gosan-ri Type Pottery and projectile points (© Jeju National Museum). On the surface of the pottery are imprints of grass and/or other organic fibers. While arrowheads may include several types, it seems that there is little change in their shape over the whole period of occupation. Similar potteries and stone tools are known in the Russian Far East at such sites as Gromatukha with C-14 dates as old as c. 15 ka.

15 ka was obtained from organic residue left on a potsherd. Direct dating of other potsherds suggests their age should lie between 10,100 and 8,700 BP. Their mean value is about 9,500 BP at the probability level of 95.4%. Discovery of the microlithic locality of Saengsugwe and a couple of other palaeolithic sites underscores the possibility of continuous human occupation of the island from the Pleistocene on [**Figure 2.4**].

Excavation revealed pit-houses and storage pits, but it is not clear whether these were left by those who made Gosan-ri Type Pottery. The C-14 dates obtained from these structures are calibrated to about 9,600 BP. It seems that these dates fit better with other pottery rather than Gosan-ri Type Pottery. The other type is called Appliqué-Decorated Pottery and also known as Raised Design Pottery [**Figure 3.9**]. Until the discovery of Gosan-ri, this pottery had been known mainly from the east and the southeast coast and regarded as the oldest pottery in Korea.

Figure 3.9 Appliqué-Decorated Pottery. A: Gosan-ri in Jejudo; B and C: Osan-ri in Yangyang; D: Sinam-ri in Ulsan; E: Dongsam-dong in Busan. Photos are not to scale. Notice that vessels of different shape, size and decoration are all lumped under the same name because of the application of thin clay bands for decoration. © Jeju National Museum (A); Seoul National University Museum (B, C); Ulsan Museum (D); National Museum of Korea (E)

It is believed that it first appeared around 8,000 BP. At Gosan-ri, its dates range between 8,650 and 8,000 BP at the probability level of 95.4% with a mean of 8,300 BP. Thus, Appliqué-Decorated Pottery here might be slightly older than similar ones in the mainland, and perhaps had appeared at least a thousand years later than the Goran-ri Type. Presence of this and other younger ones with decorations resembling Comb-Patterned Pottery suggests that interaction between the island and the mainland had been maintained throughout the Neolithic.

Early occupation of Gosan-ri as represented by the two pottery types is marked from the late episode by a stratigraphic break. Dates related to the second occupation center around 6,400 BP. A storage pit dug during the initial occupation and revealed on a profile had been completely filled in by this time. This late occupation is associated with the appearance of a new, undecorated plain pottery. By this time, Undecorated Pottery is also found in the mainland, at such sites as Dongsam-dong in Busan on the south coast [**Figure 3.10**]. Although they are sometimes treated as a chronological marker, given the size and the relative ease to shape them, perhaps they might have been made casually as simple utilitarian vessels regardless of their age or location of occurrence.

As the chronological division of the Korean Neolithic heavily relies on pottery typology, there are diverse opinions and it is difficult to synthesize them in a coherent manner. However, despite disagreements in details, perhaps many would agree that the overall sequence may be divided into four major phases, which may be named the Initial, the Early, the Middle and the Final Neolithic. The Initial Neolithic can be defined as the period of Gosan-ri Type Pottery. The following Early Neolithic is represented by Appliqué-Decorated Pottery while Jeulmun Pottery appeared and dispersed during the Middle Neolithic. The latter was replaced by various local types during the Final Neolithic but evidence in general is rare.

In considering the cultural sequence, it is known that the timing of the North Atlantic ice drifting events matches fairly well with the monsoonal events in East Asia. That is, negative change in precipitation in East Asia is closely related to the climatic deteriorations at a worldwide level during the Holocene. When compared to these events, the initial occupation of Gosan-ri somewhat coincides with the Bond Event 6 (c. 9,400 BP) which occurred during the transitional period from the Pre-Boreal to the Boreal. Then, although data is fragmentary, the initial occupation of Gosan-ri might have occurred under cooler climatic conditions than today. As seen below, boundaries between the major chronological phases of the Korean

Figure 3.10 Undecorated Pottery from the Dongsam-dong shell mound. These bowl-like vessels are similar in shape despite large variation in size. Smaller ones were made by pinching a lump of clay while large vessels were shaped by piling rims of clay and smoothing the surface. The inner surface may show marks of trimming. The rim part of the vessel may be folded and smoothed, or simply left untouched while the surface may show traces of pressing with weaved material. Such rather minor differences are often taken as the basis for typology although they might have no real temporal meaning. © National Museum of Korea

Neolithic do not seem to deviate much from climatic events. In China, the collapse of the Neolithic in the Central Plains seems to have had occurred around 4,200 BP, possibly coinciding with the so-called 4.2 ka BP Event in the Mediterranean. It might be that the climate also had played a role in bringing about culture change in East Asia. Nevertheless, a causal relationship between the climatic and culture change is far from being established as evidence is too weak [cf. **Figure 3.2**].

For the temporal boundary between the Initial and the Early Neolithic, the appearance of Appliqué-Decorated Pottery at Gosan-ri seems to match reasonably well with the Bond Event 5 (c. 8,200 BP). Such a coincidence might mean that the transition as marked by this pottery had also something to do with the change in climatic condition.

The ending of the Early Neolithic might fall around the Bond Event 4 (c. 5,900 BP). At Gosan-ri, Non-Decorated Pottery replaced Appliqué-Decorated Pottery a few hundred years earlier, at around the time of the Weak Asian Monsoon Event of 6.3 ka. But the difference appears lying within the error range. Many sites with this pottery in the mainland are dated around 6,000 BP. More importantly, Comb-Patterned Pottery had appeared at this time along with others of different shape and design [**Figures 3.5, 3.6**]. Such diversity in the manufacture of potteries during the Middle Neolithic led to the proliferation of many local sequences.

The final phase may be said to begin around the Bond Event 3. By 4,000 BP at about the same time as the collapse of the Neolithic in central China, the sheer amount of archaeological remains diminished all of a sudden and the assemblage composition had become even simpler. The ending of the phase, i.e., the ending of the Neolithic, is conventionally set in the middle of the 2nd millennium BCE, around 3,500 BP. By this time, traces of Comb-Patterned Pottery faded out and new ones of the Bronze Age emerged.

To summarize, the whole period may be divided into the Incipient (>9,500 ~ 8,000 BP), the Early (8,000 ~ 6,000 BP), the Middle (6,000 ~ 4,000 BP) and the Final Neolithic (4,000 ~ 3,500 BP) with an error range of a few hundred years for the boundaries. In this scheme, the Incipient Neolithic is set up solely with the Gosan-ri evidence. As any comparable data outside of the island is so far not known, there yet remains a gap of several thousand years to count for the Palaeolithic-Neolithic transition in the mainland.

To repeat the cultural sequence in terms of pottery, we may say that Gosan-ri Type Pottery of the Incipient Neolithic was followed by Appliqué-Decorated Pottery at around 8,000 BP. Then, Comb-Patterned Pottery appeared at around 6,000 BP in the central western Korea. This Jeulmun Pottery represents Incised Pattern Pottery in Korea which is found widely across Northeast Asia and includes a variety of forms, sharing the surface decoration by incision. Then, around 4,000 BP, pottery appeared with little surface treatment, marking the beginning of the final phase. These relatively simple vessels are sometimes considered as a precursor of Plain Coarse Ware, i.e., Mumun Pottery, of the following Bronze Age although not everybody agrees.

About the origin of these diverse Neolithic potteries, despite the long-held belief in southwardly diffusion, it remains to be seen where and when they had appeared for the first time and how they had spread. For instance, Thick-Lined Incised Pottery mainly found in the southeastern coastal area was once believed a derivative of Comb-Patterned Pottery [**Figure 3.6**]. But some C-14 dates hint at the possibility that it might have appeared independently sometime during or before the 4th millennium BCE.

The case of Thick-Lined Incised Pottery may explain why there are so many confusing typological pottery sequences. Because Neolithic potteries demonstrate a lot of variation in their shape and decoration, so many pottery types have been proposed and their subtypes as well as local chronological sequences by 'splitters'. For now, it is not realistic to expect a coherent cultural sequence agreeable to everybody, especially for the Early and the Middle Neolithic. For example, according to a somewhat popular opinion, the Incipient Neolithic as mentioned above is followed by the Initial (8,000 ~ 6,500 BP) and the Early Neolithic (6,500 ~ 5,500 BP). Likewise, the Middle phase is divided into the Middle (5,500 ~ 5,000 BP) and the Late Neolithic (5,000~4,300 BP), which is followed by the Final Neolithic (4,300 ~ 3,500 BP). It is not necessary to repeat that this is not the only alternative scheme but evidence for this or other suggestions is only weak at best.

Chronological schemes at the local level are even more confusing. For example, in the central western part of the peninsula, the period between 6,000 and 4,000 BP alone may be divided into as little as two to three and as many as six to eight sub-phases based on pottery typology and C-14 dates. As another example, in the southeastern part of Korea, depending on the opinion about the timing of the adoption of the pressing technique for surface decoration, the period between 8,000 and 6,000 BP may be divided into up to four sub-phases but with varying ideas about their temporal boundaries. It is ironic that finer chronological subdivisions do not help but rather hinder a coherent understanding. Given the simple nature of design, decoration technique and overall shape, random and independent origin of any given 'type' of pottery seems to be an open possibility.

Settlement Pattern

Settlement sites are not as conspicuous as shell-mounds, but once revealed, their configuration and distribution of various features are an important source of information about a given society and culture. However, most of the so-called Neolithic settlements consist of a few pit-houses only, and sometimes sites are found made of an isolated, single pit-house. Including such single-dwelling sites, the total number of settlement sites reported by 2021 is approximately 150, about one fifth of which are in North Korea. The total number of all the other kinds of sites including shell middens, burials, open-air hearths and camp sites appears less than 300. Among the settlement sites, those with more than ten pit-houses are less than 20. Even the biggest ones are found with 50 to 60 of them which would not have been built at the same time [**Figure 3.11**].

Such paucity of evidence is far from the picture of an affluent agrarian society. Both the density and the size of the sites suggest that Neolithic society was small in terms of population size and simple in social organization. Judging from the conditions of the structural remains, assemblage composition and the context of deposition, most settlements appear to be transient in nature, serving as a short-term base rather than a place of year-round occupation. Overall, the Neolithic society of Korea looks more like relying on provisions provided by nature rather than producing subsistence resources.

Like the settlements where they are found, pit-houses themselves are small and simple [**Figures 3.12, 3.15**]. Early ones were made as round and shallow dug-out structures and their diameter rarely exceeds 5m. Later, they tend to be square to rectangular in plan, and are slightly but not significantly larger. Floor size of most pit-houses is less than 25m², perhaps suitable for a nuclear family. Some are as small as 8 or 9m² or smaller, thus, too small to be a proper dwelling structure. Regardless of their shape and size, a simple fireplace was usually made in the middle and a few postholes around. Occasionally, at a corner of the floor or outside of the pit-house, a dug-out space for storage may be found with or without jars inserted. Their superstructure was also simple. The roof was covered with sprigs, and the space in between the thin rafters were filled with weeds and grass. Many of the round-shaped pit-houses were perhaps conical in their appearance, slanted walls serving as roof as well. The application of adobe or mud brick for wall or roof has not been observed.

The largest number of Neolithic dwellings is known at the site of Unseo-dong in Yeongjongdo, an island off the west coast where the Incheon Airport was constructed on reclaimed land [**Figures 3.5, 3.11**]. Here, a total of 68 pit-houses were revealed in two loose clusters. In the absence of reliable information to determine the timing of the occupation for each pit-house, their distribution might be interpreted in any way one would like to see. Nevertheless, what seems to be clear is that the distribution of the pit-houses appears rather random and does not demonstrate a spatially organized pattern that can be expected if they were occupied at the same time. Most probably, not all of them were contemporary but had been built in a haphazard fashion over a period by a small group of occupants. In this case, the site might have been formed from repeated visits to this particular place by a small band of foragers.

In comparison, the inland site of Daeneung-ri revealed a total of 38 pit-houses demonstrating a certain amount of spatial organization. The site is deemed to be of early Middle Neolithic from the pottery as is the case for Unseo-dong, thus, comparable to the well-known Jeulmun Pottery site of Amsa-dong in easternmost Seoul [cf. **Figure 3.3**]. Here, pit-houses were built on a south-facing slope of a low-lying hill. Apparently, they were arranged roughly along the elevation. But the pattern is not perfect so all of them may not be contemporary [**Figure 3.11**].

It is difficult to determine how long these two sites had been occupied and whether all of the pit-houses were occupied at the same time. But even if it is so, the maximum number of occupants of Daeneung-ri would be less than several hundred and the actual group size could be well below this number. For Unseo-dong, although the number of dwellings is almost twice that of Daeneung-ri, as mentioned, the site might have been formed by repeated visitation by a small group. Of course, the absolute majority of the Neolithic settlement sites could have accommodated even fewer people.

Within a radius of 20km from Unseo-dong, on islands and on the coast a few

Figure 3.11 Neolithic sites of Unseo-dong in Yeongjongdo island, Incheon, and Daeneung-ri in Paju. They represent the largest settlements of the Middle Neolithic. © National Research Institute of Cultural Heritage; Gyeonggi Ceramic Museum

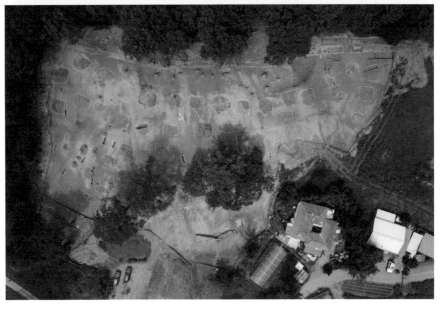

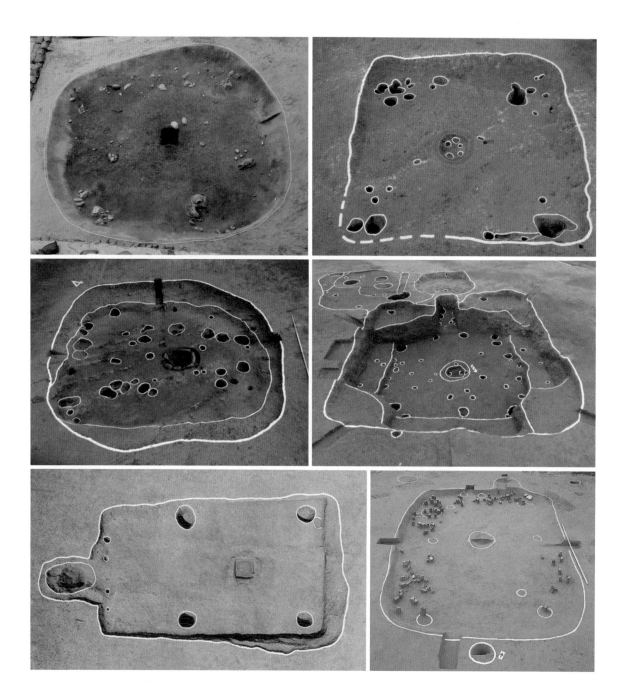

Figure 3.12 Neolithic pit-houses. From left to right and top to bottom, Osan-ri, Neunggok, Jungsan-dong, Unseo-dong, Gwanpyeong-dong and Sangchon-ri (after The Korean Archaeological Society 2010, Figure 30).

sites have been discovered with 15 to 30 or less pit-houses [**Figure 3.5**] as well as shell-mounds and outdoor hearth sites [**Figure 3.13**]. The location of these sites alone suggests that people did not come here to cultivate ground crops or to practice arboriculture. In the west central coast, assuming the contemporaneity of Unseo-dong and all the other sites, their distribution somewhat matches the expectation of a subsistence-settlement system of foragers to whom social fusion and fission were a part of everyday life. In that case, larger sites might have served as seasonal, annual or multi-annual bases for conglomeration of those who other-

Figure 3.13 Outdoor hearths found on a spit of sand bar in Youngyudo. Here, a total of 82 hearths were excavated in relation to the construction of the Incheon Airport. © Seoul National University Museum

wise were split into smaller groups for daily activities. Alternatively, they might have served as home bases of a social group whose subsistence and logistic activities had been carried out independently in small units.

As shall be discussed, agricultural activity in whatever form seems to be of limited importance during the Neolithic. There is little evidence which demonstrates otherwise despite the claim of the discovery of a cultivation field at such sites as Munam-ri. Sites are relatively rare in inland areas with soils suitable for cultivation while they are more often found on the coast as seen above. A similar concentration of sites is also noticed in the Ulsan area in the southern part of the east coast. Here, Neolithic people relied on marine resources so that, within a distance of about 30km along the coastline, more than a dozen Early Neolithic sites have been found such as Sinam-ri, Sejuk and Hwangseong-dong [**Figure 3.5**]. These sites mainly consist of concentrated features with a hearth at its center, each representing a separate episode of occupation. With the lack of discernible dwelling structures, it seems that they were formed by foraging groups who frequented these places for subsistence activities [**Figure 3.14**].

Meanwhile, if resources were plentiful, people could have spent a lot of time at one place, even forming a permanent settlement. The earliest site of Gosan-ri is an example, where excavation revealed 11 pit-houses and a number of storage pits within a confined area [**Figure 3.7**]. The overlapping relationship of these features indicate it had been occupied fairly intensively. While the site is sitting at the edge of a sea cliff, the coastline should have been at a fair distance during Neolithic times so that the location was also suitable to exploit terrestrial and avian resources. Its lithic assemblage is dominated by projectile points but with no evidence of manufacture on site, and there are surprisingly few tools related to exploiting aquatic resources.

A similar pattern of intensive and prolonged occupation may be recognized at other Early Neolithic sites on the east coast. For example, at the east coastal Early Neolithic type site of Osan-ri, sherds of Comb-Patterned Pottery are found in the upper levels, indicating the place had been continuously occupied into the late Middle Neolithic. The site is located in a coastal dune field developed next to a lagoon. Along the east coast, localities with similar conditions are often found with Neolithic sites, suggesting that brackish waters of the lagoon at such locations had provided added benefits to the littoral environment for the inhabitants, thus, more advantageous for the Neolithic mode of life.

Recent dating of the basal sand layer of Osan-ri indicates that it should have been formed during the final two thousand years of the Pleistocene. In the early 1980s, small-scale testings revealed a total of 11 dwellings and 7 outdoor hearths, and there must be at least several times more of them throughout the whole site area.

Figure 3.14 At Sinam-ri in Ulsan, residues and debris from the processing of marine resources had been accumulated for a long time. At the place of pit-house or storage facility, a number of hearths as the focus of subsistence activity had been formed densely within a limited area, hinting at the frequent visit to the place. Large stone knives found here might have been used to dismember the carcass of whale (cf. Figure 3.23). Two knives shown here are c. 44 and 7cm long, respectively. Here, clay pots much larger than usual Neolithic wares might have been used as boiling vessels to process the blubber. © National Research Institute of Cultural Heritage

While the archaeological evidence is found within sandy layers prone to stratigraphic reversals, its age has been said to be 8,000 BP because the pottery looks similar to those assigned to that date in North Korea. But C-14 dates lie between >7,000 and 6,000 BP. Nevertheless, it might be that the initial occupation indeed

Figure 3.15 At Cheoltong-ri on the east coast, Neolithic pit-houses were revealed on top of a low hill, forming a single column of six or seven small, square pit-houses along the ridge. © National Research Institute of Cultural Heritage

had occurred earlier, in the early days of the Holocene Optimum when the wind-blown sands were stabilized to allow the development of vegetation covering.

All of the dwelling structures revealed at Osan-ri are almost identical with a diameter of about 6m and a stone-lined hearth in the middle [**Figures 3.12**]. The pottery is flat-bottomed with appliqué decoration on the surface, and stone tools mainly consist of fishing and hunting gear. Almost identical dwellings as well as pottery and stone tools are found at other sites dotting the east coast [**Figures 3.5, 3.16**]. Including Osan-ri, it appears that each of these Neolithic hamlets could not have accommodated perhaps more than 50 inhabitants. The overall population size would not have changed throughout the Early and the Middle Neolithic.

At the same time, the homogeneousness of the material culture might indicate the presence of strong social bonding along the east coast. Solidarity among the coastal inhabitants would have enabled long-distance movement of rare raw materials such as obsidian [cf. **Figure 3.16**]. Baekdusan obsidian is found in larger quantities at Neolithic sites of the east coast than Palaeolithic localities. For example, at Osan-ri a large chunk of obsidian encased in a basaltic rhyolite layer and weighing over 5kg was found. To bring it from the source would not have been conceivable without some social engagement between the groups.

Incidentally, the distribution of both Baekdusan and the Kyushu obsidian appears more limited than the previous period. The former is rarely found in the area west of the Taebaek Mountains and reported mainly along the east coast all the way down to the south coast. The latter is seen mainly along the south coast so that their distribution overlaps in the southeastern coastal area. Continuous interaction between the south coast and northern Kyushu is demonstrated at many sites on both sides of the Korea Strait by the artifacts from the other side [e.g., **Figure 3.17**].

While the foraging lifeway of the Initial and Early Neolithic had been kept into the Middle Neolithic, evidence of cultivation began to appear together with Comb-Patterned Pottery. For a Middle Neolithic site with such evidence, the most frequently quoted one is Amsa-dong on the Han River. It is the first Neolithic site

Figure 3.16 Pottery and lithic assemblage from the site of Munam-ri. The assemblage composition is typical for the sites on the east coast. Notice pottery is of different sizes and shapes. Among the stone tools, there is seen a chunk of obsidian and a few flakes in the upper left corner. As is the case for other sites, there are found a number of stone stems for fishhooks. © National Research Institute of Cultural Heritage

known in Korea after flooding exposed the deposit in 1925. From repeated fieldwork conducted here, more than 30 pit-houses and other features are known to have been excavated. Unfortunately, early works until the 1960s are poorly documented and the available information is from the 1970s and 80s.

Like those known at Unseo-dong and Daeneung-ri, pit-houses here are semi-square in plan with rounded corners. The largest one is 7.9m long and 6.6m wide but the rest are less than 6 by 6m in size. Overlapping of pit-houses suggests that the site had been occupied somewhat intensively. In the space between the pit-houses were found outdoor hearths, storage pits and possible remnants of a pottery kiln.

Stone tools found here include hoes, ploughs, axes, knives and sets of grinding stones, which traditionally have been regarded as evidence of cultivation. Thus, Amsa-dong has been regarded as a site of a Neolithic 'farming community' along with some sites in North Korea where similar tools and charred grains were excavated. However, as much as we cannot tell how large and complex these sites really are and how intensively they had been occupied, there is no real evidence demonstrating the importance of agriculture for the inhabitants. It seems that these sites are not larger than Unseo-dong or Daeneung-ri in terms of the number of pit-houses. At both of these and other relatively large sites, evidence is weak at best that people depended upon ground crops. As shall be discussed later, it seems that incipient agriculture, whether that be agroforestry, swidden or shifting cultivation, had not spread before 5,000 BP at best. The mode of subsistence would not have allowed a long-term occupation of most, if not all, of the places.

Except the sites just mentioned, the Middle Neolithic settlement sites are made of a handful of pit-houses. Among them is the site of Songjuk-ri in Gimcheon where a small Neolithic community was revealed made of 10 pit-houses of usual size and shape, 15 outdoor hearths, a 'factory' for lithic production and a rudimentary kiln. The site provides an impression that it was a small community perhaps occupied by several dozens of people who might have exploited the rich floodplain soil to cultivate crops. However, it is an exceptional case, and even here the real

Figure 3.17 A Jomon pottery and obsidian fragments from northern Kyushu found at a shell midden in Ando off the south coast. Artifacts of Japanese origin are frequently encountered along the south coast. © National Research Institute of Cultural Heritage (obsidian)

importance of cultivation is not clear at all.

It needs to be remembered that many other sites are even smaller than Songjuk-ri. Sites found on tops of hills or slopes as one or several isolated pit-houses provide a picture far from communities relying on cultivation. The image of small and mobile bands for the Neolithic social groups is strengthened by the distribution of outdoor hearths and other limited activity sites. As seen in **Figure 3.13**, an outdoor hearth is a heap of rock fragments or cobbles piled within round and shallow pit with evidence of firing. Occasionally, potsherds or fragments of stone tool are found within them but nothing else. They are distributed among the pit-houses or form sites of their own especially in the coastal environment, suggesting repeated seasonal visit to the spot. Residue and remnant fatty acid left on the rock fragments demonstrate that they were indeed used for cooking so that those found nearby the sea were for cooking fish and shells. Some outdoor hearths found as single, isolated feature at unusual locations such as a steep hill slope deep inland were perhaps left by hungry foraging parties who were in search of foodstuffs.

A site on the east coast, Cheoltong-ri, provides a picture of the 'village' of such foragers [**Figure 3.15**]. Sitting on top of a low coastal hill, pottery typology puts its date to 5,000 BP or slightly after. The most interesting thing about the site is its strategic location and the arrangement of the pit-houses. Here, small square pit-houses are aligned to form a shallow arc at a vantage point to watch over the coastal plain. The place would not have been chosen were the inhabitants interested in cultivating crops. Among the pit-houses, the largest one measures 5 by 5m in size and smaller ones are less than 3m on each side. Such difference in size is common, making one wonder about the possible functional differences between the large and the small ones. Most of the pit-houses are empty of artifacts except some fragments of pottery. A total of six small stone axes were found in one and eleven stone net-sinkers and sixteen pebbles were recovered from another pit-house. The pebbles might have been procured to make net-sinkers. In all, it seems that the site was left by a small group of foragers who had occupied the place for a while perhaps using it as a base camp.

To summarize, despite the presence of a few inland sites with possible evidence of incipient agriculture, the image of Neolithic society is far from prosperous farming villages with hundreds of inhabitants busy with their own works. There are no large communal structures as seen among the contemporary Jomon sites in Japan nor such complex settlement sites as those of Chinese Neolithic, not to mention the megalithic builders of Europe or the early farmers of the Near East. Most sites consist of a few small pit-houses, each barely large enough to accommodate a few individuals. There can be found no hint of division of labor according to sex, age or class. If there were social and religious or any other organized activities, evidence is non-existing. From the general state of the structural remains and the contents

Figure 3.18 In arguing for the Neolithic agriculture, the most important evidence has been the stone implements which could have been used for digging earth or grinding grains. Nevertheless, they could also be used for purposes other than cultivation or processing grains. 'Digging stones' shown here are from Hopyeong-dong in Namyangju, an inland site to the east of Seoul. Grinding stones are from Gosan-ri in Jejudo and Bonggil-ri in Gyeongju on the east coast. The latter is shown with other stone implements. At these places, they might have been used for grinding wild resources rather than processing cultivated crops. © National Museum of Korea (digging stone); National Research Institute of Cultural Heritage (grinding stones)

of artifacts retrieved, it seems difficult to say that the settlement sites were meant for long-term occupation.

Population and Burials

Despite some variation in the shape and the size of pit-houses and settlement sites, little had changed in the mode of life throughout the period. As mentioned, the picture of the Neolithic society we can get from the evidence is an image of scattered and isolated hamlets. Sites are usually made of a few small pit-houses and other features to satisfy the most basic necessities for everyday life. Individual communities were probably too small in their population size to engage in complex social activities. Their inhabitants were semi-settled but still mobile foragers, who depended on hunting, gathering, collecting, fishing and what little they might have harvested from swidden agriculture, if there were any. To borrow an anthropological term, they can be properly labelled as a band society, small in size and fluid in organization.

For the population size, dwelling structures suggest that it could not exceed a couple of hundred even for large communities. To take the number of pit-houses as a standard, we may say that sites which had 15 or more form the top-tier, and less than twenty such sites are known including partially excavated ones. The next tier consists of such sites as Songjuk-ri or Cheoltong-ri, which were made of 6 to

15 pit-houses. They do not exceed 50 sites. The rest of the sites are made of 1 to 5 pit-houses, and these small 'villages' make more than half of the total. Sites of the last group could have accommodated individuals anywhere between several to a couple of dozen.

As these sites had been made over a period of at least 4,000 years, they would represent some 200 generations. Then, the order of 10^4 may be a scale too great to estimate the population size. Assuming that distribution of the settlement size as described above had been maintained throughout the whole Neolithic, simple mathematics says that the population size at any given time should have remained at several thousand at best even with a generous allowance for the survival rate of archaeological sites.

Physical remains of the Neolithic inhabitants are rare. Burials are found in the form of simple pit or jar burials. Most of them are known from shell-mounds where bones could have been preserved in the environment rich with calcium carbonate. Until the discovery of 48 and 15 burials in the islands of Gadeokdo and Yeondaedo, both off the south coast, the total number of identifiable skeletal remains known in South Korea had barely exceeded 10. Their stature appears

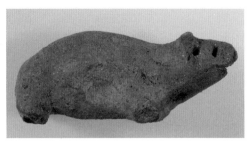
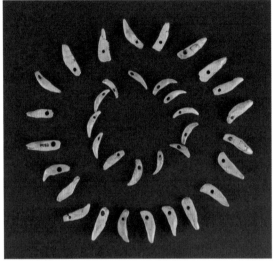

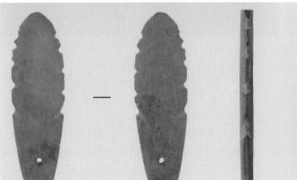

Figure 3.20 Examples of non-utilitarian objects from various Neolithic sites. A small (3.6cm) clay female torso from the site of Sinam-ri in Ulsan is the only one of its kind ever known in the prehistoric context in Korea. Two clay animal figurines might represent wild boars. They are from Yokjido and Bibong-ri. 'Anklet' and 'earring' made of animal teeth are from Yeondaedo and Dongsam-dong (© National Museum of Korea). Sometimes polished stone objects are found at both burials and settlement sites which might be amulet, talisman or token of identity. The six small well-polished ones are from the burials shown in Figure 3.19 (© National Research Institute of Cultural Heritage). The three flat items made of stone were retrieved at Daeneung-ri in Paju (© Gyeonggi Ceramic Museum).

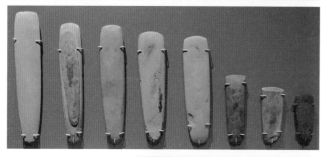

to remain within the range of modern Koreans. In average, Gadeokdo males were about 158cm tall and females around 147cm. The average height of the Yeondaedo males turns out to be 164cm [**Figure 3.19**]. Also, a male from the burial at Ando, another island off the south coast, was 165cm in height while his female partner was 160cm tall. Interestingly, these two individuals, as well as another female from Yeondaedo, had suffered from osteoma of the external auditory canal, a diver's disease caused by repeated deep diving without protection. Perhaps they were skilled divers as today's *Haenyeo*(해녀), the diving women of Jejudo, who can easily dive as deep as 30m without any protective measures. In any case, it is further evidence indicating the importance of foraging marine resources.

Art objects and personal decorations are also rare. From settlement sites, there are known simple animal and human clay figurines, stone 'amulets' and simple line drawings made on the surface of pottery. The rest are personal adornments from the burials such as arm and foot bracelets, earrings, necklaces, etc., made of shell, animal teeth, stone and jade [**Figure 3.20**]. Among the burials goods, unusually elongated stone 'axes' are known from Gyodong in Chuncheon and Hupo in Uljin on the east coast [**Figure 3.5**, Site **29** and **e**].

The discovery made at Hupo is especially unique [**Figure 3.21**]. Here, the jumbled mix of human bones found within a pit measuring 4.5 by 3.5m represents the secondary burial of more than 40 individuals. Given the estimate of the population size mentioned earlier, one cannot but wonder who they were and why they were reburied together. Some 180 pieces of elongated axe-like implements were lain on top of the burial. Most of them look like tools of no ordinary utilitarian value and perhaps made for ritualistic purposes. While purely

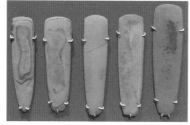

Figure 3.21 The burial site of Hupo at the time of discovery (© National Museum of Korea). Part of the stone tools are on display at the Gyeongju National Museum.

speculative, if allowed, one may wonder whether they were musical instruments.

From the distribution of sites, it seems that the importance of the coastal environment had never been diminished throughout the whole Neolithic period. In comparison, there are markedly fewer inland localities despite the introduction of ground crops around the beginning of the Middle Neolithic.

Palynological data from Jejudo indicate that climatic conditions were somewhat cooler when pottery appeared at Gosan-ri. Between 9,400 and 8,100 BP, roughly corresponding to the period between the Bond Event 6 and 5, vegetation was dominated by species of deciduous broadleaved forest mixed with some coniferous species, thus, somewhat like the vegetation composition of Zone B and C of northern Korea today [**Figure 1.3**]. It might be that the similarities shown in the Gosan-ri assemblage to the sites in the Russian Far East could have been possible under such cooler climatic conditions. Climate had become warmer in the mid-Holocene optimum. Thus, after 8,100 BP, temperate deciduous forest mixed with evergreen broadleaved species appeared so that the sub-tropical *Camellia-Magnolia* flora of the island began to be formed roughly 8,000 years ago. As already discussed, the change in the vegetation around this time coincides reasonably well with the timing of the replacement of Gosan-ri Style Pottery with Appliqué-Decorated Pottery. At many sites in the mainland deemed as the Early Neolithic, fishing gear such as net sinkers are seen frequently over arrowheads, implying a possible change in the mode of subsistence economy under warmer conditions of the mid-Holocene optimum.

It might be that the appearance of settlement sites along the east coast around 8,000 BP had something to do with warming conditions which had provided opportunity to exploit marine resources. Despite the poor survival of physical evidence of natural resources actually exploited, archaeological assemblages suggest the Neolithic coastal dwellers had exploited the same kind of resources. Especially, composite fishhooks of same design and size are found all the way from the Russian Maritime Region down to the south coast [**Figures 3.16, 3.22**].

Exploitation of marine resources is best exemplified at such sites as Jukbyeon-ri in Uljin and other east coastal localities further south such as Sejuk, Hwangseong-dong and Sinam-ri in Ulsan [**Figures 3.5, 3.14**]. These sites are with dates older than 7,000 BP, and have produced organic materials including remains of various terrestrial animals and plants. For marine resources, remains of a variety of fish and shells as well as whale and sea lion were found. Residue analysis of the inner surface of pottery identified carbonized fish fat. Such mixed exploitation of marine and terrestrial resources should have been practiced wherever possible.

At Jukbyeon-ri, some fragments of a canoe and an oar made of camphor tree (*Lauraceae* sp.), a sub-tropical plant growing only along the southern coast of Jejudo today, were preserved in a marsh deposit, an indication that the site was formed under much warmer conditions. At Sejuk, the same is indicated by the discovery of pieces of coral. Like camphor, corals grow only off the southern coast of Jejudo. Interestingly, remains of coral were also found at a site on the opposite side of the peninsula at almost the same latitude. This Gado shell midden may be slightly younger than Sejuk with uncalibrated dates around 5,000 BP. Then, we may

Figure 3.22 Exploitation of aquatic resources were important for the Neolithic people. Composite fishhooks and bone harpoons are found widely along the east and south coast. At Bibong-ri in Changnyeong, remains of two dug-out canoes were discovered. Remains of the better preserved one is shown here. The remaining length is about 310cm with a width of 60cm. Made out of a pine tree, its original length should be more than 4m at least, matching the size of some boats depicted in the engravings at Bangudae (cf. Figure 3.23). © National Research Institute of Cultural Heritage

assume that significantly warmer conditions had prevailed during the Holocene optima.

The importance of hunting whale and other marine mammals is demonstrated by their bones, some of which are found with projectile points driven into them [**Figure 3.23**]. Although its exact age is unclear yet, scenes of prehistoric whaling are vividly depicted at the famous rock-engraving site of Bangudae (Ban-gu-dae) which lies about 20km upstream from the coastal sites in Ulsan along the channel of Taehwagang. Here, in addition to various terrestrial animals, whales, dolphins, turtles and, possibly, a sea lion can be seen. As many as 58 whales of different kinds can be counted, some depicted as harpooned or chased by boats with five to about 20 people on board. In one case, a line is connecting a boat to a whale, depicting a harpooned whale and chasing boat. Given the generally small size of individual settlements, whaling should have been an organized activity which required the mobilization of more than one 'village'.

Compared to the East Sea, the Yellow Sea is shallow and tidal flats are extremely well developed at many places. While evidence of sea mammal hunting is not clear, the importance of marine resources is demonstrated by many shell middens dotting the coastline. Although they are dated generally younger than the sites of the east coast, this does not mean that the west coast was not occupied before this time. Older sites might have been inundated or eroded away. It is a familiar scene today that people collecting a variety of infauna on the exposed mud flat, which should have been the case for the Neolithic as well. For the south coast, many shell middens are found especially in its eastern part, which began to be formed from the Early Neolithic at such places as Dongsam-dong. Along with others nearby, this particular site represents the southern end of the distribution of the east coastal mode of adaptation.

Figure 3.23 Whaling during the Neolithic is demonstrated by harpooned whale bones. At Hwangseong-dong in Ulsan, bones of whales and other marine mammals were recovered (top). A whale scapula and a vertebra pierced by harpoon made of deer bone are shown as well as a humerus with a number of cut-marks on the surface (© Ulsan Museum; Ulsan Petroglyph Museum of Bangudae [middle]). Whales and scenes of whaling are vividly engraved on a smooth surface at the nearby site of Bangudae. Parts of the scenes shown here are photographed from the original ink-rubbing kept at the Seoul National University Museum. Not surprisingly, the Ulsan area has been known as a traditional whaling center with many large and small whaling ports. A beacon on the pier of the small harbor town of Jeongja-ri in the northern part of Ulsan reminds visitors the bygone days of whaling, which is also remembered by many other sculptures dotting the coastline.

As mentioned, evidence of the Early Neolithic is scarce for the inland areas. Putting those in North Korea aside, there is hardly any site older than 6,000 BP known in the area 30 to 40km or more away from the coast. In the late 1950s, with excavation of such sites as Gungsan and Jitap-ri in the north [**Figure 3.5**, Site **a** and **6**], it was suggested that Comb-Patterned Pottery and cultivation of ground crops had appeared in the Daedong River basin some 8,000 years ago. However, it is now regarded in South Korea that 8,000 BP is too early for their appearance. Instead,

6,000 BP is the generally accepted date as mentioned.

Agriculture probably began in the form of swidden or shifting cultivation of herbaceous ground crops, and relied on the slash-and-burn method even in the most favorable conditions. It is believed that agriculture in whatever form was not indigenously developed but introduced from northeast China where foxtail millet was already cultivated before 8,000 BP at the beginning of the Holocene, if not earlier. Given the geography, there is nothing surprising about its introduction to Korea at around 6,000 BP. As grains are often found with stone tools some of which look similar to those in China, it could be that plants, tools and knowledge of cultivation had been spread as a technological set, and the possibility of the migration of millet farmers cannot be excluded. In that regard, it is interesting that the timing coincides with the Bond Even 4 when the Neolithic cultures of China were in distress. In any case, however, the foraging way of life did not change a lot even after the introduction of cereal cultivation.

Analysis of fish and shellfish species found in the Middle Neolithic shell-mounds demonstrates some degree of logistic movement of people in the western coastal region. That is, the amount of different seasonal species included in the deposit varies from shell mound to shell mound. It seems to suggest that people moved around to different places from season to season in expectation of optimal return. It is not certain, however, how far, how many and how often people had moved about although it might have been a movement within certain boundaries such as seasonal exploitation of different places within an island or between nearby localities. There once appeared a hypothesis of seasonal long-distance movement from such inland sites as Amsa-dong to the west coast in order to exploit shellfish and other seasonal resources. However, it is seldom mentioned now as there is no real evidence. Whatever the movement pattern might have been, shell mound and outdoor hearth sites in the west coastal region indicate that the importance of marine resources had not diminished during the Middle Neolithic.

Meanwhile, cultivation had spread quickly once introduced. Although the total number of sites with evidence of cultivation is about a dozen or so, charred grains as well as potsherds with their impressions on the surface are found by 4,500 BP at both inland localities such as Amsa-dong and such coastal localities as Dong-sam-dong and Munam-ri [**Figure 3.24**]. Appearance of inland settlements with evidence of cultivation such as Songjuk-ri seems to suggest that attempts were made to exploit ecological niches for cultivation. However, these new inland sites are not the first tier settlements in terms of the number of pit-houses, in other words, population size. It might be that the productivity of cultivation was far below the level required to support a larger group.

Among the cultivated plants, foxtail millet (*Setaria italica* ssp. *Italica*) is most important along with its sister crops broomcorn (proso or common millet; *Panicum miliaceum*) and sorghum (*Sorghum bicolor*). Also, there are occasionally found remains and impressions of barnyard millet (*Echinochloa crus-galli* var. *frumentacea*), bean, kidney bean, wheat and barley. It was once claimed that rice was cultivated during the Neolithic or even at the end of the Pleistocene, but this view has been generally discredited. Presence of Neolithic and pre-Neolithic domesticated rice has been claimed with grains which are not free from contextual problems. As

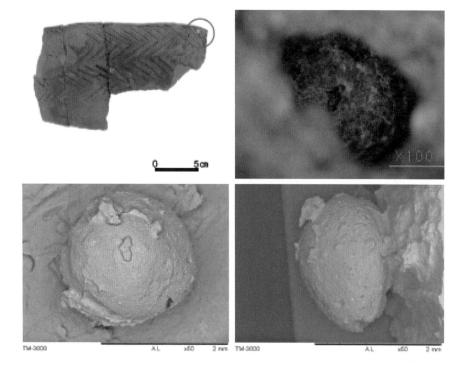

Figure 3.24 Impression of a grain of *Panicum miliaceum* on a potsherd retrieved from Munam-ri. © National Research Institute of Cultural Heritage

dates were obtained not directly from these grains, there is no compelling reason to accept such claims at their face value because of the high probability of vertical movement and stratigraphic dislocation of the grains concerned. The credibility problem of the evidence is not limited to rice alone. By the same token, the context of discovery is not entirely clear for evidence from the sites of Gungsan, Jitap-ri and Namgyeong in North Korea. Therefore, it may be questioned whether all of the domesticates listed above were actually grown during the Neolithic.

This means that many accept only foxtail millet, broomcorn, sorghum and barnyard millet as the Neolithic cultigens. But, as mentioned, their contribution to the diet appears to be limited, merely supplementing wild resources. The limited role of cultivation may have something to do with the small population size which did not allow intensive labor input required for reliable agricultural production. Or, productivity might have been so low unless plants were cultivated in exceptionally rich soil, thus, not worth to pursue at most places.

For diet, most of the necessary amount of carbohydrate should have come from various hard-seeded fruits such as chestnut, wild walnut and, especially, acorn. In Korea, edible acorns are obtained from six species of oak (*Quercus*) which are found virtually everywhere, and the acorn starch cake, *Dotori Muk*(도토리묵), is a common dish in traditional cuisine. As the Neolithic landscape had been covered by temperate deciduous forest, acorn should have been easily and plentifully available. Because of the high content of tannin acid, acorns need to be soaked and dried before grounded into powder to extract starch, and such processing is inferred from the state of acorns or their shells found at many sites. Importance of acorn and oak tree is well seen at many sites where storage pits were filled with acorns [**Figure 3.25**]. As a demonstration of the importance of acorn and other wild resources over cultivated cereals, results of the stable isotope analysis conducted at the site of Gonam-ri in Tae-an on the west coast shows that millet and sorghum, which are C4 plants, were not as important as C3 plants such as acorns and other nuts even during the late Middle Neolithic. Amino acid analysis of some outdoor hearths also indicates that they were used to process C3 plants. Although there is no direct proof of Neolithic aboriculture, it might be that oak and other nut-bearing trees had been managed carefully as known in Jomon Japan.

If the main source of carbohydrates was natural plants including acorns and other nuts, much of the fat and protein should have come from wild animals as indicated by various faunal remains preserved in shell-mounds. Despite the discovery of millet grains and other plant remains, carbon and nitrogen isotope analysis of the human bones recovered at Dongsam-dong shell-mound suggests fish and other marine animals were more important for the diet. Interestingly, some sea lion tibia bones from Dongsam-dong show a number of cut-marks near the distal end. At the same time, the C-N isotope ratio of the individuals from the Janghang shell-mound in Gadeokdo [**Figure 3.19**] suggests that sea lion (*Zalophulus californianus*) might have been important. Meanwhile, high strontium and zinc content in the bones of the Yeondaedo individuals, including those who had suffered from osteoma of external auditory canal, suggests importance of both plants and fish and shellfish.

For marine animal resources exploited, remains of whales, dolphins, sea lions and fur seals (*Callorhinus Ursinus*) have been found. For shellfish, the most commonly seen are oyster (*Crassostrea gigas*), mussel (*Mytirus corsus*), top shell (*Chlorostoma* sp.), limpet (*Lottia* sp.), turban shell (*Batillus cornutus*), creeper (*Batillaria multiformis*), worm shell (*Serpuorbis imbricatus*), murex shell (*Reisha bronni*) and venus clam (*Tapes philippinarum*), among others. Also, although it is certain that there is no chance to find the evidence, a lot of subsistence activities should have been made on the vast mud flats developed along the west and southwest coast. It must be that the mud-loving species of the family Octopodidae, such as long-armed octopus (*poulpe*; *Octopus vairabilit*) and webfoot octopus (*poulpe ocellé*; *Octopus ocellatus*), should have contributed a lot to the diet as is the case today.

Figure 3.25 Remains of acorns are often found at Neolithic sites. Photos show a cache of acorns revealed at Yulha-ri in Gimhae and those retrieved from Bibong-ri. © National Research Institute of Cultural Heritage; National Museum of Korea

For fish, there are shark (*Triakis skyllia*; Squalidae; Laminidae), ray (Dasyatidae), gray mullet (*Mugi cephalus*), mullet (*Liza haematochila*), bass (*Lateolabrax japonicas*), sea-bass (*Epinephelus bruneus*), longtooth grouper (*E. septemfasciatus*), red sea-bream (*Pagrus major*), black sea-bream (*Acanntopagrus schlegeli*), opaleye (*Semicossyphus reticulatus*), yellowtail (*Seriola quinqueradiata*), tuna (*Thunnus* sp.), cavally (*Scomber* sp.), rockfish (*Sebastes* sp.), scorpion fish (*Scomberomorus* sp.), Japanese mackerel (*Scomberomorus niphonius*) and blow fish (*Fugu* sp.). Some of the fish are large migratory species moving with the warm Kuroshio current and require as much boating skills to catch as for whaling.

Terrestrial animals are also frequently found along with bird bones. Species which might have contributed a lot to the diet include deer (*Cervus nippon*), roe deer (*Capreolus capreolus*), water deer (*Hydropotes inermis*) and wild boar (*Sus scorfa*). They continued to be important game animals until modern days. Clay figurines and the line drawings left on pottery seem to suggest that deer and wild boar were particularly important. Teeth and scapula of wild boar and antlers were sometimes worked into tools and ornaments [**Figure 3.20**]. For the other species, bones of scavengers and carnivores are also found, including raccoon, badger, tiger, bear and fox. Also, remains of domesticated dog (*Canis familiaris*) appear in the archaeological record of the Middle Neolithic next to these wild animals. Other than dogs, there is no other evidence of domesticated animals or animal husbandry, befitting to the foraging mode of subsistence which requires a high degree of mobility.

Ending of the Era

From sometime after 4,500 BP on, the archaeological record shows some interesting but baffling changes. Although we can tell little about the situation in North Korea, settlement sites disappeared so that there is hardly any of them found for the Final Neolithic. At the same time, most of the data related to the final days of the Neolithic are confined to the southeastern corner of the country. Such change led many to think that the stability of the Neolithic mode of life had been suddenly disrupted. Ultimately, no 'village' for the final few centuries of the Neolithic has been found. Although many Neolithic settlement sites might represent seasonal or temporary occupation, they anyhow should have provided a 'home base', regardless of how meager and fleeting they might be. However, no such site is known for the Final Neolithic and only 'limited activity sites' are found represented by a few thin shell middens, outdoor hearths or short-term camp sites. If there is anything similar to the settlement site, only a few tiny rock-shelters or shallow caves are found which look more like an overnight stopping place for several individuals. Distribution and spatial patterning of the sites seem to suggest that the small population had been permanently scattered or become even smaller by this time. It is around 1500 BCE that new settlements began to appear with new pottery, with which the Bronze Age began.

With scarcity of data, the ending of the Neolithic is only obscure. While fragmentary evidence must mean that some important change had occurred, we are clueless about what that would be. As far as one can glean from the published accounts, there was no abrupt change in pottery and other aspects of material culture from 5,000 BP except some minor local variations. And, on the west coast where conditions were met, the foraging mode of subsistence smoothly continued into the Bronze Age. The ending of the Neolithic might have been a quiet and slow decline of the foraging way of life due to a reason or reasons unknown.

In the neighboring northeastern provinces of China, marked assimilation to the culture of central China is observed as exemplified by the disappearance of Incised Pattern Pottery resembling Comb-Patterned Pottery. They were replaced by those made in the style of central China. In the Russian Maritime Region, the so-called Shell Mound Culture continued with little change. Thus, this sudden decline and disappearance of the archaeological record is somewhat unique to Korea. Any number of possible explanations may be suggested but nothing is certain. Potential candidates may include population failure by some unknown reasons, climatic deterioration, adoption of a different subsistence strategy or social organization to respond to changes in ecological conditions, or all of the above. If, as mentioned earlier, the last few hundred years of the Korean Neolithic were the period of poor climatic conditions roughly coinciding with the Bond Event 3 and the general collapse of the Neolithic cultures in central China, perhaps it is such environmental change that had caused such decline as it would not have allowed the maintenance of the foraging way of life. Of course, in order to draw any conclusion about the causal relationship between climatic change and the decline of the Neolithic, we need to wait for the accumulation of more detailed and well-dated palaeo-climatic and chronometric data.

CHAPTER 4

BRONZE DAGGERS AND DOLMEN BUILDERS

Bronze Age in Two Koreas

Poor visibility of the archaeological record had improved a lot in the second half of the second millennium BCE as settlement sites began to pop up here and there, marking the beginning of the Bronze Age. It is generally acknowledged that Gojoseon, the first Korean state mentioned in historical records, was established during the Bronze Age most probably in Liaodong, the region east of the Liao River in the Liaoning province of China which abuts the Korean Peninsula. However, descriptions of its society and culture are quite fragmentary so that it is difficult to determine when and where it first appeared. Therefore, much has been asked of archaeology but archaeological information so far does not provide clear answers.

Under the Japanese occupation, the presence of the Bronze Age was denied and Koreans were forced to accept racial prejudices and biased opinions about their own past. In their fight against the colonial education, intellectuals had heavily relied upon cultural evolutionism of the 19th century, especially the Engelsian notion of staged social change, which convinced them that it was critical to prove that Korea had also undergone the 'normal course of historical development'. In other words, it was felt urgent to demonstrate that the prehistory of Korea also had the stages of Palaeolithic, Neolithic and Bronze Age. Especially, to verify the presence of the Bronze Age was felt most important as the period was regarded as the stepping stone from prehistory to history. This attitude has been maintained in both Koreas after the division.

In South Korea, progress in research had been slow due to the lack of trained researchers so that it took almost 30 years to recognize the period officially. In comparison, as North Korea adopted the Soviet system, archaeological research equipped with the Marxist paradigm eagerly sought the Bronze Age almost immediately after liberation. As a result, discovery of a Bronze Age site was announced in 1949 at a shell midden on an island off the east coast, and the Bronze Age was firmly written on the chronological table with more discoveries made in the 1950s.

Figure 4.1 Bipa-shaped Bronze Daggers, spears and an axe of the Bronze Age. Unlike those found in the neighboring region of China, Bipa-shaped daggers found in Korea usually have a notch at the end of the stem (after The Korean Archaeological Society 2010, Figure 62).

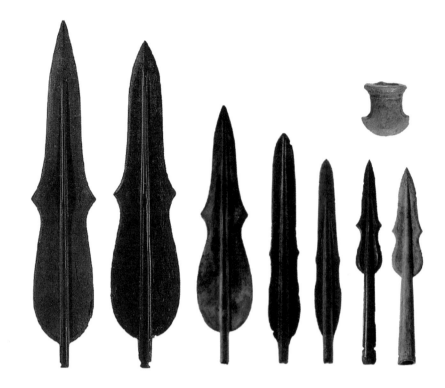

Indeed, it is fair to say that the developments made in the north had led the prehistoric archaeology of Korea for a couple of decades.

In North Korea, issues surrounding the Bronze Age and Gojoseon had been hotly debated from the late 1950s. About the Bronze Age, the North Korean opinion until the 1980s regarded that Korea and the adjoining region of northeastern China had shared basically the same culture between 2000 and 500 BCE. The whole area was divided into four sub-culture areas, each with its own cultural sequence. The most important was the Lower Amnok Basin-Liaodong Peninsula. Unlike the other three, the Bronze Age was defined in this sub-area to last until 1000 BCE, which was followed by the Gojoseon Period from 1000 BCE. It is said so because Gojoseon was defined archaeologically by the presence of the Bipa-shaped Bronze Dagger [**Figure 4.1**] and the Misong-ri Type Pottery [**Figure 4.2, C**]. The name of the dagger indicates that its shape resembles a string instrument, Bipa. Their unique shape clearly contrasts with contemporary daggers of China, which were cast as a whole piece from the tip to the hilt with straight sides. Misong-ri Type Pottery is also unique in shape, which was named after the site of its discovery in 1959.

As a chronological term, the Gojoseon Period is not yet recognized in South Korea. Nevertheless, the major point of the conclusions made in North Korea in the 1960s and the early 1970s, namely, the importance of the Bipa-shaped Bronze Dagger and its distribution for defining the Bronze Age, has been agreeable to South Korean researchers. Then, it may be said that the main difference in the opinion about the Bronze Age and Gojoseon between the two sides is chiefly about where to set the temporal boundaries of the period during the second and the first millennium BCE in addition to some technical issues such as the age estimate of individual sites and assemblages.

However, the North Korean notion of the Bronze Age and Gojoseon had suddenly changed in a bizarre way in the early 1990s, which is simply impossible to reconcile. The dramatic change is inextricably related to the efforts of deifying the leader of the regime and his family. In 1992, North Korean authorities announced the discovery of the physical remains of Dangun (Dan-gun) and his spouse, who legend says founded Gojoseon in 2333 BCE. Like in South Korea, North Korea until this time had treated him as a mere mythical figure. However, with the announcement, his godly status was degraded to a mere mortal, a real man of flesh and blood, who had a wife and six male descendants.

It was soon followed by another declaration that Gojoseon was established around 3000 BCE in Pyeongyang, thus, the preceeding Bronze Age was said to belong to the 4th millennium BCE. Naturally, the Bipa-shaped Bronze Dagger as the representative artifact of Gojoseon had to appear at 3000 BCE, some two thousand years before what had been said until this time. Moreover, it was also declared that Gojoseon had independently invented iron metallurgy, astronomy, a writing system, etc. Therefore, its level of cultural sophistication was even higher than ancient Mesopotamia, Egypt, China and India, making it one of the five, not four, ancient civilizations of the world. This alleged civilization was christened the Daedonggang Culture, following the name of the river running through the city. But of course not a single shred of reliable evidence was provided to support all these claims. Since then, North Korean literatures have been merely repeating the absurd argument. Sadly, archaeology as an academic discipline has vanished completely.

In South Korea, when the Bronze Age was first acknowledged in the early 1970s, its beginning was sought around 700 BCE. Over the years, the timeline has been continuously adjusted so that now its beginning is usually set around 1500 BCE despite some disagreements. Regardless of the date, many researchers at least implicitly think that the Bronze Age began with population influx because of the paucity of information for the final years of the Neolithic. Its ending is set around 400 BCE and followed by the Early Iron Age. Despite the introduction of iron, however, many aspects of the material culture had remained the same so that there is an opinion to treat the succeeding period as the final phase of the Bronze Age.

At least in South Korea, the earliest evidence for the Bronze Age is clearly different from the Neolithic. More than anything else, a remarkable change is seen in the distribution of the sites. Not only the number of sites increased a lot, but they are found at locations which were not exploited during the Neolithic. Instead of the coastal environment, the Bronze Age people more often chose to settle at inland localities close to flowing waters. Such difference seems to be related to the changed mode of subsistence as the Bronze Age inhabitants had relied on cultivation rather than foraging natural resources.

At the same time, the early Bronze Age settlements are much larger and individual pit-houses are also much bigger and rectangular in plan. Inside the dwelling, there are one or more hearths, usually along the central axis of the floor and closer to one end, presumably to the opposite side of the entrance. This dug-out hearth is fairly standardized in shape and size with four sides lined by stone slabs or cobbles. In the corner, storage pits were prepared. Around the walls, wooden columns were

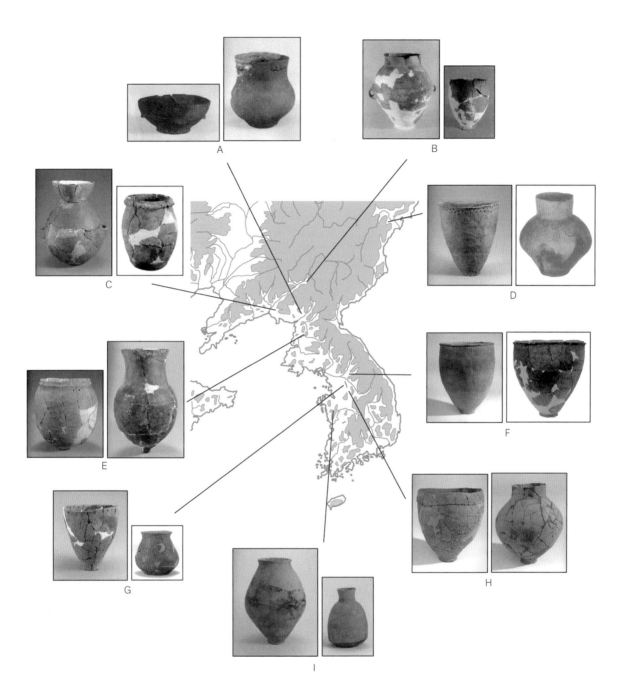

Figure 4.2 Major types of the Bronze Age pottery. They are collectively known as Mumun Pottery. The name refers to the general absence of surface decoration *vis-à-vis* those of the Neolithic period. Despite their simplicity, there are some regional and temporal variation in shape and surface treatment (after The Korean Archaeological Society 2010, Figure 58). A: Sinam-ri Type Pottery; B: Gonggwi-ri Type Pottery; C: Misong-ri Type Pottery; D: Pinhole-lined Pottery and Color-decorated Pottery, E: Top-shaped Pottery; F: Raised-and-Notched Rim Pottery; G: Yeoksam-dong Type Pottery; H: Garak-dong Type Pottery; I: Songguk-ri Type Pottery

erected densely, giving supports for superstructure. Overall, these settlements provide an impression that they were meant for year-round occupation.

In these settlements, people made new kinds of pottery collectively known as Plain Coarse Ware, or Mumun Pottery [**Figure 4.2**]. For everyday life, they relied on stone and wooden tools, using them for cultivation and hunting animals [**Figure 4.3**]. Fishing gear in the form of net sinkers and composite fish hooks are also found along with spindle whorls, needles and other tools for clothing. Despite some variation in the shape and surface treatment, pottery is typically flat-bottomed and lack surface decoration, thus, distinguishable from the Neolithic pottery usually covered with decorations of geometric motifs. In South Korea, researchers tend to equate their appearance with the beginning of the Bronze Age. However, it is not clear when they first appeared in North Korea although many in the south accept the hypothesis of southerly diffusion of Mumun Pottery.

As the idea about the location of Gojoseon implies, common cultural traits of the Bronze Age occur widely across Korea and beyond. Many consider that such sharing of material culture means the formation of a culture area, which can be called the Korean Culture Sphere and was made of the core area of Gojoseon and

Figure 4.3 A Bronze Age tool-kit of wooden and stone tools on display at the National Museum of Korea. There are shown tools for ploughing, wood-working, harvesting and husking, etc. Below are photos of stone knives and net sinkers exposed on the floor of a pit-house at the early Bronze Age settlement site of Auraji. © National Research Institute of Cultural Heritage

its peripheries. Much of the Korean Peninsula, including the whole of South Korea, belonged to the latter. In this southern periphery, the Bronze Age was a period of increasing sociocultural complexity as it moves from egalitarian to stratified society. As evidence of burgeoning inequality among the indigenous groups, daggers and other bronze artifacts are found. Most of them were probably not locally produced but imported and inherited for generations as prestige goods. As social stratification had progressed, large settlement centers emerged in the late years of the period, which is also suggested by change in mortuary practices.

Time and Space - Bronze Age without Bronze?

In South Korea, it is generally agreed that the first bronze evidence so far known in the Korean Peninsula may be represented by a small hand knife reported in 1966 in North Korea at a site in the downstream area of the Amnok River (Yalu in Chinese). This 10cm-long artifact was found together with a round bronze button. They are similar to those reported from a tomb excavated in Yinxu, the famous Shang capital site in central China, as well as a couple of other sites in

Figure 4.4 The early Bronze Age settlement site of Auraji and Pit-house No. 1 where pieces of tubular and discoidal jade and four small pieces of bronze were collected. Each of the bronze pieces is about 1cm in length. The whole site is much larger than the area under excavation seen in the photo. © National Research Institute of Cultural Heritage (scenes of excavation); Cheongju National Museum (beads)

Liaoning and Inner Mongolia, which are dated to the 13th and the 12th century BCE. Therefore, their age is believed to be about 1200 BCE at the maximum.

Bronze artifacts known in South Korea are regarded younger than these two but there are a couple of potentially older, controversial examples. One is discovered from the settlement site of Auraji (A-u-ra-ji) deep in the mountainous region of Gangwon-do. Here, four small ornamental pieces were found in a pit-house [Figure 4.4]. Two C-14 dates suggest their age would lie between c. 1250 and 1050 BCE. But there is a suggestion that they could be as old as 1500 BCE because the associated pottery should be of that age. The other evidence is a bronze dagger retrieved from a pit-house at Hakpyeong-ri in central South Korea [Figure 4.5]. Depending on one's view about the typological change of the bronze daggers, the date for the specimen is regarded either c. 1200 BCE or younger than 1000 BCE.

These two discoveries are rather exceptional not only because of their possible age but also their context of discovery. That is, except these two and another one or two, bronze artifacts of the Bronze Age in South Korea are found as mortuary goods from the burials of the 1st millennium BCE, most of them estimated to be younger than 700 BCE. On the other hand, there are settlement sites with Mumun Pottery which are older than 1000 BCE. Quite a few of them are believedly of the 15th or the 14th century BCE like the case of Auraji. It means that virtually all of the bronze artifacts had appeared after Mumun Pottery.

At the same time, bronze artifacts are rare. Regardless of their type, size, condition of preservation or provenance, those properly reported are less than 100. The number will be even smaller when we count only the pieces with detailed information about their context of discovery. Moreover, there is virtually no direct evidence related to their manufacture. In fact, a large-scale production of bronze artifacts had occurred only after around 400 BCE when iron was known to southern parts of the peninsula. From such background, the beginning of the Bronze Age was, and is, defined by the appearance of Mumun Pottery, not with the evidence of use or manufacture of bronze artifacts. That is, the appearance of Mumun Pottery is taken as the proxy to define the beginning of the period as bronze artifacts are rare. When we take a closer look, such practice appears to be related to the conception of the Korean Culture Sphere [Figure 4.6].

As mentioned, Korean researchers regard that the Korean Culture Sphere during the Bronze Age had been formed across Korea and much of northeast China. As such, many have believed that the whole area can be treated with a single chronological framework. It led to another belief that the appearance of bronze in any place within the sphere means the beginning of the Bronze Age for the rest of the sphere. In that context, during the 1970s and 1980s when information was poor, dates known for the bronze artifacts from the China side of the sphere were important for setting up the date for the Bronze Age in Korea. Incidentally, these dates

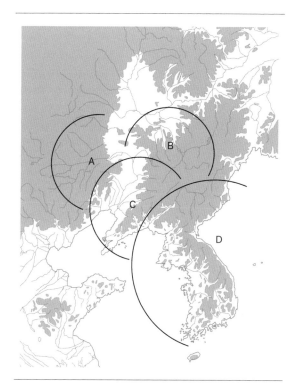

matched closely to those few reported from the settlement sites with Mumun Pottery. Because it was well known that bronze artifacts were found with Mumun Pottery, it was further considered that such dates could be taken as the evidence to define the Bronze Age beginning. While the validity of the reasoning has not been carefully thought over, dates for Mumun Pottery have been continuously updated, pushing back in time the beginning of the Bronze Age.

The date of 1500 BCE may be a correct estimate for the earliest Mumun Pottery in South Korea despite some questions. However, it is not quite so for the bronze artifacts as mentioned. There are only a couple of controversial examples of bronze evidence older than 1000 BCE. Also, there is a fundamental question whether it is reasonable to define the Bronze Age of Korea with evidence outside of the Korean Peninsula. Moreover, 1500 BCE looks like a date too old even for the oldest bronze in the whole Korean Culture Sphere. It seems that the assemblages with the Bipa-shaped Bronze Dagger in China are seldom dated earlier than the 13th century BCE.

Whatever problem there might be, the beginning of the Bronze Age is customarily defined in South Korea with the oldest date for Mumun Pottery, not with bronze artifacts. Pottery is also regarded as the key to define the cultural sequence of the period.

Figure 4.6 The Korean Culture Sphere of the Bronze Age as defined with the distribution of the Bipa-shaped Bronze Daggers (after The Korean Archaeological Society 2010, Figure 61). From the difference in assemblage composition, four sub-culture areas may be defined. A: Xiajiadian Upper Layer Culture; B: Xiduanshan Culture; C: Liaodong Bipa-shaped Bronze Dagger Culture; D: Korean Peninsula Bipa-shaped Bronze Dagger Culture

Daggers and Dolmens

Polemical issues aside, as mentioned already, many features in the material culture are shared across a large area from the Liaohe basin all the way to the Maritime Region of Russia and the Korean Peninsula during the Bronze Age. The most notable aspect is the occurrence of the Bipa-shaped daggers from burials, with which there was coined the term Bipa-shaped Bronze Dagger Culture Area. The term may be regarded as another expression of the Korean Culture Sphere. This culture area, or sphere, may be divided into four sub-areas on the basis of assemblage composition [**Figure 4.6**]. Definition of the sub-areas is somewhat similar to the above-mentioned North Korean thoughts before the early 1990s. But it is different in that it incorporates a large part of western Liaoning province. Also, the Korean Peninsula and Liaodong are treated separately despite the possibility that the territory of Gojoseon might have included both Liadong and northwestern Korea.

Overall, the appearance of the Bipa-shaped daggers may look similar wherever they are found. However, they are not uniform in size, shape or method of manufacture [cf. **Figure 4.1**]. For example, those found in Korea usually have a notch at the base of the stem to which hilt is attached, which is rare among those known in China. On the other hand, pommels in the shape of a reversed T are common in China but not so in Korea. Such differences may mean localized production of daggers under a common idea about the general shape of the dagger. Their shape had changed through time, and there are two contrasting opinions about the sequence of change. One is that they had become shorter and slimmer with diminished protrusion of the side edges, and the other sees that the opposite had

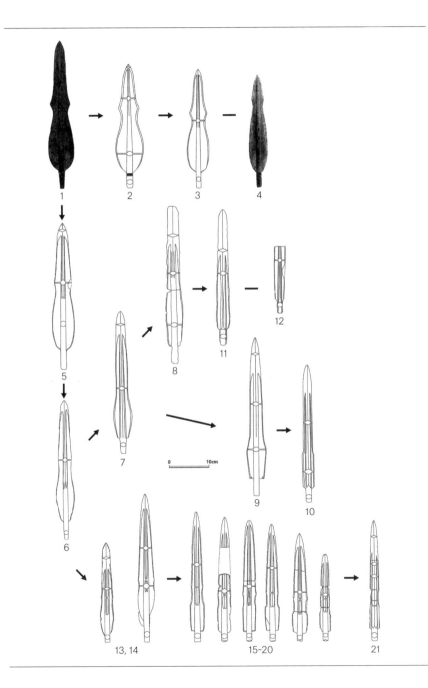

Figure 4.7 A suggestion on the typological change of the bronze daggers in the Korean Culture Sphere (modified after Oh 2020, Figure 3). In this scheme, the 'classic' Bipa-shaped dagger had 'evolved' into two directions; one getting shorter, the other getting narrower. Numbers indicate the order of appearance of each type. The Korean-style Bronze Dagger of the Early Iron Age is viewed as the final product along this line of change. A contrasting opinion differs in that the 'classic' form of the Bipa-shaped Bronze Dagger had evolved out of shorter one so that the direction of morphological change shown in the top row needs to be reversed.

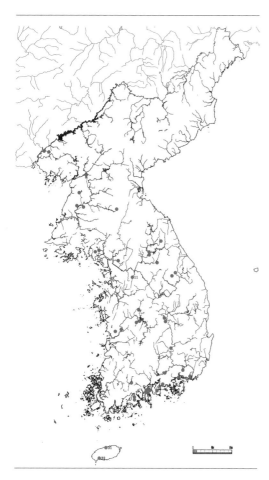

Figure 4.8 Distribution of the Bipa-shaped Bronze Daggers. © Cheongju National Museum

occurred [**Figure 4.7**]. What these two opinions mean is that it is difficult to tell the exact age of the daggers and their age estimate is subject to personal judgment about their appearance and associated artifacts. Nevertheless, it is generally accepted that they had become gradually straighter and slimmer to become the Korean-style Bronze Dagger of the Early Iron Age. The latter was also known as the Sehyeong Donggeom, the Narrow-shaped Bronze Dagger, in consideration of their narrow and slim body.

As of 2020, about 40 pieces of the Bipa-shaped Bronze Daggers are known from 37 sites with varying degrees of contextual information. In addition, there are several more 'collected' items [**Figure 4.8**]. They include both typical ones with markedly protruded sides as well as atypical ones with slightly curved side edges, implying they are not contemporary products. Most of these daggers are dated between 700 and 500 BCE. However, it is not always clear in the writings whether such age estimates mean the timing of its manufacture or its inclusion in the archaeological context. All of those known in South Korea are from dolmens and stone-cists except two. One is the Hakpyeong-ri specimen mentioned already, and the other is from a late Bronze Age site with much reduced curvature of the side.

Given their limited number and the context of discovery, it might be that the bronze daggers were more of a prestige good buried with the owner than a tool for practical purposes. Also, they might have been inherited over generations. On the surface, visible signs of wear and tear are not detected although microscopic examination may tell otherwise. In some burials where organic materials are well preserved, these daggers are surrounded with remnants of wooden sheath varnished with *Ot*(柒), the traditional lacquer of dark vermilion luster obtained from the sap of *Rhus verniciflus*. Although it is an allergic substance to the sensitive, it has been continuously used from the prehistoric times on in East Asia in treating the surface of wood, ceramic, iron, etc. for the enduring protection of the material beneath.

Much of what has been said above may be applied to the other bronze artifacts such as spearheads, arrowheads, fan-shaped socket axes and mirrors. Including fragments, their total number barely exceeds 200. Many were collected before 1945 with poor information about their provenance, and the context of discovery is known for less than one third of this number. They also are found across the Korean Culture Sphere.

Among them, mirrors are next to the daggers in their importance. They are decorated with a simple geometric pattern on the back [**Figure 4.9**]. Decoration had become refined in time so that, by the time iron was spread, mirrors with remarkably fine decoration were made [cf. Chapter 5]. So far, there are known 50+ specimens with cruder decoration which are distributed across Korea, northeast-

Figure 4.9 Mirrors of the Bronze Age. It is believed that they first appeared around 700 BCE somewhere in the Liaodong Peninsula and soon spread widely. There are two, and rarely three, small knobs with holes for attachment, which is different from Chinese mirrors which have only one knob. Also, their backside is decorated with crude geometric motifs, thus, named the Roughly Decorated Mirror, the Jomungyeong (Jo-mun-gyeong), as shown by two examples on the right side. Decoration on the back had gotten refined throughout the Bronze Age and into the Early Iron Age during which there were made mirrors with exquisitely fine decoration. They are named the Jeongmun-gyeong, the Finely Decorated Mirror (cf. Figures 5.4, 5.12). Both of them may be found together in the burials of the Early Iron Age © National Museum of Korea

ern China and the Russian Maritime Region. For mirrors with finer decoration, a similar number is known in Korea with another dozen or so reported in Japan. These mirror would have been important prestige goods with some kind of symbolic or ritualistic meanings.

About the manufacture of the bronze artifacts, evidence of foundry or mining facilities are not found. The evidence is limited to a few casting moulds made of stone. Although experimental study has provided answers for the manufacture of many bronze artifacts, there still are left unanswered questions for their production. Despite the possibility of local manufacture hinted by them, the general scarcity of bronze artifacts has led many to think that they were not made locally but somewhere else, perhaps somewhere in the core area of Gojoseon, i.e., in Liaodong or northwestern Korea, and obtained either by trade or exchange or provided as gifts.

In addition to pottery and bronze artifacts, the assemblage of the Bronze Age includes another important element. That is, ground stone tools for daily activities. They include axes, plows, hoe blades, mattocks, club heads, plane blades, chisels, knives, spindle whorls, net-sinkers, etc. Their manufacture began by chipping off the raw material to shape a rough outline, and is completed after a number of grinding stages. Among them, the most conspicuous is the Polished Stone Dagger. The stone dagger had been produced in quantity and various shapes through-

Figure 4.10 Distribution of bronze mirrors of the Bronze Age and the later periods. Circles indicate those with rougher decoration on the back such as shown in Figure 4.9. Squares are for those with more refined decorations (cf. Figure 5.3). Triangles indicate the mirrors of Chinese style imported during the Early Iron Age and the Proto-Three Kingdoms Period. © Cheongju National Museum

out the period, whose origin had been discussed by the intellectuals of the Joseon Period as mentioned in the introductory chapter.

These Polished Stone Daggers are usually classified into two basic groups depending on the presence/absence of the hilt. Thus, they may be called as the Hilt Type and the Stem Type, respectively [**Figure 4.11**]. Some of the latter group may look like an oversized arrow or spearhead, whose stem tends to get shorter in time. They would have required a wooden handle to be attached for use. For the Hilt Type, its hilt is sometimes grooved horizontally in the middle. Also, a pair of 'blood grooves' may be made on the surface. All of these daggers served both as tools of practical purposes and mortuary goods. Engravings of the outline of the daggers with hilt are sometimes found on dolmens, which might indicate that they were symbolically important to their makers as well [**Figure 4.12**]. For the Hilt Type, those with grooves on the hilt had appeared earlier than those without but they were made side by side for a long time.

As blood grooves are also a characteristic feature of the Korean-style Bronze Dagger, some stone daggers with similar grooves on the body were taken as evidence by the early Japanese archeologists to argue that they had to be a copy of the bronze dagger. It is followed by another assertion that the bronze daggers were made only after the Chinese invasion of 108 BCE so that they are the physical evidence that the state of stone age had continued long into the historical times and there was no proper Bronze Age. It is such assertions as this one that had made the Korean intellectuals of the early 20th century to seek after the evidence of the Bronze Age eagerly as mentioned earlier.

Other stone tools also demonstrate some degree of morphological variation according to time and place. For example, those flat and triangular stemless arrowheads of the earlier period were later replaced by elongated and stemmed pieces [**Figure 4.13**]. Shapes of the arrowhead also vary, perhaps reflecting functional diversification and specialization. The stem part of the arrowhead may be long or short, and their shape may be stepped or tapered. In this case, the stepped stem appeared earlier than the tapered one. Those with tapered stem are often found together with stemless, laurel leaf-like arrowheads.

Morphological variation is also seen in the so-called Semilunar Stone Knife. Stone tools grouped under this name are quite diverse but none of them really looks like a half moon. These stone knives have two characteristic holes in the middle for tying knots for a grip. They are believed to be tools for harvest [**Figure 4.14**]. In general, their width had become shorter in time to form a triangular shape. This Triangular Stone Knife is frequently found in southern parts of the

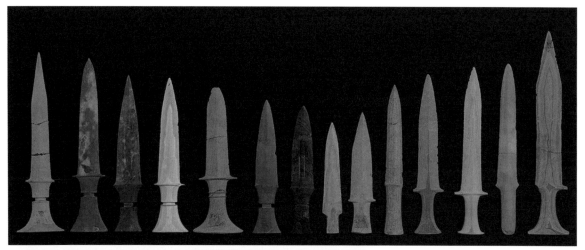

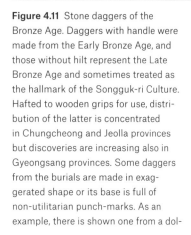

Figure 4.11 Stone daggers of the Bronze Age. Daggers with handle were made from the Early Bronze Age, and those without hilt represent the Late Bronze Age and sometimes treated as the hallmark of the Songguk-ri Culture. Hafted to wooden grips for use, distribution of the latter is concentrated in Chungcheong and Jeolla provinces but discoveries are increasing also in Gyeongsang provinces. Some daggers from the burials are made in exaggerated shape or its base is full of non-utilitarian punch-marks. As an example, there is shown one from a dolmen in Mugye-ri, Gimhae. Its length is almost twice the normal length of common stone daggers. But most of the daggers from the burials are the same ones found in the dwellings. Those shown in the top row are on display at the Jeonju National Museum. Below are the daggers on display at the Gyeongju National Museum. Large ones on display are about 30cm long. Despite the differences in raw material, they demonstrate that stylistic elements were widely shared across Korea. © Jeonju National Museum; National Museum of Korea (Mugye-ri)

peninsula during the Late Bronze Age.

Finally, in addition to Mumun Pottery, the Bipa-shaped Bronze Dagger and the Polished Stone Daggers, there is another important and highly conspicuous relic of the Bronze Age, which is the dolmen [**Figure 4.15**]. As briefly mentioned in the introductory chapter, in a memoir written in 1201, Yi Gyubo left a comment

Figure 4.12 An engraved capstone of dolmen at Orim-dong in Yeosu. A stone dagger is engraved upside down next to two human figures. The dagger is about 35 cm long. © Chonnam National University Museum; National Research Institute of Cultural Heritage

about his experience of visiting a famous dolmen, mentioning that "people say it was erected by a great man in the past, and it indeed was a curious and extraordinary relic".

Until industrialization and urbanization took off in the 1960s in South Korea, dolmens were a thing that one could not miss in the landscape. Even though most of them are long gone, the name of Jiseok-ri, literally meaning the dolmen village, has survived on the map at many places. It is estimated that there once were at least 40,000 of them in the southwestern province of Jeollanam-do alone where the landscape has been less disturbed [**Figure 4.16**]. Such estimates may suggest that there once were possibly as many as three to five hundred thousand dolmens across South Korea. It should be that the Bronze Age landscape had been domi-

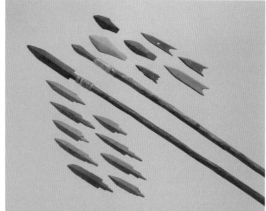

Figure 4.13 A wooden base of quiver and arrows with willow stem and stone point excavated at Cheonjeon-ri, Chuncheon. © National Research Institute of Cultural Heritage; Chuncheon National Museum

Figure 4.14 Semilunar Stone Knives on display at Gyeongju National Museum. In Jejudo where suitable raw material is scarce, abalone shells were used to make the knives. © Jeju National Museum (shell knives)

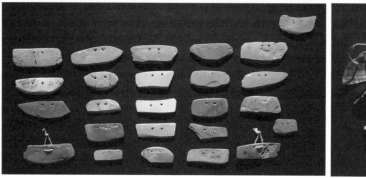

nated by these stone burials. Now, well-preserved dolmens in three municipalities are designated as UNESCO World Cultural Heritage sites.

In sum, the Bronze Age of Korea is represented by Mumun Pottery, the Bipashaped Bronze Dagger, the Polished Stone Dagger and dolmens. Much of the discussion about the Bronze Age in Korea has been about how these important archaeological remains had changed in relation to other aspects of the material culture.

Figure 4.15 A Table Type dolmen in Unhwa-dong, Eunyul. It is probably the dolmens like the one shown in this undated photo of the early 20th century that had impressed the western visitors. © National Museum of Korea

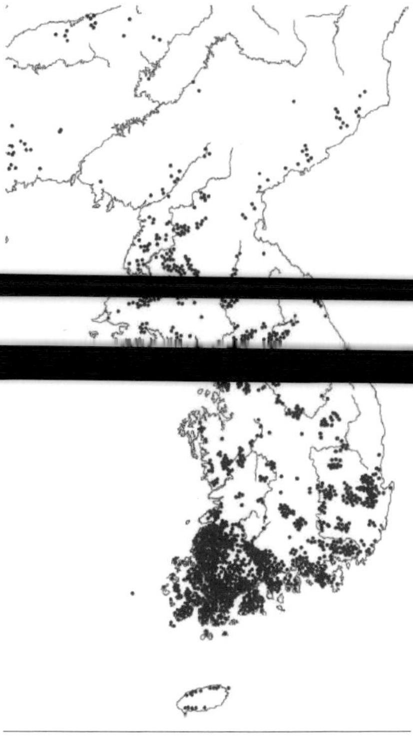

Figure 4.16 Distribution of dolmens (modified after National Museum of Korea 2010, p. 70). They are found wherever settlements of the period were formed.

Chronology and Periodization

As mentioned, the Bronze Age is regarded to cover the period between 1500 and 400 BCE although some think that the Earl~~~~ ~~~~ ~~~~should be~~~~ ~~~~ ~~~~ ~~~~ of the Bronze Age, a topi~~ ~~which will be discussed later. To repeat, in the 1970s and 80s when radiocarbon ~~~~ ~~~~ ~~~~ ~~~~ ~~~~ ~~~~ ~~important in the chronological discussion. Therefore, the beginning of the Bronze Age was set at 700 BCE mainly in consideration of the reported dates for some related artifacts in China and Siberia. In the late 1980s, absolute dates obtained from settlement sites with Mumun Pottery pushed the date back into time by a couple of hundred years. Then, the beginning of the Bronze Age was set around 13th century BCE in the 1990s, which was soon followed by a suggestion of 1500 BCE with older dates from the settlement sites.

Over the years, as different dates for different types of pottery had been accumulated, the sequence of change and typology of pottery has become important for chronological discussion [Figure 4.17]. For that matter, it is usually taken as granted that Mumun Pottery in South Korea had appeared as a result of diffusion. However, it is yet to be understood exactly where, when and how it was made

Figure 4.17 Basic pottery sequence of the Bronze Age in South Korea (after The Korean Archaeological Society 2010, Figure 45). In the top row are shown two types of the Raised-and-Notched Rim Pottery of the Initial Bronze Age, <1> preceding <2>. Below are finds from Garak-dong<3>, Heunam-ri<4> and Yeoksam-dong<5> of the Early Phase. The bottom row shows those of the Song-guk-ri Culture<6>.

for the first time. The idea was proposed originally in its explicit form in a 1970s article arguing that Mumun Pottery in South Korea appeared in the mid-Han River basin as a result of diffusion. At that time, little had been known about the rest of the country. We may call this pottery known in the mid-Han River basin 'classic' Mumun Pottery. It is represented by those simple, deep bowl-like specimens with a wide-open mouth, more or less straight or slightly curved body and a small, flat bottom. Usually 30 to 60cm in height, they were probably used as storage jars. From their shape, the term Simbalhyeong, i.e., the Deep Bowl Type, was coined to indicate them. For example, vessels shown as <5> in **Figure 4.17** can be all classified as this type. In time, the term began to be applied to those known outside of the area or of different age. For example, in **Figure 4.2**, those shown on the left side of D, F, G, H are typologically different but all of them can be described as Simbalhyeong.

The suggestion of diffusion proposed in the 1970s emphasized the similarity between some attributes of those shown as G and H of **Figure 4.2** and the others reported in North Korea. In the mid-Han River basin, their rims are decorated with simple notches and/or perforated to form a line of pinholes or tiny bulges. It was suggested that these characteristics reflect diffusion from two different directions. That is, perforation along the rim should have come from the Perforated Rim Pottery of northeastern Korea [**Figure 4.2, D**], and the small bottom associated with notching of the rim from the Top-shaped Pottery of the northwest [**Figure 4.2, E**]. This rather handy 'explanation' was an immediate hit, and even today remains influential in the discussion about the origin of Mumun Pottery. But of course this and any other argument of diffusion have not been supported by evidence that such actually had occurred, and perhaps will remain so.

From the 1990s, aggressive application of various dating methods began to indicate the presence of types older than the 'classic' Mumun Pottery. As the latter had been regarded to represent the Early Phase of the Bronze Age, or the Early Bronze Age, the name of the Initial Bronze Age or the Initial Phase of the Bronze Age was assigned to the new evidence, which is represented by the Raised-and-Notched Rim Pottery [**Figure 4.2, F**]. The name describes that it has a thin coil of clay attached along the rim just below the edge and short parallel lines are notched on it. Based on the shape of the protrusion, there are recognized two sub-types of allegedly different age [**Figure 4.17, <1> and <2>**].

This oldest Mumun Pottery was first reported in the early 1990s at Misa-ri on the Han River just outside of Seoul, which is more famous as a Neolithic site. More discoveries soon followed at many settlement sites, including Auraji mentioned earlier. Unlike those of the previous period, these sites are located deep inland. Sitting on a natural levee, their location should have allowed easy access to the rich alluvial soil where successful cultivation was possible. With C-14 dates as old as 1500 BCE, the pottery has become the hallmark of the beginning of the Bronze Age.

Much attention has been paid to its origin, and some pointed out the morphological similarity in the shape of the rim to the pottery of the final Neolithic. While proponents of this argument implicitly emphasize the continuity from the Neolithic to the Bronze Age, others see little or no similarity and continuity. To them, the pottery and the other elements of the assemblage had appeared as a group of people had moved into the Korean Peninsula from somewhere outside, who had spread rapidly.

To those who support the population movement hypothesis, the progenitor of the earliest Mumun Pottery and associated assemblage can be found in the upper reaches of the Taizi River in Liaodong or on the opposite side of the Duman River. Nevertheless, it needs to be determined how much similarity other than some morphological traits really exist between these places and South Korea. Incidentally, these Chinese sites are large and complex enough to infer the presence of a certain degree of social stratification, which cannot be found among the sites in South Korea.

The validity of the concept of the Initial Bronze Age has been under challenge since the mid-2010s as mixed results have been obtained from radiocarbon dating. More importantly, the overall assemblage composition of the Initial Phase does not look really different from those of the 'classic' Mumun Pottery. It led some to argue that the so-called oldest Bronze Age pottery is not actually older than the Simbal-hyeong pottery of the Early Phase. The dispute will require time to be settled.

The Early Phase following the problematic Initial Bronze Age is the period that the characteristic elements of the Bronze Age, i.e., Mumun Pottery, the Bipa-shaped Bronze Dagger, Polished Stone Dagger and dolmens, had spread widely. Regardless of the problem about the Initial Phase, many seem to accept that the Early Phase began somewhere around 1200 BCE. However, as C-14 dates are not completely reliable because of the fluctuations in the atmospheric C-14 level as well as the contextual problems of some samples, there is no firm consensus about its beginning date. Rather, the situation is somewhat confusing as some set it around 1100 while others argue 800 to 700 BCE. And of course, there are still other opinions. Nevertheless, there is a general agreement that this was the period during which agriculture was fully established and social stratification had progressed a lot. Settlement sites small and large are found virtually at every corner of the country. People lived in rectangular pit-houses, and their size and number suggest continuous population increase [**Figure 4.18**].

Traditionally, the Early Phase has been marked by the 'classic' Mumun Pottery excavated in the 1960s and the 70s at the three type sites of Yeoksam-dong, Garak-dong and Heunam-ri. Yeoksam-dong and Garak-dong are in what is southeastern Seoul today, less than 10km apart from each other. The latter is some 60km away from them to the southeast, sitting on a hilltop on the Namhan River, or the South Han River, one of the two main tributaries of the Han River. It was here that domesticated rice grains were discovered for the first time at a Bronze Age site in 1977. They were retrieved again from a partial re-excavation made in 2019 along with charred grains of beans and perilla seeds.

The assemblage composition reported at these sites has led researchers to suggest there were two cultural traditions during the Early Phase, one the Yeoksam-dong/Heunam-ri Type, the other the Garak-dong Type. The main difference between the two is said to be in the shape of the pottery, which was argued to reflect diffusion from two different directions as mentioned. The former is characterized by the Simbalhyeong pottery often perforated along the rim while those of the latter have

Figure 4.18 The early Bronze Age pit-houses are rectangular in shape. Densely packed pit-houses demonstrate that the site of Yongam-ri in Hwacheon had been occupied for a prolonged period. Larger and longer rectangular pit-houses are generally older than small, square ones. Large ones are found with multiple storage pits and hearths inside, and postholes or supporting stones are found along the walls where posts were erected. © National Research Institute of Cultural Heritage

folded rim with small bottoms. Nowadays, these 'classic' Mumun Pottery types are reported from places far south, challenging the hypothetical notion about their origin.

Including those of the Early Phase, Mumun Pottery demonstrates many different shapes and sizes but there are two typical forms. One is the Simbalhyeong which is already mentioned, and the other is the Hohyeong, i.e., the Jar Type. As is the case for the former, the latter is a descriptive term indicating the overall shape of a vessel, which can be applied to any large and round-bodied, somewhat globular jars with or without neck. such as the one on the right side of <3> in **Figure 4.17**. Sometimes, large jars of this type are found standing along the wall of a pit-house with rice and other grains inside, demonstrating the importance of crop cultivation during the Bronze Age.

Cultivation of ground crops and other plants had become ever more important in the Late Phase. To our confusion, this Last Phase of the Bronze Age is called the Middle Phase by those who refuse to recognize the Early Iron Age and regard it as the Late Phase of the Bronze Age. It is true that pottery, stone tools, dolmens and other elements of the Bronze Age material culture did not disappear overnight at the end of this phase. Mumun Pottery was continuously made and little had changed in other components of the material culture as well. The only noticeable difference is the appearance of some iron and refined bronze artifacts. Therefore, arguments have been raised to devise an alternative chronology.

However, as already mentioned in the introductory chapter, devising a new framework can never be easy because sociocultural change had not occurred equally and evenly between different parts of the country. While acknowledging the problems, to avoid confusion, the conventional framework is adopted here so that the Bronze Age is divided into the Initial, the Early and the Late Phase, followed by the Early Iron Age.

The Late Phase of the Bronze Age is also referred to as the period of the Songguk-ri Type Culture. Often shortened as the Songguk-ri Culture, the name takes after the type site where there were known pottery [**Figure 4.17**, <6>] and pit-houses of a unique shape [**Figure 4.19**]. The site became famous with the discovery of rice grains in the early 1970s. Excavation has been ongoing but only a small portion of the estimated 53 hectares of the site area has been tested so far.

It seems that to equate the Late Phase with the Songguk-ri Culture is not entirely correct because its presence is still poorly reported above the 37th parallel. Of course, sites with the Songguk-ri style pit-houses are being discovered slowly in Gyeonggi-do and Gangwon-do. For example, there are several sites in the outskirts of Seoul and even only a few kilometers away from the DMZ on the east coast. Nevertheless, it is still unclear what came after the 'classic' Mumun Pottery in the central part of the peninsula. Most of the Songguk-ri sites are in the southern provinces of Chungcheong, Jeolla and Gyeongsang. It might be that the material culture of the Early Phase had not changed much for a long time in the central part of the peninsula but it is not certain at all how the Early Phase had ended and what came next.

In the core area of the Songguk-ri Culture, a clear change can be seen in the assemblage composition with its appearance so that it is popular to say that the culture had appeared as a result of diffusion. Nevertheless, even if that is the case, both the origin and the timing of diffusion is not clear at all. Until the 1990s, its appearance was usually set around 500 BCE or later. Now there are many suggestions but no clear winner due to the obscurity of the radiocarbon dates.

Except such extreme views that it had appeared before or around 1000 BCE, there are two major opinions about the boundary between the Early and the Late Bronze Age. One is to hold on to the notion of 500 BCE while the other sets it around 700 BCE. In other words, the Songguk-ri Culture had lasted either only 100 years or about 300 years as far as the Early Iron Age is set to begin around 400 BCE. Also, followers of the latter view tend to regard that the Early Phase had begun before 1000 BCE. But this date is too early for the proponents of the former. To them, 1500 BCE is also too early for the beginning of the Bronze Age and 1300 to 1200 BCE, if not later, should be more or less appropriate.

Both of the views have problems, however. In order to accept 700 BCE as the beginning date of the Late Bronze Age, there must be more supporting evidence. For the date of 500 BCE, the problem is that bronze daggers from the alleged burials of the Songguk-ri Culture are considered much older than this date. At the same time, the duration of one hundred years appears too short for the culture to be spread widely.

Despite the disparity of some 200 years between the two views, however, argu-

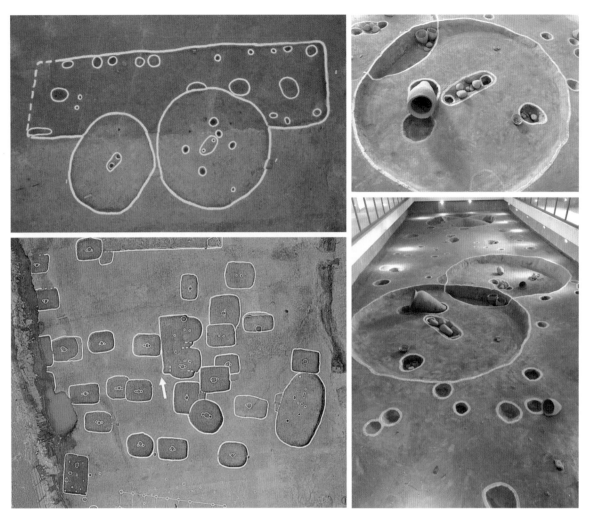

Figure 4.19 The so-called Songguk-ri type pit-house is usually round in shape with a diameter around 5 meters. In the middle of the structure is made a shallow depression with or without two round holes. When postholes are found inside, there are usually 4 to 6 of them. At Buldang-dong in Cheonan (top left), two Songguk-ri pit-houses were built over an earlier rectangular pit-house. Densely packed and overlapped pit-houses at Jinra-ri in Cheongdo (bottom left) suggest the prolonged occupation. To the right are seen the Songguk-ri type pit-houses at Samyang-dong in the Jeju islnd where they had been continuously made into the historical times despite changes in pottery and other aspects of material culture, © Chungnam Institute of History and Culture (Buldang-dong); The Yeongnam Institute of Cultural Properties (Jinra-ri)

ments are often made with a wide margin of error. Given the overlapping dates and the vague spatial boundary of the Songguk-ri Culture, it might be that the material culture of the Early Phase had diversified to produce different forms in different areas at different times, some with more of the old characteristics and others with more of new ones.

In any case, the Songguk-ri Culture is quite striking because virtually the same pottery, stone tools and structures for dwelling were made across a large area. Typical jars of the Songguk-ri Pottery may be anywhere between 20 and 100cm in height but demonstrate remarkably similar profile. Likewise, the pit-houses are quite standardized. They are usually round in plan with a diameter of about 5m, demonstrating little variation in size and shape [**Figure 4.19**]. They also share a peculiar feature made at the center of the floor, the so-called 'work space', which is a shallow and somewhat elliptical depression with or without a pair of small holes inside. Change in the shape of this feature is taken as a clue to determine the relative age of a given pit-house.

Population had rapidly increased during the Late Phase and many villages had sprung up, thanks to the increased agricultural productivity, which is the result of the adoption of irrigation for rice cultivation. Although there had been contacts and movements of people between the mainland and Jejudo throughout the Holocene, clear evidence of population influx is seen in Jejudo for the Late Bronze Age as rapid population increase in the mainland inevitably caused emigration across the sea. It is demonstrated by the sudden appearance of the villages of the Songguk-ri Culture [**Figure 4.19**]. These immigrants had brought with them a full set of material culture. Although the original Songguk-ri assemblage gradually had evolved in Jejudo in its own way, construction of the Songguk-ri style pit-house had continued for a long time as late as the 6th century CE or so, centuries after it had disappeared in the mainland. Waves of migration also had reached northern Kyushu, and the arrival of the Songguk-ri Culture and immigrants was crucial in establishing rice cultivation and the Yayoi Culture in western Japan.

To summarize, the Bronze Age in South Korea is usually divided into three phases when the Early Iron Age is discounted. However, such periodization is based upon rigid application of pottery typology. As it relies upon the presence/absence of a few pottery types, it may not successfully take into consideration the real complexity in the data. Naturally, pottery types might have appeared at one place and later spread widely and mixed with others, a simple possibility not well considered in the chronological discussion. Although we may know a little about the gross trend of change during the Bronze Age, it is a moot point how to define the boundaries between the phases as well as between the Bronze and the Early Iron Age. The boundary between the Initial and the Early Phase is often set around 1300 to 1200 BCE but we cannot be completely sure and may question whether it is appropriate at all to differentiate the two. Likewise, the relationship between the Early and the Late Phase is not free from the problem. Regardless of the opinions about the timing of the appearance of the Songguk-ri Culture, there remain many questions about its beginning and ending. Moreover, we know little to tell about what had been going on outside of its core area.

Village and Community

Despite problems in chronology, there is no doubt that the Bronze Age society and culture were very different from the previous period. If the Neolithic society was small-scale and semi-settled, mainly relying on a foraging economy, the Bronze Age society was much more populous and made of permanently settled agrarian communities. During the period, both the number of settlements and dwellings per settlement had steadily increased. Frequent overlapping of structures and/or their compact distribution is a clear departure from the Neolithic settlements.

A systematic tabulation of dwellings and settlements of the Bronze Age has not been attempted. To make an educated guess, a cursory examination of various source materials would allow one to say that at least 20,000 or more pit-houses have been excavated between 1990 and 2020, the majority of which are of the Late Bronze Age. Those of the Initial and the Early Bronze Age seem to make about 10 and 30 percent of the total, respectively. These numbers suggest rapid increase of population by at least an order of magnitude, which should be related to the spread of successful farming.

With continuous growth of population, settlements of the Early Bronze Age had spread to low-lying hills and slopes, whose relative elevation is usually less than 50m, allowing easy access to the field below. Locations of many Bronze Age settlements had been reoccupied over and over for a long time so that it is not a complete exaggeration to say that there used to be found a Bronze Age site nearby a village everywhere in the countryside.

Spatially the Bronze Age farming communities had become larger and complex in time. Sites are found with many dwellings and functionally specialized structures such as kilns and workshops. In the Late Bronze Age, differences in size and complexity of the sites had become clear enough to postulate the possibility of hierarchical organization of the settlements. Those of the highest tier are often taken as the political and economic center of a burgeoning complex society.

The size and the shape of the dwelling structures had changed also although the basic structural elements had remained much the same. These pit-houses are usually shallow enough not to require a ladder or any other facility for entrance. The roof is supported by the columns erected in the corners and/or along the four walls and the midline of the floor. There is no evidence of adobe or wattle and daub walls. Perhaps empty spaces between the columns were filled with thatches and grasses.

Pit-houses of the Initial Bronze Age are usually 9 to 12m long and the length-to-width ratio is about 2 to 1 or less [e. g., **Figure 4.3**]. This means that the floor size of the smallest one is still large enough for a family made of two or three generations. Some larger ones found with multiple hearths were perhaps large enough for more members.

During the Early Bronze Age, on average pit-houses had become larger [**Figure 4.18**]. Among them, particularly interesting are elongated ones which are more than 20 to 25m in length but with a width of only a few meters [**Figure 4.20**], the length exceeding 5 to 6 times of the width. Their shape contrasts with other contemporary pit-houses whose length to width ratio runs below 3 to 1. These elongated pit-houses are usually found with multiple hearths along the center line of the floor at intervals.

Such distribution of hearths led some to speculate co-habitation of multiple households, each huddling around a hearth. Although interesting, however, any number of alternative hypotheses can be proposed. For example, as they are often found as pairs or trios running parallel to each other among many rectangular pit-houses, it might be that they were not structures of a mundane household. While no conclusion can be drawn, what seems to be clear is that they could not have been built without a sizable population.

Evidence of uneven distribution of wealth is not clear in the settlement sites of

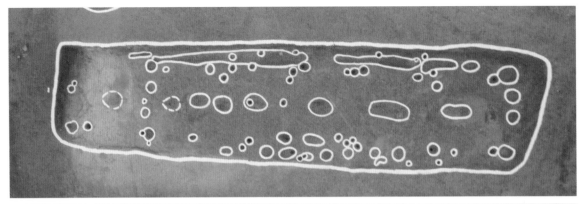

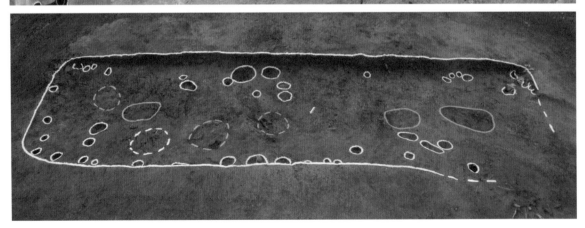

Figure 4.20 Elongated pit-houses of the Bronze Age. As also can be seen in Figure 4.21, some of the early pit-houses may be more than 25m long with a width around 4 to 5m. Three examples shown here are from the sites of Buldang-dong in Cheonan, Godae-ri in Yanggu and Ssangsong-ri in Hwaseong. © Chungnam Institute of History and Culture (Buldang-dong); National Research Institute of Cultural heritage (Godae-ri and Ssangsong-ri)

Figure 4.21 A partial aerial view of the complex site of Jungdo in Chuncheon. Notice different shapes of the pit-houses representing different periods and their overlapping relationship. Once the community was protected by trenches on four sides. © Joint Excavation Research Team of Jungdo-dong Site, Chuncheon

the Initial or the Early Bronze Age. There is no telltale sign of social inequality such as marked difference in the assemblage composition or floor size between the dwellings. Hierarchical relationship among the settlements is also not clear as settlements appear to be of similar overall size and contents of discovery. Although discovery of a bronze dagger at Hakpyeong-ri [**Figure 4.4**] might mean that social differentiation had emerged early in time, other evidence which hints that such really was the case cannot be found. Settlement sites of the period have not revealed a clue of advanced social complexity in terms of spatial organization of individual pit-houses and the composition of artifacts recovered.

Evidence for possible social stratification at a community level can be seen only rarely. **Figure 4.21** is a partial view of a settlement site which occupied rich alluvial soil. The picture shows complex overlapping of the pit-houses from different periods of the Bronze Age. At one point, a community was surrounded by trenches protecting it on all four sides. In relation to social stratification, what is interesting is the discovery of a bronze dagger and an axe from two pit-houses. Like Hakpyeong-ri, they are not different from the other pit-houses except the presence of these two bronze artifacts. The fact that one or two households could have kept bronze at home might be indicative of the presence of individuals who had wielded authority over the others. Perhaps the successful farming community might have required more organized control of the society.

In comparison, there is clearer evidence of social stratification for the Late Bronze Age. First of all, there were settlements of very large size such as Song-

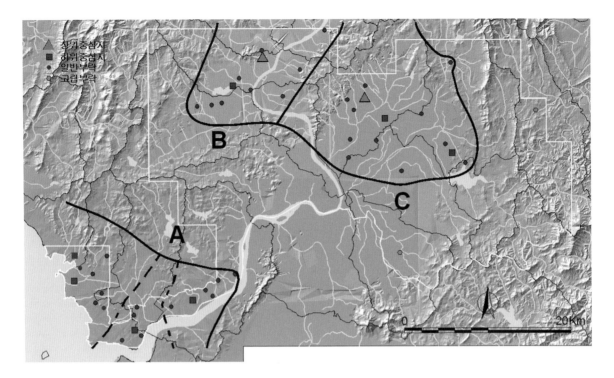

Figure 4.22 Settlement system of the Songguk-ri Culture in western Chung-cheongnam-do (after Kim 2005). Settlements are believed to be made of three tiers, and spatial boundaries may be drawn for each settlement group. The site of Songguk-ri is shown as the triangle in C.

guk-ri. With complex communal structures and special factory shops, the site represents the 'mega community' of the period, overwhelmingly larger than all the others. Such contrast is interpreted as demonstrating some kind of hierarchical settlement system which consists of center and peripheries. Judging from the settlement size, the system might have been a three-tiered hierarchical organization, reflecting the function of individual communities. Settlement distribution would have been organized across the space with its center surrounded and supported by the lesser ones.

For example, the settlement system of the Songguk-ri Culture in the western part of Chungcheongnam-do might have consisted of several competing centers, each surrounded by lower-level settlements within a loosely bounded territory [**Figure 4.22**]. The most prominent center of Songguk-ri was enclosed by wooden fences within which dwellings, kilns and other facilities were arranged. On the contrary, small sites on the periphery consist of only a few pit-houses but with a number of storage pits. In this settlement system, production and distribution might have been centrally controlled while provisions for the center were provided by the communities of the hinterland. Such centers would also have wielded political power over the lesser ones as social stratification had intensified. The appearance of such sociocultural organization might have not been possible without success in rice cultivation. Increased surplus would have encouraged population growth and increased social complexity as well as the development of large settlement centers where political elites could have risen gradually as evidenced by burials with bronze and other prestige goods.

Functional specialization of settlements is also suggested by their location. It seems that some of them were deliberately located for controlled exploitation of important raw materials. For example, in the upstream area of the Taehwagang in Ulsan, settlement sites were located at strategic locations to exploit the fertile floodplain as well as high quality hornfels. Stone tools of remarkably similar shape are found at many nearby sites which, to the naked eye, appear to be made of the identical raw material found in this particular place. Perhaps there were other similarly important places for procurement of various raw materials. Although a provenance study has not been attempted, remarkable resemblance in color and shape of stone daggers of the Songguk-ri Culture provides an impression that they might have been centrally produced and systematically distributed during the Late Phase. In that case, location of settlement should have been chosen strategically after careful consideration.

Increased social complexity as reflected in the settlement system is accompanied with an interesting change in the design of the pit-houses. As mentioned, rectangular pit-houses were replaced by round ones as small as Neolithic pit-houses. They are standardized in shape and size and perhaps accommodated fewer people than the earlier ones [**Figure 4.19**]. Certainly, the change reflects that the membership of individual household had been diminished, suggesting a change in social organization at the level of family and kinship. Possibly, the nuclear family had become the basic social unit and replaced some sort of extended family of the past who shared larger structures.

Such change in social organization, if indeed it had occurred, is sometimes explained by referring to the spread of rice cultivation. As today, careful maintenance of rice paddies should have been critical for successful farming, especially, the timely control of water. As the Bronze Age rice paddies were small in size and irregular in shape, they had to be tended separately by the individuals while communal work could have been made for large dry fields [cf. **Figure 4.23**]. It follows that individualized attendance of the paddies might have resulted in changes in the mode of labor mobilization, ultimately bringing about social organizational change beginning at the household level. As the extended family had been dissolved and shifted to nuclear family, there should have occurred concomitant change in architecture of the dwellings to make smaller pit-houses. Although not everybody agrees to this straightforwardly materialistic view, it remains as a working hypothesis in the discussion of the Songguk-ri Culture.

With reduced floor size of the Songguk-ri pit-house, indoor storage disappeared along with dug-out storage space or storage jars. Instead, storage was prepared outside so that evidence of structures with lifted floors is frequently seen [**Figure 4.24**]. Judging from the distribution of the postholes, sometimes some very large storage structures were constructed. Their construction should have been necessary to manage agricultural surpluses at the community level. Fairly large beaker-shaped underground storage pits with narrow openings are also found. They might have been needed to store durable foodstuffs or artifacts. Disappearance of indoor storage and construction of large storage structures are sometimes viewed as reflecting the communal sharing of the agricultural products or the monopolized control of the surplus by the elites. The opinion is closely related with the thought that the society was multi-tiered and political power was in action.

Organized use of space is clearly seen at many Bronze Age sites. For example, in

Figure 4.23 Cultivation fields of the Bronze Age are often found within easy reach from the village as revealed at Daepyeong on Nam River in Jinju, Gyeongsangnam-do. Here, furrows of the dry field prepared next to the village appear the same as what we can see today. In comparison, rice paddies were divided into small units suitable for a single individual to work inside like those revealed at nearby Pyeonggeo-dong shown at the bottom. Here, the smallest one barely exceeds several square meters in size. © National Research Institute of Cultural Heritage

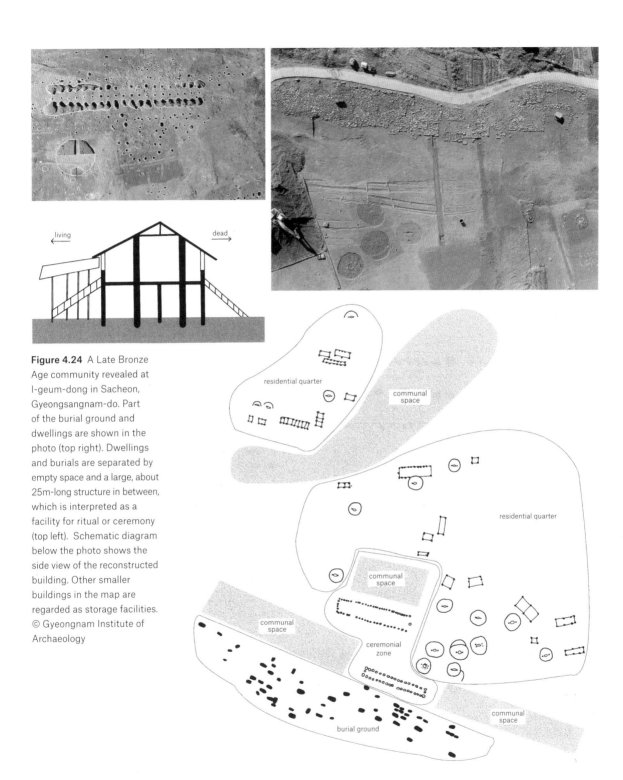

Figure 4.24 A Late Bronze Age community revealed at I-geum-dong in Sacheon, Gyeongsangnam-do. Part of the burial ground and dwellings are shown in the photo (top right). Dwellings and burials are separated by empty space and a large, about 25m-long structure in between, which is interpreted as a facility for ritual or ceremony (top left). Schematic diagram below the photo shows the side view of the reconstructed building. Other smaller buildings in the map are regarded as storage facilities. © Gyeongnam Institute of Archaeology

Figure 4.24, functional organization of space in and around a community can be detected. Also, many communities were protected from potential threats from wild animals or enemies by ditches or wooden fences so that large settlements of the

Songguk-ri period were surrounded by trenches and/or fences [**Figure 4.25**]. The enclosed space should have provided protection in times of emergency for those residing nearby, which should have occurred from time to time with intensified inter-group competition as told by the burials with evidence of traumatic death. Also, from the early Bronze Age are found pitfall traps with sharpened woods erected at the bottom. They seem to be distributed rather randomly at settlement sites of earlier times but in quite organized fashion by the time of the Songguk-ri Culture [**Figure 4.26**].

Organized use of space is also suggested by the presence of an empty lot in the middle or at a corner of a settlement site, which was probably for communal activities such as harvest festivals or ceremonial gatherings. Also, in large settlement sites, production facilities such as factory shops and kilns are not randomly distributed but assigned to a certain section of the village. While evidence is not clear for the Initial and Early Phase, like the one in **Figure 4.24**, large buildings built on the ground are found at many Late Bronze Age sites, which are interpreted as some sort of public building, possibly to perform religious rituals [**Figure 4.27**].

In relation to religious practices or ritual activities, interesting discoveries are

Figure 4.27 At a corner of the Songguk-ri site, there were found a number of post holes and ditches which testify there once were built large buildings and walls. The place shown in the photo is presumed to be a space reserved for special ritual or ceremony. © National Research Institute of Cultural Heritage

being made. The site of Ssangsong-ri in Hwaseong is an example. At this Early Bronze Age site to the southwest of Seoul, two groups of pit-houses were found on top of a low hill. Between the two on the highest point was found a round circle of trench with three exits. Slightly elongated in N-S direction, its inner diameter is about 25m. A number of postholes were found in the middle of the encircled area, which suggests that poles were once erected [**Figure 4.28**]. Similar features are now known at other Early Bronze Age sites.

One may be allowed to speculate that this enclosure would correspond to the sanctuary as described in *Dongyichuan* (Chapter of Eastern Barbarians) of *Weishu* (Book of Wei) in *Sanguozhi* (Records of Three Nations), a Chinese historical record written in the late 3rd century. A chapter about southern areas of Korea mentions that people served Spirits and performed rituals in a sacred space named *Sodo*(소도). Within it, poles were erected, from which bells and drums were suspended. The place was so sacred that even a thief could not be apprehended once he entered inside so that it had made people to develop a habit of stealing and thievish propensity. Perhaps what this peculiar structure says is that such tradition described by a Chinese historian started from the Bronze Age, many hundreds of years before it was recorded. Although its meanings are completely lost to modern Koreans and it is very hard to find nowadays, fragments of such prehistoric tradition have survived in the form of *Seonangdang*(서낭당), a place of prayer and offering usually marked by prominent trees and/or rocks decorated with colorful strips of cloth and guarded by *Jangseung*(장승) and *Sotdae*(솟대).

About the domestic life, there is little evidence with which we can make inferences about activities at the household level. Of course, distribution of artifacts and

Figure 4.28 Occupying a hilltop, an encirclement was made betwen two groups of pit-houses. It might be a sacred place as described by Chinese historians. © National Research Institute of Cultural Heritage

structural features allows one to make rudimentary guesses about sexual division of labor and differential use of space, but not much. For the dwellings themselves, despite the difference in size and shape, all of them are basically simple subterranean pits with a roof. After a pit was dug out, wooden columns were erected for roof and walls covered by grass or thatch. The floor was sometimes treated with a burnt and hardened layer of clay or covered with woven matts made of tree bark or grass. Where drainage is poor, narrow trenches were dug around the floor and sometimes extended out of the house.

Another chapter in *Dongyichuan* provides a hint about life in pit-house when it depicts the Eumnu people who had lived somewhere north of Korea if not in the northeastern corner of the peninsula. Although they were separated in time from the Bronze Age inhabitants of Korea, it helps to imagine what the life of the latter might have been like:

Eumnu lies to the east of Buyeo(부여), more than one thousand *li* away, next to the Big Sea, neighboring Bukokjeo(북옥저) to the south, but its northern limit cannot be told. The land is mountainous and rugged. People look like Buyeo people but the language is different from Buyeo and Goguryeo. For production, there are five grains, cow, horse and hemp cloth. People are brave. There is no Big Chief and each village has its own chief. They live in between mountain forests and always reside in pits. Larger houses are deep with nine steps of ladder, and people favor deeper houses. Climate is cold, even colder than Buyeo. In their custom, they raise pig, eat its meat and make clothing with its skin. In the winter, people cover their body with pig fat as thick as several inches. By doing so, they defend themselves from the coldness of the wind. In the summer, they are naked but covering the front and the rear with a piece of cloth about a foot long. People are unclean, and make toilets in the middle (of the house) and live around them.

Evidence of Farming

As the location of the settlement suggests, people of the Bronze Age had relied on cultivation from the very beginning. Charred remains of grains found on the floor of the pit-house or within storage jars indicate they planted rice, millet, foxtail millet, sorghum, barley, wheat and beans. These various crops seem to be of equal importance at first and rice had become more important in time. Since the discovery of charred grains of rice in the 1970s, physical evidence of cultivated crops has been discovered as charred grains, husks and impressions on the pottery surface with additional information provided by palynological and phytolith analysis of soil samples. For example, from starch residue left on the edges of potteries, grinding stones and stone knives collected from Heunam-ri in 2019, there were isolated 12 starch grains from millet (*Setaria italica* ssp. *italica*), 148 grains from another species of the subfamily Panicoideae and 12 grains of Pooideae. Especially, the latter was found on the edge of a Semilunar Stone Knife, which seems to confirm that the tool was used to collect ears of rice.

From the 1990s, archaeologists began to pay attention to the cultivation field itself to learn about the technology of farming. Large-scale excavations often revealed that crops were cultivated close to the residential area. However, rice paddies were prepared in back swamps or valley bottoms where water supply and control could have been relatively easy. They were prepared following the contour and the topography in order to guarantee the smooth flow of water. As a result, their shape and size cannot but be irregular and small [**Figure 4.23**]. It seems that such small size had remained unchanged until animal power was exploited. Historical records show that cattle were introduced for ploughing in the early 6th century CE in Silla.

Excavation of rice paddies often reveal simple water control facilities such as small-scale dams, waterways and wells [**Figure 4.29**]. Sometimes potsherds and wooden figurines in the shape of a bird are found within wells. Perhaps they were offerings to wish for stable supply of water. Water-logged wooden tools are also found in the rice paddies [cf. **Figure 4.3**], whose shape had little changed so that the very same ones had been used unchanged until mechanization took over in the late 20th century. What has not been found so far are thrashing tools for harvest and winnowing trays or something similar to separate stalks, leaves and foreign matters once ears cut by stone knives were collected.

If rice paddies were small and irregular in size and shape, dry fields were usually tidily arranged as large units, which led some to suggest that they were perhaps shared by the whole community. In **Figure 4.23**, furrows look remarkably familiar. Perhaps it is not surprising that the same plants were cultivated as today in the field. If the Bronze Age farmers cultivated other kinds of seed-bearing therophytes, evidence has not been found yet. Also, like their predecessors and modern Koreans, people of the Bronze Age exploited chestnuts, acorns and Manchurian walnuts (*Juglans* sp.).

One important aspect of the Bronze Age agriculture in relation to diet and nutrition is that pulses were cultivated across the country. Thus, at least three kinds of beans were included in the diet which are red bean, mung bean and soybean. Among them, particularly interesting is soybean. It goes without saying that, without soybean, there would be no *Ganjang*(간장), the quintessential flavor-enhancing condiment in Korean cuisine. Making of this traditional soy source starts with boiling soybeans, and boiled beans become blocks of *Meju*(메주), the base for *Ganjang* after fermentation. Moreover, without *Meju*, there would be neither *Doenjang*(된장) nor *Gochujang*(고추장), two other quintessential condiments. Likewise, *Cheonggukjang*(청국장) with its smelly but delicately delicious taste requires fermenting of soybean, and it is not necessary to mention what Tofu is made of. The oldest record about soybean-based condiments in Korea goes back to the late 7th century, but soybean had been already around for a very long time, thus, possibly, various condiments. Until the 1970s, when sparrows returned to their old nests on wooden beams underneath the eaves of roof-tiled houses, the narrow alleys of Seoul used to be filled with the warm and sweet smell of brewing fresh *Ganjang*, now only a faint memory.

There of course is no evidence to tell what the Bronze Age cuisine was like. What little we can say is simply that the size of cooking vessels and the residues left on their inner surface suggest that rice and other grains were cooked in small amounts, perhaps prepared separately in individual jars for each member of the household, not in a large vessel to be shared by the whole family which is a tradition in Korea. Also, it might be that boiling was the rule for cooking. The Bronze Age pottery assemblage lacks utensils for steaming. *Siru*(시루), the common steaming utensil in Korea with multiples holes on the bottom, appeared in its current form perhaps in the 1st century CE. It has become indispensable in preparing Korean cuisine and rice cakes, or *Ddeok*(떡), cannot be made without it.

Meanwhile, compared to the continuous update of information about plant cultivation, evidence is virtually nil about animal husbandry. Although faunal remains are generally rare for any period in Korea, they are especially hard to find for the Bronze Age, a situation exacerbated by the general absence of shell middens where organic materials might have survived. At the same time, presence of pens or cages as indirect evidence of animal domestication and husbandry is not reported, either. Perhaps animal fat and protein had been obtained from wild resources as implied

Figure 4.29 Charred remains of rice and other grains are frequently discovered from dwellings and storage pits of the Bronze Age. Rice grains (top left) are from Songdam-ri in Yeon-gi, and others are from Okbang in Jinju. As water control was important for rice cultivation, facilities were made to divert and contain water within the paddy during the growing season. Photos show remnants of a dam revealed at Jeojeon-ri in An-dong (bottom left). To its right, remnants of a wooden conduit are shown running along the edge of a stream beyond which is seen a settlement site of Songguk-ri Culture under excavation at Bongsan-ri in Gochang. Below is an outlet of irrigation ditch revealed at Manggok-ri in Masan.© National Research Institute of Cultural Heritage

by frequent occurrence of fishing and hunting gear throughout the period. Also, hidden traps set around the village perimeters might have provided an occasional bounty in addition to protection of the inhabitants. For animal resources, water deer and wild boar could have been important as had been the case for the Neolithic. Even today, they are frequently encountered in the countryside, and quite a few of them fall as victims of road kill annually.

Burials and Social Stratification

While there are relatively few cases in which burials and residential quarters are found in close proximity for the Initial and the Early Bronze Age, many burials are found close to pit-houses during the Late Bronze Age and often cemeteries comprise a part of a settlement system as seen in **Figure 4.24**. Thus, dolmens and stone-cists, which are closely related burials, may be found in the space between residential quarters, in a corner of a settlement site, or even immediately next to the pit-houses. Jar coffins or small stone-cists are frequently placed close to the living, perhaps in memory of the deceased. Also, jar-coffins may be found below the dolmen or within the stone-cist. They are more frequently reported for the Late Phase, usually found standing upright or slightly tilted [**Figure 4.30**]. No special mortuary pottery was made to be used as a coffin, and domestic jars were used for the purpose. Given their size, most of them were probably burials for premature deaths. In some rural areas, the practice had survived until the 1960s so that domestic jars were used as coffins for infants and stillborn babies.

Among these burials, dolmens are of course highly visible features in the landscape as mentioned earlier. From their appearance, they may be classified into several types [**Figure 4.31**]. Among the dolmens, some stand out as imposing and impressive structures and their capstones may weigh easily over hundreds of tons [**Figure 4.15**]. But many are much smaller and form a cluster [**Figures 4.32, 4.33**]. It appears that, when dolmens are clustered, they were built one after another,

Figure 4.30 Jar coffin No. 1 discovered at Pyeongchon-ri in Dalseong. It is 54cm tall with a maximum body width of 32cm. Here, three jar coffins of different size and shape were found next to 28 stone cists, one of which is shown in Figure 4.35. © National Research Institute of Cultural Heritage

Figure 4.31 Dolmen are usually classified into several basic types based on the presence/absence of supporting stones, their number and shape as well as overall appearance. Dolmens may be accompanied with 'standing stone' of various sizes which might have been erected to designate the burial ground. © Gwangju National Museum (dolmens); National Research Institue of Cultural Hewritage (standing stone)

their infrastructures being attached to each other. Burials below the capstone are sometimes protected by neatly prepared stone pavements which also could have provided space for ritual or ceremony. Also, pole-like stone(s) may be found standing next to them, somewhat similar to the so-called Menhir of western Europe or the 'deer stone' guarding the Bronze Age burials in Mongolia.

One interesting aspect of the Korean dolmens is that their appearance betrays the expectation of what can be found below. Thus, those of the most unassuming appearance may produce such prestige items as the bronze dagger while massive burials are left with only a few fragments of pottery or stone tool. The largest Bipa-shaped dagger found in the whole Korean Culture Sphere was found in one such dolmen [**Figure 4.33**]. These relatively smaller dolmens are usually dated to the Late Bronze Age as pit-houses of the Songguk-ri Culture are often found in close proximity. Occasionally, some of the dolmens were 'recycled' many years later as told by

the offerings found below the capstone. Also, there may be seen engravings of stone daggers as mentioned [**Figure 4.12**] or geometric patterns the meaning of which is not understood.

Since the first dolmen was excavated in 1915, hundreds, if not thousands, of them have been investigated. Until the 1970s, however, investigation was hindered due to the lack of physical means to deal with them. Only from the 1980s, systematic data collection has been possible, thanks to the introduction of heavy machinery in the field. Nevertheless, there is still a lot to be desired in our understanding of these monuments. We cannot answer such innocent questions as when and where they first appeared, how they were built and who were buried there. They still remain an enigmatic monument of the past.

About the question when and where dolmens first appeared, it is said that they likely appeared during the Early Phase somewhere in the 'north'. But below the surface of this casual response, opinions are truly diverse, a situation largely due to differences in evaluating the age of the burial goods, especially the bronze daggers. Indeed, there is little evidence other than these daggers which can be used to estimate the age of the dolmens despite their rarity. Different ideas about their age do not allow researchers to reach an agreement about where and when the dolmens first appeared. On the other hand, there is a wider agreement about the question when dolmens ceased to be constructed. It is believed that the dolmen and its sister burial the stone-cist had not been built from around the

Figure 4.32 Many dolmens are found as a cluster. In the top photo are shown dolmens revealed at Yeoeuigok (Yeo-eui-gok) in Jinan after the area under excavation was cleared of soil and vegetation cover. Often there are found stone pavement below the capstone presumably to protect the burial itself and/or to be used as a space to perform ritual. The original structure below the capstones is well preserved at Maechon-ri in Sancheong as shown below. © Jeonbuk National University Museum; National Research Institute of Cultural Heritage

beginning of the 4th century BCE in most places. In other words, they were not made largely by the time when iron was known although their construction had not ended completely until the late Early Iron Age in isolated places such as the

Figure 4.33 At the site of Sangchon at Wolnae-dong in Yeosu, dolmens were found next to the pit-houses of the Songguk-ri Culture. A Bipa-shaped Bronze Dagger was intentionally broken into two before burial. © National Research Institute of Cultural Heritage

Seomjin River basin. In Jejudo, it seems that they were not abandoned even during the Three Kingdoms Period, hundreds of years into historical times.

Once, dolmens were regarded as evidence of a 'chiefdom society' which were built for ruling elites. The problem, however, is that there simply are too many of them so that not every dolmen could be for 'chiefs' or their households. In other words, many dolmens look more like burial for an average person.

Nevertheless, some dolmens do appear to be special burials for the powerful, especially for the Late Bronze Age. Perhaps it is not surprising given the possibility of the multi-tiered social system of the Songguk-ri Culture. Most interestingly, massive structures were built within a narrow belt of distribution along the south

Figure 4.34 Massive dolmens within a walled 'courtyard cemetry' at Deokcheon-ri in Changwon (left). Diagram is schematic cross-section of one of the dolmens. Below it, a partially destroyed dolmen of similar size at Dongchon-ri in Boseong shows what lies below the massive capstone. © Kyungnam University Museum (Deokcheon-ri); Gwangju National Museum (Dongchon-ri)

coast. It seems that they were originally built inside a stone-walled 'graveyard'. Special structures were also made presumably to conduct some kind of ceremony or ritual [**Figure 4.34**]. In some cases, these massive dolmens were connected to each other by stone pavements and/or surrounded by lesser dolmens and stone-cists.

Contrary to their impressive appearance, these so-called Graveyard Type dolmens are extremely poor with burial goods. It might be that the power and the wealth of the buried were meant to be demonstrated by the appearance of the burial and/or the process of their construction. The paucity of burial goods is in sharp contrast to the burials of the immediately succeeding period which are poor in appearance but rich with mortuary offerings. If these massive dolmens indeed are the status burials for the elites who were able to wield the power to mobilize the labor for their construction, their distribution implies that a number of more or less politically independent groups began to appear which later developed into the peer polities of Samhan.

The appearance of these dolmens is quite impressive and in marked contrast to those plain dolmens found in the same area. But, as mentioned, it is the latter where such precious artifact as the Bipa-shaped Bronze Daggers are found, which are usually considered older than the massive Graveyard Type dolmens. It might be that frenzied construction of massive dolmens had swept the south coastal region in the 5th century BCE just before the arrival of iron there when the modest farming hamlets of the early Bronze Age communities had grown populous enough to engage in such civil works. It had to be that the process of social stratification was accelerated in this cul-de-sac of the peninsula towards the end of the Bronze Age.

In the early 20ᵗʰ century, dolmens were classified into two groups, one the Table Type, the other *Baduk*(바둑)-board Type. The Table Type was named after those with a large and flat capstone and slabs of supporting stone, thus, resembling the shape of a table like the one shown in **Figure 4.15** [**Figure 4.31, top**]. Many of them are taller than an average person and stand aloft to dominate the landscape. The *Baduk*-board Type indicates those whose thick capstone is supported by stumpy supporting stones [**Figure 4.31, middle**], somewhat like the shape of the board of the chess-like game of *Baduk* (Gō in Japanese).

These two types were once called the Northern and the Southern Type, respectively, because the former was believed to be distributed in northern Korea and Liaodong while the latter is restricted to southern Korea. Later, it turned out that the so-called Northern Type dolmens are also distributed far south. Then, in the 1960s, dolmens lacking supporting stones for the capstone were identified [**Figure 4.31, bottom**]. These Atypical or Capstone Type dolmens are sometimes found mixed with the others. Especially, those of the *Baduk*-board and the Capstone Type are often found together [**Figures 4.32**].

So far, no evidence has been found that a body was buried underground in the case of the Table Type. It is assumed that the body was laid on the ground below the capstone as the supporting stones make four walls of a coffin. For the Southern and Atypical Type, the burial space was prepared underground [**Figures 4.31-4.34**], which could be a simple shallow pit, a neat stone coffin made of well-trimmed stone slabs, or anything in between.

For dolmens outside of the Korean Peninsula, there are some massive Table Types in Liaodong. Although evidence is weak, they are regarded as burials of the Initial and/or the Early Phase and are thought to be related with Gojoseon because the Bipa-shaped Bronze Dagger are found in them. Meanwhile, Southern Type dolmens in Jejudo and northern Kyushu tend to have smaller capstones but with many supporting stones, and are regarded as the remains left by the immigrants of the Songguk-ri Culture.

As mentioned, often no artifacts are found beneath the massive structure, thus, suitable dating material is hard to come by. As a result, many have tried to assess their age by establishing the typological change of dolmens on the basis of their shape and structure. However, such attempts achieved little success. This is because there is a very large range of variation in their details so that it is hard to tell which of the attributes are really meaningful variables for a successful typology.

As the sister burial of dolmens, stone-cists also appeared in the Early Bronze Age and became popular during the Late Bronze Age with the expansion of the Song-guk-ri Culture [**Figure 4.35**]. They were built as independent burials or to form a burial complex mixed with dolmens. At the same time, many of them might have been built originally as coffins underneath the dolmen whose original capstone was removed or destroyed. Like dolmens, their structure and shape demonstrate a lot of variation. For example, while some are found as a box-shaped coffin whose six sides were made with well-worked slabs of stone, many others were made of layers of river cobbles or roughly hewn stone blocks. If stone-cists were built for the elites, they may lie inside a lot demarcated by a long trench as shown in **Figure**

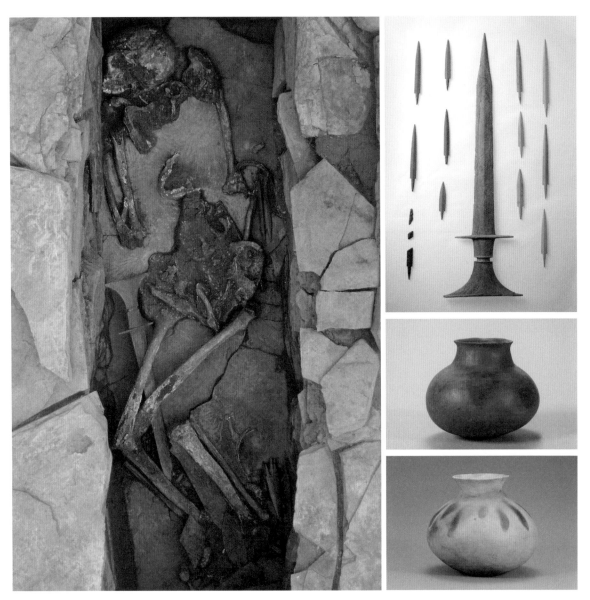

Figure 4.35 Stone-cist No. 20 excavated at Pyeongchon-ri in Dalseong and mortuary goods. Although not discovered at this particular burial, stone-cists of the Bronze Age, especially those of the later period, are usually found with the Red Burnished Pottery or its variant form the Eggplant Motive Pottery. Beads and stone tools are also common findings. As burial goods, stone daggers may be in exaggerated shape, extravagantly decorated by making a number of pinholes or deliberately broken before laying in the burial. The dagger shown here is 63cm in length, one of the largest ever found, and perhaps was not made for everyday use. © National Research Institute of Cultural Heritage (burial and stone tools) National Museum of Korea (pottery)

4.36. In this case, the length of the largest lot is over 40m. However, the burials themselves lying in the middle are quite humble, comprising plain-looking stone-cists or pit-burials.

When human remains are found within the stone-cist, the body was laid either stretched or flexed. In rare occasions, there is evidence of *in situ* cremation. Com-

Figure 4.36 Stone-cists at Cheonjeon-ri in Chuncheon. Here, parts of a complex site consisting of a settlement, burials and agricultural fields were excavated in relation to the construction of a highway interchange. The location of the photographed stone-cists is indicated by the red arrow. They were constructed separately from dolmens, perhaps implying the special status of the buried. © National Research Institute of Cultural Heritage

pared to dolmens, mortuary goods are seen relatively frequently, represented by Red Burnished Pottery [**Figure 4.35**]. This small pottery is round-bottomed and burnished in a reddish texture and often found together with a Polished Stone Dagger and/or a few arrowheads, among others. Also, it is not uncommon that both the Red Burnished Pottery and stone artifacts were intentionally broken or smashed and their fragments were spread inside or over the burial, suggesting a ritual had been performed at the time of burial.

Most of these artifacts are the same ones found in settlement sites. However, some stone daggers demonstrate exaggerated shape and size or are excessively decorated with a number of tiny holes or carvings. Interestingly, burials with such artifacts seem to appear within certain geographical boundaries. For example, many of the large and non-functional daggers are found mainly along the south coast, somewhat matching with the distribution of those massive Graveyard Type dolmens.

A Step Closer to History

Throughout the history of archaeological research in Korea, the importance of the Bronze Age has been emphasized as a preparatory stage for the rise of early statehood. The period is believed to start with simple and small agrarian villages of the late second millennium BCE, which gradually had become more complex and populous. The period is also seen to be defined with the manufacture of Mumun Pottery. After appearing, the Mumun Pottery tradition had survived long after the introduction of iron, and did not disappear completely even in the early years of the Christian Era. In comparison, bronze artifacts are rarely found for the late second millennium BCE, if any. As the most representative artifact of the Bronze Age, the Bipa-shaped Bronze Dagger is usually believed to be included in the archaeological record in Korea sometime after 1000 BCE but perhaps not later than 700 BCE.

During the Bronze Age, bronze artifacts were extremely rare and daily activities were carried out with stone and wooden tools. These tools proved satisfactory enough to maintain the thriving society which relied on agriculture. Among the crops, rice had become increasingly important. Its high productivity ensured continuous population growth, resulting in emigration across the South Sea during the Late Bronze Age. Given the number of sites, population size of the Bronze Age might have started slightly larger than the final days of the Neolithic and increased a lot during the middle of the first millennium BCE as evidenced by tens of thousands of dolmens and numerous settlement sites. The population size of the Late Bronze Age would require a scale much larger than the Neolithic. Perhaps it might have reached or exceeded a hundred thousand by this time.

Population increase could have acted as a pressure for social stratification. During the Late Bronze Age, social inequality is manifested in the construction of burials. Also, difference in the size of settlement sites suggests that the society was multitiered and centers and peripheries appeared. Centers could have accommodated a large number of inhabitants with provisions supplied by the peripheral communities. Construction of communal buildings, storage facilities, defensive structures, controlled management of cultivation fields, evidence for ritual or religion, centralized production of stone tools and the widespread sharing of stylistic elements in various aspects of the material culture all suggest that the Late Bronze Age had witnessed the birth of social stratification in much of the Korean Peninsula. Of course, a lot more about what the society was really like must be understood.

It needs to be emphasized again that this description is mainly for the southern parts of the Korean Peninsula. More than anything else, Gojoseon had appeared in the north. By the time that the Late Bronze Age began in the south, it had to be that Gojoseon was feeling the ripples from the conflicts between the warring states in China. Unfortunately, we can tell little about what the society and culture were like in the northern areas of Korea and beyond when Mumun Pottery had appeared and changed in South Korea.

In any case, at least a couple of centuries before Gojoseon was invaded around 300 BCE, southern parts of the Korean Peninsula were teeming with thriving communities of rice farmers. They were ready to receive the new technology of iron and to produce exquisite bronze artifacts. The archaeological record would change a lot soon.

CHAPTER 5

EMERGING PEER POLITIES

Arrival of Iron

As reviewed in the previous chapter, many small agrarian communities flourished in the southern parts of Korea in the middle of the first millennium BCE. There are clear signs of population growth, which must have had something to do with the success of rice farming as suggested by storage jars filled with rice. The period looks like a peaceful time with no signs of conflict. By this time, to the east and north of Gojoseon, the Goguryeo and Buyo states were soon to appear, one in the mid-Amnok basin, the other in the mid Songhua basin in Jilin province of China today. Thus, the stage was set for the introduction of iron to the indigenous communities of the southern parts of Korea at the beginning of the 4th century BCE.

On the other hand, however, the time was full of turmoil in China as the Seven Warring States were relentlessly fighting against each other. Conflicts of the Warring States period finally settled down as Qin unified China in 221 BCE. But turmoil ensued after the death of the First Emperor in 210 BCE, which were subdued when the new dynasty of Han emerged as the winner in 202 BCE.

It is obvious that ripples from the events in China were felt by its neighbors. Even before Qin's unification, at around 300 BCE Gojoseon had lost a large chunk of territory to Yan, one of the Seven Warring States. It forced Gojoseon to relocate its center to the south, probably to the Pyeongyang area. Two hundred years later, Emperor Wudi of Han destroyed Gojoseon in 108 BCE. He absorbed the conquered territories into the administrative system of his empire, and the Commandery of Lelang, or Nangnanggun(낙랑군) in Korean (Nangnang[낙랑] in short), was established with its center on the southern shore of the Daedong River in Pyeongyang. Despite dynastic changes in China, Lelang had survived more or less as an independent political entity until the early 4th century. As such, the northern parts of the Korean Culture Sphere had faced many troubles in relation to China, and indigenous groups in the south would also have been influenced at least indi-

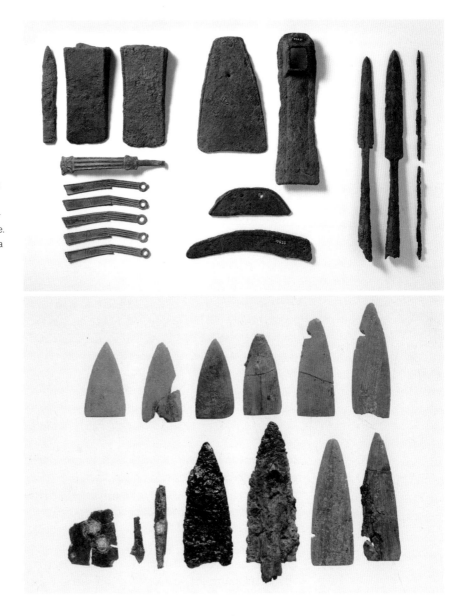

Figure 5.1 Early Iron Age artifacts. Hoarded artifacts have been discovered occasionally on the shores of the Amnok River at such places as Yongyeon-dong in Wiwon (top). Farther to the south, pit-burials of the period may produce stone and iron arrowheads as known at Manjeong-ri in Anseong, south of Seoul (bottom). Iron was rare for most of Korea at the time, and many arrowheads were still made of stone. © National Museum of Korea (Yongyeon-dong); Gyeonggi Cultural Foundation (Manjeong-ri)

rectly by what was happening in the north.

The introduction of iron has been explained by referring to such a volatile historical background. Since the early 20th century, researchers have tended to believe that the arrival of iron is announced by hoarded artifacts discovered on both shores of the Amnok River. A typical discovery includes a set of iron implements put in a jar with a bunch of knife-shaped bronze money of Yan China [**Figure 5.1, top**], which were taken as evidence indicating that the introduction of iron is somehow related to the Yan invasion around 300 BCE.

Coining of the term Early Iron Age in the 1970s reflects the thought of the time that, despite its arrival, iron was known only in limited scale and did not affect the lives of many living in the southern parts of Korea immediately so that much of the

Korean Peninsula had entered a sort of incipient stage of the Iron Age. The period was thought to have ended with the beginning of the Christian Era as changes in mortuary practice and material culture were detected. Especially, there were ceramics made in the southern parts of Korea fired under higher temperatures, which was interpreted as the result of the introduction of advanced technology from Lelang. This frame of thought has not changed much and only the dates for this period have been pushed back in time. Thus, the Early Iron Age now covers the period between 400 and 100 BCE. This means that iron was known to Korea before the Yan invasion and that it had been fully incorporated into the material culture by the end of the 2nd century BCE.

Arrival of this new and powerful technology had little meaning to the lives of the general populace. Iron was rare. There is no indication that iron implements had been manufactured and used casually for cultivation and other daily activities. People kept using stone tools. Iron artifacts are found as mortuary goods in very limited quantity. At the same time, bronze was more important as mortuary goods. Manufacture of bronze artifacts had reached its peak during the Early Iron Age. They were distributed widely and buried with the deceased. Iron had remained precious until ore was discovered, which does not seem to have occurred probably until the 2nd century BCE. According to more conservative estimates, perhaps the mastery of iron production was achieved only at the end of the period, around 100 BCE.

Bronze Age Extended

By the time iron was introduced, as mentioned, dolmens had disappeared in most places, replaced by relatively simple pit-burials which should have been much less costly to construct [Figure 5.2]. Once a wooden coffin was laid inside a narrow pit, the space between the coffin and the pit might or might not be filled or lined with chunks of stones, sometimes even covering the coffin to form a low stone mound. These burials are not visible on the surface, perhaps due to the small size of the original mound which had been eroded away. Because of their inconspicuous and unassuming appearance, their discovery is often accidental or consequential to large-scale salvage excavation. The custom of putting stones within or over the burial had slowly disappeared in time, ending the tradition of stone burials of the Bronze Age.

Ironically, despite the name of the period, it is Mumun Pottery which is important for the chronology of the Early Iron Age because of the rarity of iron. At the same time, some iron and bronze artifacts of the period had been continuously made and buried in the burials of the succeeding period, making it difficult to determine the age of a given site with these artifacts alone. Despite some disagreements, it seems that there had appeared two new kinds of Mumun Pottery sometime around 400 BCE and they had spread quickly across South Korea. They were made as late as the beginning of the Christian Era although technologically advanced pottery began to appear from around 100 BCE, more or less coinciding with the timing of the Han invasion of Gojoseon.

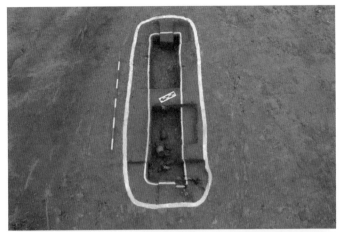

Figure 5.2 Pit burials revealed at Sinpung in Wanju, Seonje-ri in Gunsan and Mundang-dong in Gimcheon. © National Research Institute of Cultural Heritage

These two pottery types are called Attached-rim Pottery and Black Burnished and Long-necked Pottery (Black Burnished Pottery in short) [**Figure 5.3**]. They are treated as the chronological marker of this period in the absence of better evidence. These two are often found together most often in mortuary contexts. Also, they demonstrate remarkably little variation in shape.

Attached-rim Pottery is a rather plain-looking jar. It is named so because of a coil of clay running around the rim. Black Burnished Pottery is a vase-like vessel with a round body and straight or slightly curved neck. Despite the name, its surface may not be burnished. They may have a pair of grips attached to the body, which are named the Oxbow-shaped Grip and made by joining two pieces of small, horn-like lumps of clay. This peculiar grip had been made for a long time especially in the Gyeongsang Basin if in a somewhat changed form for later examples.

Mainly based on some morphological traits of the two types, the Early Iron Age may be divided into two 150 year-long sub-periods. The most important attribute is the cross section of the rim part of the Attached-rim Pottery. It is believed that its round shape had become flatter and triangular in time. The shape of Black Burnished Pottery also had changed but less prominently and predictably. Many believe nowadays that these two pottery types had originated in the Liaodong region to the north of the Amnok River. This is because the pottery and associated bronze artifacts from the burials there are almost identical to those found in the southern provinces of Korea. Therefore, it is hypothesized that their appearance might have something to do with emigration or evacuation of the Gojoseon elites to the south as implied by the written accounts of crisis. Otherwise, the occurrence of identical sets of artifacts between two faraway places would be difficult to explain.

In relation to the origin of these artifacts, the most frequently cited evidence

Figure 5.3 A typical set of the Early Iron Age mortuary goods from Deok-dong in Wanju. The Attached-rim and the Black Burnished Pottery in the back row are used as the key to determine the Early Iron Age status of a site. © Jeolla Munhwayusan Yeonguwon (downloaded at https://ko.wikipedia.org/wiki/)

is the burial site of Chengjiawozi in Shenyang, Liaoning province. Here, there were reported not only the two important pottery types described above but also bronze artifacts frequently found in Korea, such as daggers, mirrors and other ritualistic or decorative items [**Figures 5.4**]. Also, overall structure of the burial itself looks similar to those of the Early Iron Age as seen in Figure 5.2. Therefore, it is hypothesized that those who made the Chengjiawozi burial and the likes had arrived in the southern parts of Korea with various artifacts. From the distribution of the burials, it is suspected that they might have landed on the west coast somewhere below the 37th parallel.

For their age, Chengjiawozi and other related sites were reported not younger than c. 500 to 400 BCE, thus, leading many to think that 300 BCE is too late a date for the beginning of the Early Iron Age. Incidentally, in the 1990s, the age of some early Yayoi sites in western Japan was readjusted to be older than 300 BCE. This means that the Early Iron Age artifacts found in Japan should have been made before this date in Korea. Thus, the beginning of the Early Iron Age was reset.

More recently, some have argued that the Early Iron Age began around 500 BCE at least in the northern parts of South Korea, i.e., in the Imjin and the Han River basin, implying that iron was spread gradually from north to south. Though interesting, we cannot tell whether such was the case. Evidence is still

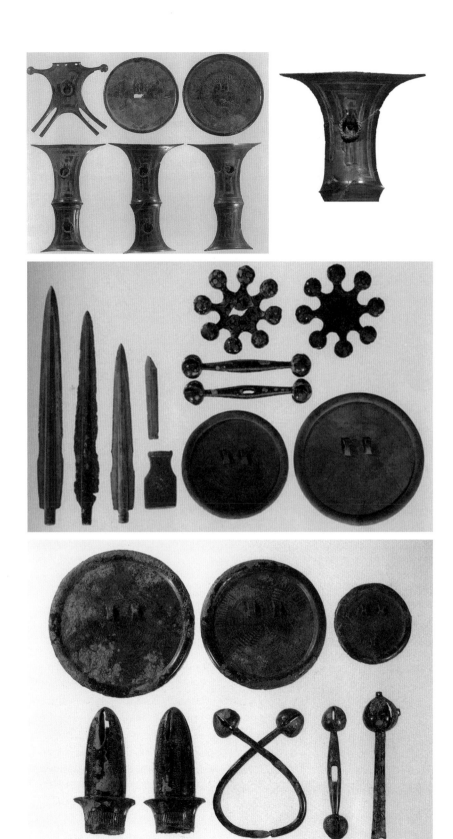

Figure 5.4 Bronze artifacts from the Early Iron Age burials of Namseong-ri in Asan, Daegok-ri in Hwasun and Chopo-ri in Hampyeong. The mortuary assemblage usually includes a few additional pottery and iron implemets. Their sudden appearance in southern parts of Korea are often said to be the result of the southerly movement of the Gojoseon elites. © National Museum of Korea

too weak, and there is no information from the adjoining region of North Korea to evaluate the opinion.

Regardless of the temporal definition of the period, as mentioned, many researchers agree that the concept of the Early Iron Age is problematic because its material culture appears little changed from the Bronze Age, and, thus, regard it as the last stage of the Bronze Age. To repeat, when the term of the Bronze Age II was renamed in the 1970s, it was intended to emphasize the introduction of iron to southern parts of Korea. However, those rare iron objects of the period were status items buried with elites, and had little or no meaning for the culture and the people in general. Moreover, it is questionable whether iron was known at the same time across the whole of Korea. At the same time, the upper boundary of 100 BCE is also arbitrary as there is no real difference in the archaeological data immediately before and after this point in time. Thus, the concept of the Early Iron Age does not satisfactorily summarize the nature of the material culture during the period between 400 and 100 BCE even for the southern parts of Korea, not to mention the whole Korean Culture Sphere, so that both terms, the Early Iron Age and the succeeding Proto-Three Kingdoms Period, are inadequate. At best, they may serve for some parts of the southern Korean Peninsula but fail to represent a complex situation. Nevertheless, redesigning the chronological framework for these years in the dawn of history requires the development of a totally new perspective in interpreting the archaeological data. It is of course an enormous task, exacerbated by the North Korea problem. So far, alternative suggestions often repeated the same mistake of over-simplification that they meant to criticize.

Given the problems surrounding this unwieldy period, the term the Early Iron Age should be used very carefully, keeping in mind the possibly misleading connotations and implications that those words, 'Early', and 'Iron Age', may conjure. It will be used merely as a term of convenience to indicate the period between 400 and 100 BCE while acknowledging the arbitrariness of the temporal boundary.

Changes in Culture Sphere

During the period under consideration, the southern parts of Korea became involved in the East Asiatic world system for the first time. As evidence, there are exotic items such as the glass beads made in Southeast Asia [**Figure 5.5**]. From this time on, various aspects of culture, society and environment were known to China and put into writing later. Meanwhile, early forms of the stratified society of the Late Bronze Age in southern parts of Korea slowly and steadily had developed into more complex forms during the Early Iron Age, approaching closer to statehood. Yet, its material culture had remained quite homogeneous throughout South Korea.

As mentioned, the Early Iron Age had been an unnerving and volatile time for the northern parts of the Korean Culture Sphere. According to Chinese records, Gojoseon had been threatened not only externally but also internally, and a

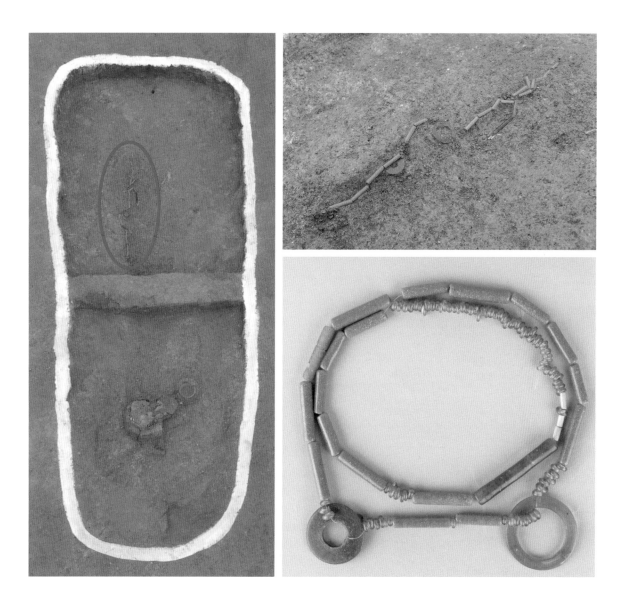

Figure 5.5 Glass beads from a pit-burial at the site of Sinpung in Wanju. With a total of 81 burials and various artifacts, this cemetery of the elite burials was formed between the early 2nd and the mid-1st century BCE. The beads represent the oldest glass artifact found in Korea. They are of lead-barium glass and believed to have been made in Southeast Asia. © Honam Cultural Property Research Center (excavation scenes); National Museum of Korea (beads)

dynastic change had occurred in 194 BCE with the rise of Wiman the usurper. The expelled ruler Junwang fled to the south, perhaps following the footsteps of those who had fled at the time of the Yan invasion or some other upheavals. He was received warmly in Jin-guk, a leader of small polities in southwestern Korea. Wiman's last dynasty of Gojoseon was a short-lived one as it was subjugated by the Han empire during the reign of his grandson. The same record also indicates the presence of many indigenous groups in the southern parts of Korea. Political and military upheavals in the north would have influenced them a lot and accelerated the sociopolitical process which had been already going on.

With such historical events, the Korean Culture Sphere now had shifted somewhat eastwardly [**Figure 5.6**]. When compared to the Bronze Age [**Figure 4.6**], the region west of the Liao River is now excluded from the map, reflecting the expansion of Chinese influence. On the other hand, the southernmost part of the maritime

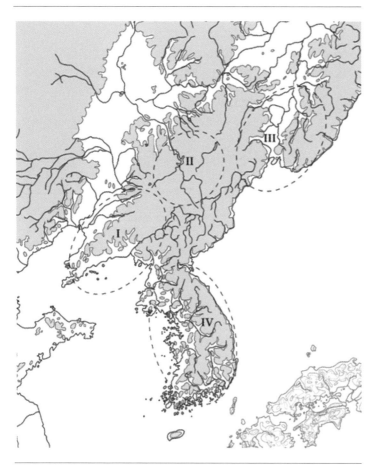

region of the Russian Far East is now included in the map. Mainly based upon mortuary evidence, the sphere may be differentiated into four areas of "Culture Types". Named after the type sites, they are called the Sejukri-Lianhuabao, the Dahaimeng-Paoziyan, the Duanjie-Kronovka and the Namseongri-Chopori Type.[1] Their location is shown as I to IV in **Figure 5.6**. However, the spatial extent of the first three types cannot be defined clearly due to paucity of evidence so that the boundaries shown in the map are better taken as a rough approximation. The territorial extent of Gojoseon, Goguryeo or Buyeo is also not shown.

The Sejukri-Lianhuabao Type covers the Liaodong Peninsula and the lower reaches of the Amnok River. Its distribution corresponds roughly to the territory of Gojoseon. To its east, the Dahaimeng-Paoziyan Type covers the mid- to upper Songhua River Basin. Next to it, the Duanjie-Kronovka Type is found in the lower Duman River basin and the neighboring coastal area. In the area between the Sejukri-Lian-

Figure 5.6 The Korean Culture Sphere of the Early Iron Age (after The Korean Archaeological Society 2010, Figure 71). During the period, early states of Goguryeo and Buyeo were rising in the eastern edge of I and the northern part of II. Gojoseon was not completely collapsed yet and was perhaps controlling parts of I and II.

huabao Type and the Dahaimeng-Paoziyan Type, early Goguryeo burials appeared in the mid- to upper reaches of the Amnok River in the 4th century BCE.

Many South Korean researchers regard that the Dahaimeng-Paoziyan Type as having developed out of the Xiduanshan Culture of the Bronze Age [**Figure 4.6**], and correspond it to the culture of Buyeo. Likewise, the Duanjie-Kronovka Type is regarded to represent the culture of Okjeo, another ancient entity but only vaguely described in the records. Further to the north of the two cultures, the Guntuling Culture in the Sanjiang Plain is recognized where the two mighty rivers of Songhua and Amur meet. Sometimes it is regarded as the remains of Eumnu mentioned in the previous chapter. These cultures continued to exist into the early centuries of the Christian Era corresponding to the Proto-Three Kingdoms Period in the chronology of Korean archaeology.

Below the Sejukri-Lianhuabao Type lies the Namseongri-Chopori Type. It is defined by mortuary goods from pit-burials as shown in **Figures 5.3** and **5.4**. Strictly speaking, the unsatisfactory concept of the Early Iron Age would better

......

1   Place names of Sejukri, Namseongri, and Chopori are transliterated as Sejuk-ri, Namseong-ri and Chopo-ri. However, hyphens were deleted here in consideration of the possible confusion caused by multiple hyphens.

be applied only to this type. Its northern boundary is blurry but perhaps would run roughly along the 39th parallel. Both of the type sites of Namseong-ri and Chopo-ri are isolated burials located in similar settings in Chungcheongnam-do and Jeollanam-do. More of them have been discovered in the southwestern part of the peninsula. With gently rolling hills and well-developed drainages, the land is suitable for agriculture and movement across the terrain is not difficult at all. Their proximity to the coast is one of the reasons behind the argument of the arrival of the Gojoseon elites there and the subsequent dispersal of remarkably similar burials.

Where Are They?

As much as the concept of the Early Iron Age relies on mortuary evidence, there are very few sites other than burials. While there are at least 200 burials including poorly reported ones, the number is less than 50 for all the other types of sites. Most of them are known as 'settlement sites', but it is customary to call a site a 'settlement' as long as a 'pit-house' is found regardless of its size, location and the assemblage composition. These sites are made of a few 'pit-houses' in which only some pottery and stone toolsare found, making them a poor source of information. Overall, they suggest that life had little changed since the Bronze Age.

But what is really interesting is that these so-called settlement sites are in no sense comparable to the farming villages of the previous period. They are not found at the locations favored during the Bronze Age or the later periods. Instead, almost all of them are located at high elevations. Moreover, none of them can be a match against the large Bronze Age settlement sites or those of the later period in terms of the number of pit-houses or spatial extent and complexity.

The 'pit-houses' are usually square to round in plan and tend to be small, about the same as those of the Songguk-ri Culture. Twenty to thirty or less of them are found at a given site and overlapping indicates that not all of them were occupied at the same time. Presence of Attached-rim and Black Burnished Pottery suggests that they are of the Early Iron Age. Otherwise, they may be regarded as those of the Bronze Age. In essence, they look hardly different from those of the Bronze Age. However, if they are genuine settlement sites, their small number and size mean that population size had been abruptly and remarkably reduced with the beginning of the Early Iron Age, which makes little sense.

The sudden disappearance of so many thriving Bronze Age communities is difficult to comprehend unless the population was wiped out due to some disaster. Even if so, there must be some evidence but nothing is found. Engravings on bronze artifacts suggest agriculture was important [**Figure 5.7**], but not a single site of a farming community has been excavated. It is more mysterious because so many prosperous farming communities are found immediately after the Early Iron Age, consisting of scores or hundreds of dwellings. Therefore, the sudden disappearance of settlements at around 400 BCE after steady population growth defies commonsense and requires an explanation. After all, the

Figure 5.7 Engraved bronze artifact from Goejeong-dong, Daejeon. A scene of ploughing is seen on one side and an engraving of *Sotdae* is on the other side. © National Museum of Korea

production and distribution of iron and bronze mortuary goods could not have been possible without a sufficiently large population that had engaged in various activities related to their production. Moreover, the presence of such burials suggests a strengthened social hierarchy, which also could not be maintained with a depleted population. Elites in any period, past or present, need those to rule.

It may be that much of the problem can be blamed on the archaeologists. Perhaps what is not right is the chronological scheme in use. The problem might have something to do with the fact that archaeological periodization has relied on the assumption of the stepped and discontinuous change of pottery. In doing so, they seem to forget that the latter part of the first millennium BCE had been a dynamic and volatile period so that the old and the new cultural traits could be found randomly together. It is also possible that different types of pottery might have served different functions so that household utensils might have been different from those for ceremony or ritual. Given the possibility, some of the settlement sites assigned to the late Bronze Age or the Proto-Three Kingdoms Period could in fact be of the same age as the elite burials of the Early Iron Age. Or, by the same token, 'settlement' sites of the period might be either older or younger than the perceived age. For example, at least several cases of fragments of Attached-rim Pottery are reported from Songguk-ri Type pit-houses.

If this is the case, we need to think about the nature of the so-called 'settlement'

sites of the Early Iron Age. For that matter, one may begin with asking why almost all of them, except several, are located on high ground with limited space. Most of them are reported on tops of mountains and buttes with altitudes of about 300m above the sea level. They are not really difficult to climb but look fairly imposing, commanding a fine view of the surroundings.

While not all of these sites were fully excavated, they are usually surrounded by circular or oval trenches covering an area with a diameter of about 30m or so. Within the encircled area, there may be found 'pit-houses' and/or postholes for the structures built above the ground. They may also be found outside the encirclement [**Figure 5.8**]. Within the trench itself, fragments of bronze artifacts or pottery may be found, suggesting the possibility of ceremonial or ritual activities. As suggested for the case of the Bronze Age [**Figure 4.28**], one may wonder whether these enclosed 'settlements' might be the sanctuary of *Sodo* in a more evolved form, now separately located from the villages down in the valley.

Figure 5.8 An Early Iron Age 'settlement' site of Banje-ri in Anseong. © National Research Institute of Cultural Heritage

Although hypothetical, if this is the case that these sites are in fact contemporary to some sites of the Late Bronze or the early Proto-Three Kingdoms Period, the mystery of the missing inhabitants may be answered. To speculate further, those characteristic pottery types of the Early Iron Age might have been used more often as mortuary artifacts and/or for ritualistic or ceremonial purposes.

Meanwhile, it is reported that dwellings in the northernmost parts of Korea are equipped with heating facilities which can be said to be an incipient form of *Ondol*(온돌), a quintessential element of Korean-style housing. It is also found in contemporary dwellings in the Russian Maritime Region and the northeastern provinces of China abutting Korea. The central feature of this new system is the smoke way connecting the hearth and chimney. It was built on the floor along or toward the wall so that heat radiates from a section of the house to warm up the inner space. Therefore, it is different from the modern variety which heats the floor to warm the space from the bottom up, and also can be regarded as the ancestor of *Kang*, the traditional heating system of northern China. Despite its structural simplicity, its adoption was quite a departure from the hearths made on the floor of pit-houses. But it is during the following Proto-Three Kingdoms Period that this new heating system was popularized [cf. **Figure 6.21**].

A Theocratic Society?

As the burials of the Early Iron Age are of simple structures without large mounds, many of them had been destroyed unnoticed. However, when they are discovered, a full set of mortuary goods is occasionally found, which was the case for the type sites of Namseong-ri and Chopo-ri. In recent years, large-scale salvage excavations have revealed many such burials. Occasionally, a number of them are found together to form a cemetery. Earlier and later burials are sometimes distinguishable as the former tend to have more bronze artifacts over iron.

As these burials are built in a relatively simple way, little attention has been paid to their structure *per se*. Instead, most attention is given to the artifacts so that most of the publications are about the typology and chronology of bronze and iron artifacts, mainly focusing on their origin and dispersal as well as regional differences. Another important topic is the technology of their manufacture and use. A lot has been learned about them from experimental study and scientific analysis of artifacts.

Among the artifacts of the period, the one which has received the most attention is the bronze dagger. As mentioned in the previous chapter, those of the Bronze Age had become the Korean-style Bronze Dagger of the Early Iron Age, which are found across Korea [**Figure 5.9**]. Gradually, iron replaced bronze so that iron daggers of simpler form had appeared. Like the Bipa-shaped Dagger, the Korean-style Dagger has a separable hilt. Pommel fittings and other parts of the hilt were made of bronze even when the main body was made of iron. For bronze mirrors, decoration on the backside had become ever more elaborated in time [**Figures 5.4, 5.12**]. Although we still do not know clearly how those extra fine lines on the mirror were made, the occurrence of stone molds means that bronze artifacts were manufactured in different places during the period [**Figure 5.10**]. For other bronze artifacts, there are also spearheads, dagger-swords, chisels, engravers, etc. [**Figure 5.11**]. Sometimes, broken pieces of daggers and other weaponry are found hoarded in a ceremonial manner.

Additional artifacts include probable gadgets for rituals like the lid-shaped discs as well as bells of various forms [**Figure 5.4**]. As bronze daggers, mirrors, disks and bells have been a part of the typical shaman's paraphernalia in Korea and other areas of Northeast Asia, it is often inferred that, if these artifacts were buried together with its owner, the elites of the period may have functioned both as religious and political leaders at the same time. Also, bronze artifacts are often found together with jade jewelry and stone arrowheads [**Figure 5.4**]. Those three artifacts, bronze daggers, bronze mirrors and jade, are known in Japan as the Three Divine Artifacts, the so-called *Sanshujinki*.

When compared to bronze, iron artifacts appear more mundane and utilitarian in nature and axes, ploughs, weaponry and ingots are frequently found. Iron implements were, however, rare and precious and only elites could have owned them. Thus, it was only at the end of the period that iron replaced bronze for weaponry.

Contents of the mortuary assemblage, or its mere presence, contrast with the

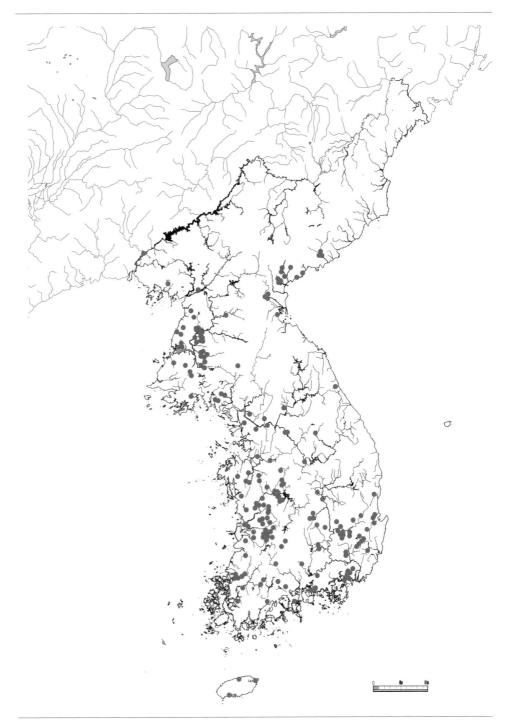

Figure 5.9 Distribution of the Korean-style Bronze Daggers. Because they are found as mortuary goods, their distribution may be taken as a proxy in considering the political geography of the time. With some 187 reported locations of the discovery, the number is more than four times greater than that of its predecessor, the Bipa-shaped Bronze Dagger. ©Cheongju National Museum

 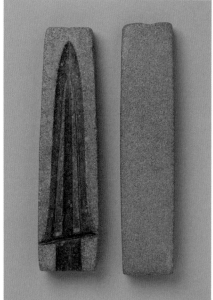

Figure 5.10 Stone molds for casting bronze artifacts of the Early Iron Age. Often they were carved with more than single implement to maximize their use. Thus, dagger and spearhead may be carved on different sides of the mould such as the one excavated at Galdong in Wanju shown here. © National Museum of Korea

general absence of burial goods among those massive dolmens of the previous period. Such differences might mean that the structure and organization of the society had somehow changed. If the paucity of mortuary goods of the dolmens suggests that social wealth had been spent in erecting the heavy structure itself, the less costly burials of the Early Iron Age seem to emphasize the wealth of the buried. Such differences might suggest a concentration of political power to the elites who had technological knowledge and could control the production of elaborate artifacts. Those Gojoseon refugees might have brought with them such resources, allowing them to occupy easily the upper echelon of indigenous society.

From the distribution of the burials, we may be allowed to infer the presence

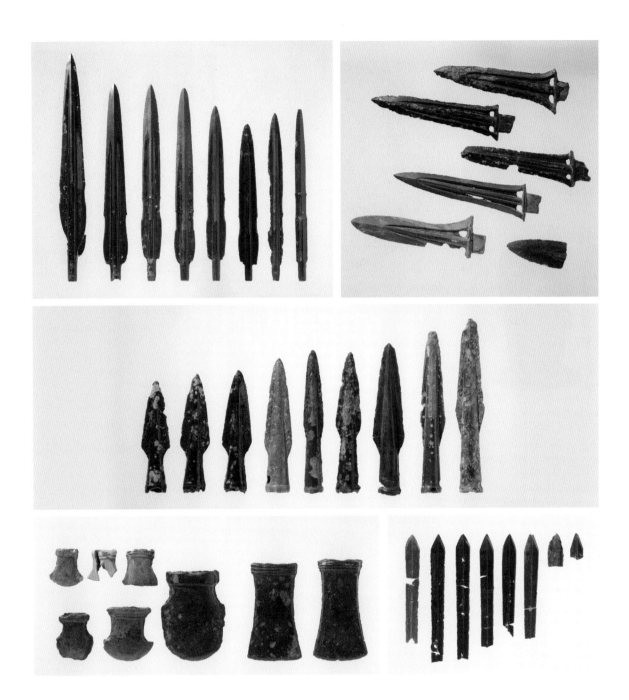

Figure 5.11 Korean-style Bronze Daggers, dagger-swords, spearheads, axes, engravers and chisels of the Early Iron Age. Daggers were retrieved together from a single burial at Dongseo-ri in Buyeo. © Cheongju National Museum

of a number of small-scale peer groups and take their distribution as an indirect guidance for drawing a rough political map of the time. From **Figure 5.9**, their distribution in South Korea appears more or less clustered and not evenly and randomly distributed, perhaps hinting at the rise of the polities of Samhan as shall be discussed in the next chapter. The territory of these early polities perhaps did not exceed several hundred square kilometers at best, thus, about the size of a Myeon, which is the lowest administrative unit in South Korea with permanent government office. The aforementioned *Sanguozhi* lists 78 "nations" constituting

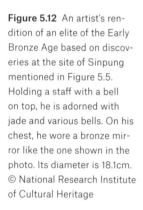

the Samhan, or the Three Hans, in southern Korea in the early years of the Christian Era. The distribution of burials seems to indicate where their seeds were sown during the Early Iron Age.

Figure 5.12 An artist's rendition of an elite of the Early Bronze Age based on discoveries at the site of Sinpung mentioned in Figure 5.5. Holding a staff with a bell on top, he is adorned with jade and various bells. On his chest, he wore a bronze mirror like the one shown in the photo. Its diameter is 18.1cm. © National Research Institute of Cultural Heritage

CHAPTER 6

DAWN OF HISTORY

Early Polities

As the Korean Culture Sphere was in turmoil at the end of the Early Iron Age, Wiman's dynasty collapsed in 108 BCE. His grandson, the last Gojoseon king, had fled to Samhan as many before him. Soon, the culture and history of Korea began to be recorded in more detail. As all of the forthcoming dynasties and kingdoms in Korean history had left their share of archaeological remains, historical archaeology is thriving in South Korea and much more active than prehistoric archaeology. Researchers are dealing with all kinds of remains that one can think of. Sites being excavated are various, which include ruins of palaces, temples, urban centers, villages, burials, production facilities, roads, bridges, fortresses, agricultural fields, etc. At the same time, underwater archaeology is most active in Asia ever since the discovery of a 14th century shipwreck in 1976, thanks to many remains scattered on the bottom of the shallow sea along the west coast.

With plenty of remains, many works for each historical period are being conducted. For example, as of August 2010, some 1,200 monograph-sized technical reports describing excavations for the Goryeo and the Joseon period have been published. By July 2020, the number had shot up to 3,500 and continues rising. For the Three Kingdoms Period and the Unified Silla Period, there must be much more but it is hard to tabulate the exact number because of their overwhelming amount. Perhaps more than 80% of all the archaeological fieldwork carried out in South Korea pertains to various historical periods. This and the next chapter are an extremely short and simple, bare-boned description of such works. Readers are reminded of the immense amount of information and the diversity of research topics.

This chapter is about the Proto-Three Kingdoms Period. As mentioned earlier, it is a term that was coined to cover the period between 100 BCE and 300 CE based on the understanding that Silla and Baekje had remained in the incipient stage of statehood until around the beginning of the 4th century. Its beginning

Figure 6.1 Barbarian groups around the Korean Peninsula during the Proto-Three Kingdoms Period (after The Korean Archaeological Society 2010, Figure 6.9).

roughly coincides with the invasion of Gojoseon by the Han empire of China. The period ends with the appearance of the large mound burials of Baekje and Silla, which signifies that sovereign power was well established. During the period, many polities had appeared so that, besides the tripodal kingdoms of Goguryeo, Baekje and Silla, there were many large and small polities some of which had survived until the 6th century.

It was already mentioned that the concept of the Proto-Three Kingdoms Period has been criticized so that its application would better be limited to describing the archaeological data of the area where Silla and Baekje were born and rose to their strength. Then, as is the case for the Early Iron Age, it may best be regarded as a mere term of convenience to indicate the period between 100 BCE and 300 CE.

Figure 6.1 shows roughly where the major political players were located during the period as described in historical records. The territory of Gojoseon now belonged to the Liaodong and the Lelang Prefecture of China. To their north and east were Goguryeo, Buyeo, Eumnu and Okjeo. To the south of Okjeo was Ye(예) or Yemaek(예맥) somewhere in the mountainous northern Gangwon-do and southern Hamgyeongnam-do, but descriptions are vague and short for Eumnu, Okjeo and Ye. The southern parts of the Korean Peninsula were the territory of Mahan(마한), Byeonhan(변한) and Jinhan(진한), collectively known as Samhan, the Three Hans. Also, the island of Jejudo is mentioned separately as the nation of Tamna(탐라), and Japan was known as Wa, the nation of short-statured people.

Each of the three Han groups consisted of dozens of peer polities which together maintained loose federations so that the southern parts of Korea were teeming with many pre-state level societies whose rise is foretold by the pit-burials of the Early Iron Age. As the oldest historical record about them, *Sanguozhi* describes Mahan as consisting of 54 such 'nations'. It also mentions that Byeonhan and Jinhan consisted of twelve polities each, shared the same tongue and were similar in various aspects of everyday life. Like Baekje, which began as a small Mahan polity, Silla originally started as the minor Jinhan polity of Saroguk(사로국). Also, polities of Byeonhan had developed to become the many small kingdoms of the Gaya(가야) federation.

But historical records are sometimes vague, speculative or unrealistic in their description. Although archaeological findings are filling the gap, there nevertheless are limitations. Information about Lelang is a good example. In North Korea, its presence has been vehemently denied since the 1960s, and remains excavated after 1945 are reported as those of Gojoseon in its terminal phase. Seals, stamps and any evidence with inscriptions related to Lelang are categorically stigmatized

Figure 6.2 Exotic artifacts found in the Proto-Three Kingdoms Period burials in southeastern Korea (after The Korean Archaeological Society 2010, Figure 145). Bronze jar and iron kettle on the left are the products of the nomads of Inner Asia, probably related to Xiongnu. Bronze mirrors in the middle are from China, either directly or via Lelang. Spearhead on the right is from Japan.

as forgeries by the Japanese imperialists. Therefore, the only available evidence about Lelang is limited to a few photographs and brief notes as well as artifacts kept in Seoul from the pre-World War II excavations made in and around the Lelang Earthen Wall in southwestern Pyeongyang, which is believed to be the location of the Lelang administrative center.

In South Korea, archaeological data has increased particularly a lot for this period. As a result, we can now see regional differences and variations in material culture. There are known sites deemed to be political centers of the period, while the return of shell middens along the southwest and south coast implies a rapid upwardly shift in demography. At the same time, there is a lot of evidence indicating craft specialization and long-distance contact.

According to historical records, iron was a highly important export item of Jinhan and Byeonhan so that traders from Lelang and Wa came to obtain it. Remains of piers and quays indirectly suggest the active movement of people and goods. People of Jinhan and Byeonhan perhaps traded iron for prestige goods, which had found their way into burials as mortuary goods. As shown in **Figure 6.2**, they include bronze mirrors, coins and ornaments from China, some perhaps via Lelang, as well as bronze weaponry from Japan and utensils from the nomadic barbarians roaming the steppes in the north of China. Imported artifacts are also found in the territory of Mahan, many at the places close to the coast, sometimes hoarded or intentionally discarded perhaps after ritual or ceremony. Glass beads of Southeast Asian origin are reported from burials across South Korea [**Figure 6.3**; cf. **Figure 5.5**]. Beads are also made of crystal, jasper, agate, amazonite and

Figure 6.3 Imported glass beads are found widely and frequently from the burials of the period. Examples shown are from Unyang-dong in Gimpo to the west of Seoul (top), Deokcheon-ri in Gyeongju (borrom left), and Sangun-ri in Wanju (bottom right), each representing central, southeastern and southwestern part of Korea, respectively. A pair of golden earrings found at Unyang-dong resemble those of Buyeo. © National Research Institute of Cultural Heritage (Unyang-dong, Sangun-ri); Yeongnam Institute of Cultural Properties (Deokcheon-ri)

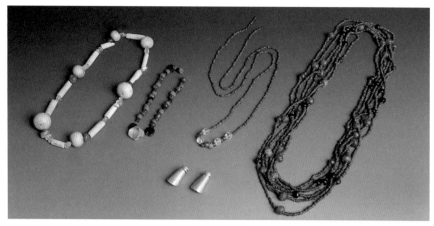

amber, some of which were produced locally. Their frequent occurrence reminds one the description in *Sanguozhi* that the people of Samhan loved beads more than gold and silver.

Organic materials preserved in swampy environments testify that the time was prosperous in the southern parts of the Korean Peninsula. The best example is seen at the site of Sinchang-dong, Gwangju, in southwest Korea. Here, all kinds of wooden objects were recovered, including a musical instrument, hair combs, writing brushes, umbrella ribs, shoes and shoe frames, door pieces, chariot and cart parts, to name a few [**Figure 6.4**]. Pieces of hemp and silk clothes, oracle bones and bundled coils of tree barks for packaging were also found. Various grains and even seeds of gourd and cucumber were also retrieved. The evidence allows us to imagine that the agrarian society of the Songguk-ri Culture of the Late Bronze Age continuously prospered, adding another piece of indirect evidence to suspect the validity of the concept of the Early Iron Age as mentioned in the previous chapter.

Inter-regional differences in the composition of material culture are well illustrated by pottery. By around 100 BCE, pottery began to diversify regionally and Mumun Pottery had been replaced by those produced by more advanced pyro-technology although it did not disappear overnight as seen in **Figure 6.5**. As a result, while their common ancestry may be visible among the early pottery of the period, it becomes harder to recognize for later ones. Likewise, dwelling

Figure 6.4 A musical instrument discovered at Sinchang-dong, and oracle bones from the shell-mound of Gungok-ri, Haenam, in southwest Korea. Reconstructed instrument demonstrates it is ancestral to traditional string instruments. © Gwangju National Museum (instrument); National Museum of Korea (oracle bones)

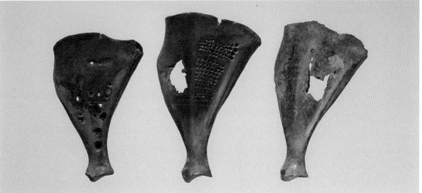

structures also demonstrate regional differences. For example, those found in Gyeonggi-do and Gangwon-do tend to be larger and steadier with rectangular or pentagonal floors, and usually equipped with well-defined entrances and primitive *Ondol* in many cases. They are in marked contrast to the round or square pit-houses known in Chungcheong and Jeolla provinces, which are little different from the Late Bronze Age. Although relatively few settlement sites are known in southeastern Korea in the region of Jinhan and Byeonhan, those discovered there also tend to be small and round.

Despite such differences, other evidence demonstrates continuation of the interaction between the regions. The best example would be the bronze buckles in the shape of horses or tigers found frequently in burials [**Figure 6.6**]. It seems that many were manufactured by the same hands and distributed across cultural and political borders of the time.

Figure 6.5 Early ceramics of the Proto-Three Kingdoms Period demonstrate regional differences although they still retain the characteristics of those of the previous period. Representing northern, central, southwestern and southeastern South Korea, there are shown samples form Janghyeon-ri in Namyangju (top left), Sin-gi-dong in Mun-gyeong (top right), Sinchang-dong in Gwangju (bottom left), and Daho-ri in Changwon (bottom right). All except Daho-ri are settlement sites. Daho-ri potteries are typical mortuary wares of the Gyeongsang Basin. © National Research Institute of Cultural Heritage (Janghyeon-ri, Sin-gi-dong and Sinchang-dong); Gimhae National Museum (Daho-ri)

However, the structure of burials with these buckles is markedly different between the regions. In the territories of Jinhan and Byeonhan, burial traditions of the Early Iron Age only became more luxurious and elaborated. Thus, the pit-burials with wooden coffins were buried with many more prestige goods. In time, they had become larger and adopted the outer receptacle which allowed space for more offerings [**Figure 6.7**].

On the other hand, burials in western South Korea in the territory of Mahan consist of one or two simple pits with or without coffins. Often with fewer and simple mortuary offerings, they were prepared under a low earthen mound, and the whole mound is usually surrounded partially or completely by shallow ditches [**Figure 6.8**]. These Low Mound Tombs are found to form a cemetery in many cases, sometimes neatly arranged in their distribution [**Figure 6.9**].

In addition to these Samhan burials, there are very different types of burials in eastern Gyeonggi-do and northern Gangwon-do, which may delineate the territory of Ye [**Figure 6.1**]. Here, there are stone mounds with multiple burial spaces [**Figure 6.10**]. Also, evidence of cremation is known at settlement sites in this part of the country which is so far not seen anywhere else.

In the following review, evidence related to Goguryeo during the period will be dealt with in the next chapter for the sake of convenience as it had appeared before the beginning of the Proto-Three Kingdoms period but lasted until the 7th century. In this chapter, discussion will first touch upon the evidence related to Buyeo, which was absorbed by Goguryeo in the 5th century. Then, a very short mention

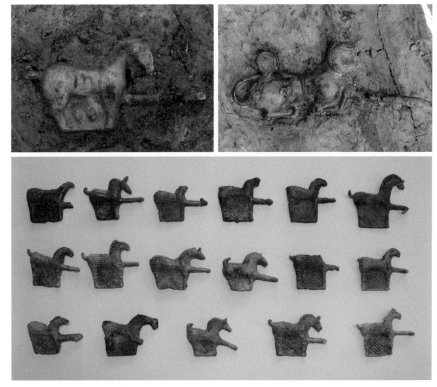

Figure 6.6 Bronze buckles in the shape of horse and tiger are found in the burials of Samhan across South Korea except in parts of Gyeonggi-do and Gangwon-do. Often only a single piece was buried but sometimes many of them are found together. Shown on top are buckles revealed at Sindae-ri in Gyeongsan. Seventeen pieces of the horse-shaped buckles are from Buksu-ri in Asan. Among them, seven pieces were found together. © National Research Institute of Cultural Heritage

Figure 6.7 Distribution of Wooden Coffin Burials in the Gyeongsang Basin. As the burials of the Jinhan elites, their presence is not detected on the surface because of the absence of mound or any other visible sign. Burials shown are those discovered at Yangji-ri in Gyeongsan (left) and Sara-ri (right, top) and Tap-dong (right, bottom) in Gyeongju. © National Research Institute of Cultural Heritage (Yangji-ri, Tap-dong); Yeongnam Institute of Cultural Properties (Sara-ri)

will be given to Eumnu and Okjeo, about which evidence is scanty, especially for Eumnu. The Early Iron Age culture in northeastern Korea and its neighboring region continued as late as the 3rd or the 4th century, which should be related to Okjeo. Evidence of Lelang will follow Okjeo. Many think Lelang had become a

Figure 6.8 Low Mound Tombs are distributed in western South Korea along the coast from Gimpo down to the Yeongsan River basin. The shape and size of the ditches surrounding the burial may vary from place to place. Burials shown here are Unyang-dong in Gimpo (top and middle), and Yecheon-dong in Seosan (bottom). © National Research Institute of Cultural Heritage

Figure 6.9 Burials of the Proto-Three Kingdoms Period in the region of Mahan are usually found to form a cemetery, sometimes demonstrating highly systematic arrangement of individual burials. Examples shown are Giji-ri in Haemi (top), Munseong-ri in Chungju (middle) and Osong in Cheongju (bottom) © National Research Institute of Cultural Heritage (Giji-ri and Munseong-ri); Central Institute of Cultural Heritage (Osong)

political entity of its own by absorbing the indigenous culture and social structure soon after it was established as a commandery. After these four, central and southwestern Korea, i.e., Mahan, Jinhan and Byeohan will be reviewed.

During the period under consideration, Baekje and Silla had gradually dis-

Figure 6.10 Stone mounds with multiple burials are known along the major drainages in northern central part of South Korea. The one shown above is at Hakgok-ri in Yeoncheon on the Imjin River. At Gonjiam to the south of Seoul, a stone mound measuring 55 by 34m at the base was excavated to reveal a total of 80 burials (bottom). © Cultural Heritage Administration (Hakgok-ri); National Research Institute of Cultural Heritage (Gonjiam)

tinguished themselves among their cohorts. Nevertheless, archaeological evidence does not tell us about their or any other's territorial boundaries. What we can see is the presence of gross regional differences between central, southwestern and southeastern Korea with some minor local variations. During this several hundred years of growth and change, regional differentiation had progressed a lot so that even the kinds of sites most frequently encountered look different between the regions. For example, settlement sites are numerous in central and western South Korea but they are rare in the southeast where Silla and Gaya had been growing. Here, most of the information comes from burials.

Buyeo, Eumnu, Okjeo and Lelang

Buyeo is known to be the ancestral homeland of the rulers of both Goguryeo and Baekje. As such, Buyeo was also the family name of the Baekje royalty. It was located in the Songhua Basin in Heilongjiang province of China, and absorbed by Goguryeo in 494 CE. As said in the previous chapter, the Dahaimeng-Paoziyan Type Culture of the previous period is believed to be remains left by the Buyeo people. Results of field research made at its center began to appear in the 1980s, according to which the earthen-wall site of Nanchengzi on the Songhua River nearby Jilin city was the residence for Buyeo elites. The most important discovery so far is known at Laoheshen in Yushu. Here, 129 burials were excavated, which were dated to c. 100 BCE to 100 CE. However, it is a moot point who the buried are as some believe the burials should belong to the nomadic people of Xiongnu or Xianbei, not Buyeo. The question about the identity of the buried is also raised for other burial sites such as Xichagou, which is said to predate Laoheshen. Among the artifacts recovered at these sites, there are some iron long swords with rounded antennae-shaped pommels. Similar pommels are known among some bronze and iron swords of contemporary artifacts in Korea [Figure 6.11].

For Eumnu, although scanty, evidence is for the most part from settlement sites. If the Guntuling Culture represents the remains of Eumnu as mentioned earlier, its sites are distributed on both sides of the Amur River because the so-called Poltse Culture seems to be the Russian version of the Guntuling. The

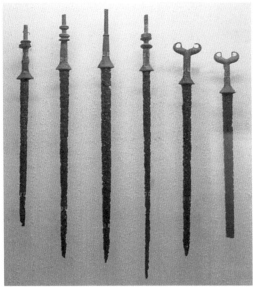

Figure 6.11 Reconstruction of body armor and iron swords from Laoheshen, Yushu, in display at the local museum. (after The Korean Archaeological Society 2010, Figure 100).

Figure 6.12 A pit-house with primitive *Ondol* and pottery revealed at the site of Chernyatino 2 in the Russian Maritime Region. Some researchers believe the pottery should have something to do with similar ones found in northern South Korea such as shown in Figure 6.17. © National Research Institute of Cultural Heritage

beginning date of these cultures is not clear but they seem to have existed several centuries into the Christian Era. Settlement sites were made on high ground and protected by defensive structures, and found with various iron weaponry, which reporters interpreted as demonstrating a high degree of inter-group competition and conflict. Chinese historical records say that Eumnu did not use the cup attached to a slim stand. Its presence is not reported from the Poltse Culture.

Okjeo is said to be represented by the Duanjie-Kronovka Culture, which means that its territory covered both sides of the lower Duman River bordering Korea, China and Russia. In recent years, Korean archaeologists have participated in excavations in the Russian Maritime Region and noticed that some dwelling

Figure 6.13 Ruin of the Lelang Earthen Wall and remains of brick pavement and building. Photographs were taken around 1931. © National Museum of Korea

Figure 6.14 Lelang burials. Early wooden coffin burials (top left) had changed to wooden chamber burials (top right), and bricks replaced wood later (bottom left). Within the chamber, various artifacts were orderly arranged as exemplified by the Tomb No. 9 of Seokam-ri (bottom right). The golden buckle of Figure 6.15 was found here. (after The Korean Archaeological Society 2010, Figure 103)

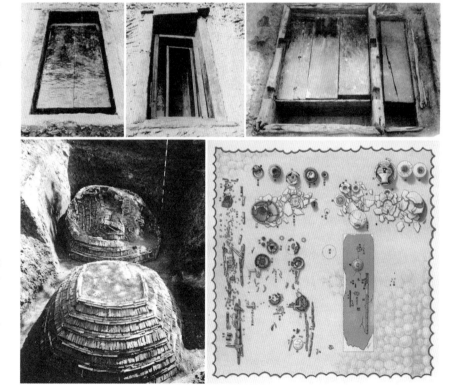

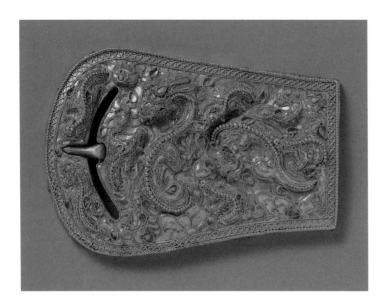

structures and ceramics look similar to those of the Proto-Three Kingdoms Period in central Korea [**Figures 6.12, 6.17**].

Lelang was among the original four commanderies of the Han empire, but the other three were soon disbanded or relocated. Lelang had become strong enough to control much of the northern parts of Korea. In the late 2nd century CE, the central government of China lost its grip over the provincial powers. Lelang submitted to the warlord of the Liaodong region, who in the early 3rd century divided Lelang and established Daebang County in its southern half in order to cope with the indigenous powers. In 313, Goguryeo annexed Lelang, and Daebang next year. While the location of the Lelang center is known [**Figure 6.13**], its counterpart for Daebang is not clear but ruins of an earthen wall in Bongsan in Hwanghaebuk-do could be its location.

Major archaeological remains of Lelang are represented by burials and architectural ruins. For the latter, roof tiles and bricks were found bearing inscriptions indicating their function. A number of clay seals for official documents were also found at such ruins. More spectacular discoveries came from the burials. Among the hundreds of burials found outside of the earthen wall, scores of them were excavated between the early 1910s and the mid-1930s. Only a fraction of them were reported, however, and the remains and field notes kept at the National Museum of Korea are being published one by one.

The early Lelang burials are of a single wooden coffin. Both their structure and burial goods, which include the Korean-style Bronze Dagger, are similar to the pit-burials of the Early Iron Age. Thus, it is usually said that ethnic Chinese were rather minor constituents and the ruling class should have incorporated a

Figure 6.15 Golden buckle excavated in 1916 from the Tomb No. 9 of Seokam-ri. Its length measures 9.4cm. © National Museum of Korea

Figure 6.16 Influence of Lelang ceramic technology is demonstrated by the appearance of new pottery types and kilns in the northern parts of South Korea. © National Research Institute of Cultural Heritage (pottery); Cultural Heritage Administration (kiln)

lot of the local elites. However, as burials had sinicized in time, multiple coffins for closely related family members were laid within a wooden chamber, and, later, a brick chamber [**Figure 6.14**]. Rich with burial goods, these chamber burials had produced glittering personal effects [**Figure 6.15**]. An excavation of 1936 made headlines around the world with the discovery of exquisite burial goods including a lacquered wooden box covered with delicate and vivid paintings. It turned out that this and other lacquer wares were made in Sichuan province in southwestern China today, which was another outpost at the opposite end of the Han empire thousands of kilometers away from Lelang.

But it is not these dazzling artifacts which attract archaeologists' attention nowadays but the plain pottery of everyday use. Including the adoption of the closed kiln, the advanced technology of Lelang stimulated the appearance of new pottery to replace Mumun Pottery [**Figure 6.16**]. Given the geography, it could be that the wave of influence first hit the Mahan polity of Baekje.

Early Baekje and Its Mahan Peers

According to Samguksagi, Baekje was established by two sons of the founder of Goguryeo. They had left Goguryeo in search of their own realms once they realized that neither of them could succeed the throne. The elder of the two chose to settle down nearby the coast but soon joined his brother who settled somewhere in the Seoul area north of the Han River. Together they moved to the south of the river and declared the kingdom as Baekje. It is further said that they were able to settle down with the permission of Mokjiguk, the head polity of the Mahan federation. It is believed that the Mahan polities were distributed in the western lowlands of Gyeonggi-do, Chungcheongnam-do, Jeollabuk-do and northern parts of Jeolla-nam-do [**Figure 1.1**].

It is generally accepted that Baekje began as a mere minor polity but became the leader of Mahan in the middle of the 3rd century. The Proto-Three Kingdoms Period roughly coincides with the first 300+ years of written history of Baekje until its domination over the other Mahan polities. With the emergence of Baekje, in northern Gyeonggi-do and Gangwon-do, two new types of pottery made by different methods appeared. It seems that they were made to accommodate the functional differences, such as cooking versus storage.

One is shaped basically in the tradition of Mumun Pottery but fired under higher temperatures to make it harder and more resistant to fracture. This is called Hardened Mumun Pottery or Jungdo Type Pottery, following the name of the type site [**Figure 6.17**]. Some suggest its diffusion from the northeast as they demonstrate similarities with those of the Kronovka Culture mentioned earlier.

Adoption of new pyro-technology from Lelang is more clearly visible in the other one, Stamped Pottery. As the name indicates, its surface was stamped with a paddle after shaping by potter's wheel [**Figure 6.18**]. Paddles were perhaps made of wood and thinly carved with several kinds of simple geometric designs. Thus, the surface of the pottery looks as if it was intentionally decorated. Unlike Jungdo Type Pottery, this Stamped Pottery is a complete departure from traditional pot-

Figure 6.17 Jungdo Type Pottery from Pungnap-dong in Seoul and Seongsan-ri in Hongcheon. © National Research Institute of Cultural Heritage

Figure 6.18 Stamped Pottery of the Proto-Three Kingdoms Period. Examples are from Daeseong-ri in Gapyeong. A Lelang pottery is shown in the middle. © National Research Institute of Cultural Heritage

tery-making. In general, it is made of a fine, more homogeneous paste with thinner walls and a grey-blueish surface. Firing was done in a closed kiln. While their manufacture is usually believed to be related to the adoption of new technology from Lelang, some suspect that it might have been known already during the 2nd century BCE or even earlier.

For settlement sites, a number of large and small farming communities have been found across the country. Their size varies a lot, from only a few to several hundred pit-houses. Regardless of the number of dwellings, they are located to exploit the rich floodplain soil, following their Bronze Age forefathers [**Figure 6.19**]. More complex sites are also known which look like the center of the Samhan polity recorded as *Gukeup*(국읍). **Figure 6.21** shows one such site known at Seoktae-ri in Hongseong, Chungcheongnam-do. Here, a special residential sector is protected by trenches on top of a low hill, separated from a cemetery to the west and craft shops and commoner's dwellings to the east. The protected area measures roughly 150 by 60m, about the size of the infield zone of an Olympic track. Inside were revealed 174 pit-houses as well as a number of other structures, and 80% of the pit-houses are overlapped. It had been occupied perhaps by a few hundred permanent residents.

In relation to daily life in the village, it seems that small iron implements had been routinely forged at the household level. However, there were villages that specialized in iron work. Now, many dwellings are equipped with *Ondol* [**Figure 6.21**]. By this time, this heating facility had been spread as far south as the islands off the south coast [**Figure 6.26**]. There is no doubt that its propagation would have helped wintering the bitter cold. At the same time, in the absence of fossil fuel, its adoption should have resulted in widespread deforestation, perhaps leaving a major human-induced impact on the environment of Korea for the first time.

Regarding social organization, if we can take the number of dwellings as a proxy, three or four tiers in the settlement hierarchy may be recognized, the site of Seoktaek-ri and the likes sitting on the top. But it is not possible to specify what polity such sites may represent except one.

That is, it is believed that the area surrounded by the earthen wall of Pungnap

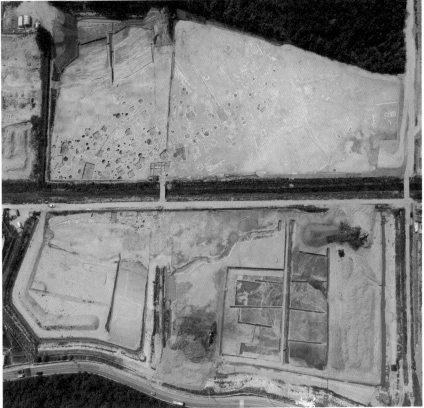

Toseong was where Baekje had started. The wall is in southeastern Seoul abutting
the Han River [**Figure 6.22**]. While more shall be mentioned in the next chapter,
despite an argument for an earlier date, the current wall seems to have been built
most probably not before the early 4th century. Inside the wall, a portion of a large

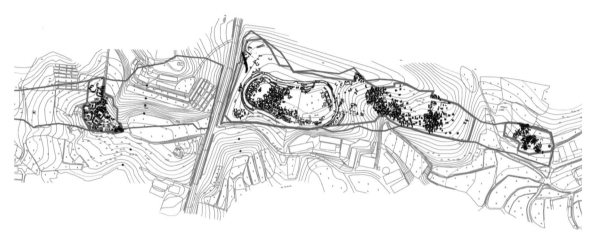

Figure 6.20 The site of Seoktaek-ri. The map shows that the space was divided into several zones. The burial ground made of Low Mound Tombs is on the left side of the map, sitting on a separate hilltop (top right) away from residential areas. At the high ground lies the central residential area presumably for elites where hundreds of dwellings and various facilities were protected by double trenches (bottom). Down the slope were workshops and residential areas of presumably common people. © National Research Institute of Cultural Heritage

Figure 6.21 Primitive *Ondol* and hearth found inside the pit-houses of the Proto-Three Kingdoms Period (after The Korean Archaeological Society 2010, Figure 117)

settlement site was revealed at the Proto-Three Kingdoms Period level. Like the other contemporary pit-houses in Gyeonggi-do and Gangwon-do, they are polygonal in plan, preferably hexagonal, with a characteristic entrance. The average floor size is between 60 to 70m² [**Figure 6.23**]. Out of this humble village, there emerged a bustling royal town surrounded by the intimidating earthen walls.

In the southern part of the Mahan territory, material culture of the Proto-Three Kingdoms Period had been continuously kept until 300 CE. Then, with the southwardly expansion of Baekje, its influence began to appear among the archaeological record. Nevertheless, the southernmost province of Jeollanam-do and its vicinities had maintained their own identity in material culture until its subjugation to Baekje in the late 6th century. Across the sea, life in the volcanic island of Jejudo had little changed since the late Bronze Age. Such 'stagnancy' might have something to do with the lack of metal and other raw materials and/or the arable land to support large populations.

Figure 6.22 It is believed that Baekje appeared as a Mahan polity in the fertile floodplain on the southern shore of the Han River. The place is what is today southeastern Seoul dominated by one of the tallest skyscrapers in the world. Arrows indicate Pungnap (left) and Mongchon Toseong (right; cf. Figure 7.11). Although not shown in the photo, the royal burial ground of Seokchon-dong lies just below the photographed area (cf. Figures 7.9, 7.10). Courtesy Seoul Baekje Museum

Jinhan and Byeonhan

Jinhan and Byeonhan were in the Gyeongsang Basin. The main channel of the Nakdong River was the rough boundary between the two but Byeonhan polities occupied the estuary on both shores. As if to confirm the historical record that they shared customs and language, archaeological remains demonstrate strong homogeneity across the whole basin while showing marked contrast with the other parts of the country. Such characteristics may have something to do with the geography. On one hand, the basin is somewhat isolated as it is bounded by the sea and the Sobaek Mountains [**Figures 1.4, 1.5**]. On the other hand, there is no real topographic barrier to hinder transportation within the basin. At the same time, the Nakdong River provided convenient waterways leading to many corners of the basin, which should have contributed a lot to maintaining cultural homogeneity.

A unique characteristic of the archaeological remains is best seen in the ceramic assemblage, especially in mortuary pottery [**Figure 6.24**]. With thin walls and fine, homogeneous texture, these new wares are collectively called Wajil Togi, Like the case of Stamped Pottery, they are often interpreted as the result of the adoption of the new technology from Lelang. At first, they retained the shape of Black Burnished and Attached-Rim Pottery of the previous period [**Figure 6.5**, lower right]. Soon various forms were made in time and the products were later fired under higher temperatures.

Figure 6.23. Pit-houses of the Proto-Three Kingdoms Period. Those found in Gyeonggi-do and Gangwon-do are large enough to be occupied more than a single nuclear family. However, those of the southern provinces are square or round in shape and as small as the Songguk-ri Type pit-houses of the Late Bronze Age. Hexagonal pit-houses shown here are from Gorim-dong in Yongin south of Seoul (top left), Woncheon-ri in Hwacheon (top right), and Jungdo in Chuncheon (middle left). The others are from Daeppyeong-dong in Sejong (middle right), Taemok-ri in Damyang (bottom left) and Bongmu-dong in Daegu (bottom right). Notice the eighteen people lying to make a cross inside the Gorim-dong pit-house. © National Research Institute of Cultural Heritage

Figure 6.24 Wajil Togi as mortuary pottery appeared in the 1ˢᵗ century BCE in its characteristic shape as shown in Figure 6.5. It is known from the burials such as the one revealed at Deok-cheon-ri in Gyeongju. Many new types were made in the middle of the 2ⁿᵈ century CE. They began to be replaced by Silla and Gaya Pottery from the late 3ʳᵈ century. The timing coincides with the beginning of the construction of large mound burials. © National Museum of Korea (pottery); National Research Institute of Cultural Heritage (burial)

As pottery diversified and new ones appeared, any development was almost immediately spread across the basin. In the 2ⁿᵈ century, some pottery was painted with *Ot* in stripe patterns. Also, duck-like figurine vessels appeared at this time [**Figure 6.24**]. Their production had continued until the early 4ᵗʰ century as they began to be replaced by Silla and Gaya Pottery at the end of the 3ʳᵈ century.

Interestingly, the absolute majority of archeological sites of this period in the

Figure 6.25 The burial site of Yangdong-ri, Gimhae. Here, burials are found from top to bottom largely in chronological order (© Dong-eui University Museum).

Gyeongsang Basin are made up of burials with Wajil Togi. Settlement sites are so rare that a mere 20 or so of them were known by 2020. In comparison, although the exact quantity of the burials cannot be presented, there must be more than several thousand of them and one can easily recount the names of at least twenty sites with hundreds of burials [e.g., **Figure 6.25**]. Such disparity between the two is difficult to explain but a hint might be found in a phrase of historical writing, which says that the region was "the land of reedy thickets". One might suspect that many settlements occupied riverine, marsh or swampy environments so that dwellings were constructed as buildings with a raised floor. Indeed, sites full of post holes and foundations of wooden structures in the form of stakes driven into the ground have been discovered.

Although it is hard to determine whether such sites were genuine settlements, from what we can see at the few settlement sites with pit-houses, life of ordinary people had remained the same as the Late Bronze Age. Dwellings are small, usually less than 25m^2 or so, and in square or round shape. However, towards the end of the period, there were large ones with a floor size of more than 40m^2 and equipped with *Ondol*. Also, some settlements were protected with wooden fences and/or trenches. In the meantime, shell-mounds came back. While those on the west coast are rather small in scale, others on the south coast and the southern islands are relatively thick and large. The best example can be found on Neuk-do island. Here, pit-houses equipped with *Ondol*, jar-coffins and pit burials were found side by side within the shell-midden deposit which once covered the whole island [**Figure 6.26**].

Figure 6.26 The small island of Neukdo off the south coast is covered with archaeological deposits. Excavation of shell middens revealed dwellings and burials of the Proto-Three Kingdoms Period. Foreign artifacts found here indicate sea-faring had been quite active at the time. Photos show an aerial view of the island, burials, dwellings with *Ondol*, Yayoi pottery from Japan, potsherds from Lelang and Chinese coins. © Cultural Heritage Administration

Figure 6.27 The Proto-Three Kingdoms Period iron implements of the Gyeongsang Basin (after The Korean Archaeological Society 2010, Figure 138). Tools for cultivation, weapons and horse fittings are seen.

While burials known at Neukdo and some other places are poor with mortuary goods and appear to be those of commoners, elites were buried with rich diverse offerings. Among such artifacts are chunks of ferriferous rock, which seems to symbolize the importance of iron in society. Likewise, many of the burials are found with a number of iron ingots or swords, demonstrating the riches brought by its trade [**Figure 6.7**]. Locally produced iron weaponry appeared for the first time in some burials of the late 2nd century BCE [**Figure 6.27**]. It might be that iron was obtained at first by processing iron sand, but mining of iron ore began by the 1st century BCE. Furnaces and other evidence for smelting and forge welding began to be found here and there at the same time. If the early production of iron had remained at a somewhat domestic level, it had become more systematic by the 2nd to the 3rd century [**Figure 6.28**].

In addition to iron ingots, other luxury items found as mortuary goods are similar to those found in the burials of the previous period. In fact, the overall mortuary practice had not changed at all and rather strengthened. The Korean-style Bronze Daggers were put in lacquered wooden scabbards to be offered as burial goods along with writing pens, fans and diverse imported artifacts.

Early burials of the Proto-Three Kingdoms Period are called Wooden Coffin Burials [**Figure 6.29**]. Continuing the tradition of the previous period, the space between the coffin and the pit is sometimes filled with chunks of rock but rather rarely. These burials are usually found to form a cemetery of elites. One of the best examples is the site of Daho-ri in Changwon [**Figure 6.30**]. In this remarkably well-preserved cemetery, coffins were made out of dug-out trunks of tree, in this case oak, their top and bottom parts put together by wooden tongue and groove.

Figure 6.28 Evidence of iron production during the Proto-Three Kingdoms Period (after The Korean Archaeological Society 2010, Figure 135). Pictures show a mining site at Dalcheon, Ulsan (top), furnaces revealed at Hwang-seong-dong, Gyeongju (middle), and artifacts and byproducts of iron production such as blastpipe, casting mould, fragments of furnace wall, pieces of slag and ore (bottom).

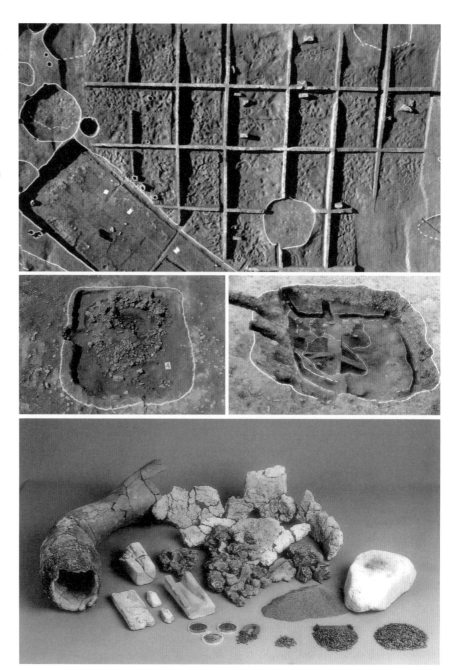

Disassembled Daho-ri coffins look a lot like the Neolithic canoe found at Bibong-ri, which is only about 10km away on the other side of the Nakdong River.

In time, coffins became larger and wooden boards and planks replaced dug-out trunks. By the middle of the 2nd century CE, as elite burials became more luxurious and bigger, coffins were laid within larger wooden receptacles to accommodate more goods [**Figure 6.7**]. These Wooden Receptacles seem to be found in close proximity to the political center as exemplified by the one shown in **Figure 6.25**. By now, it seems that the elites had solidified their political power. However, the griz-

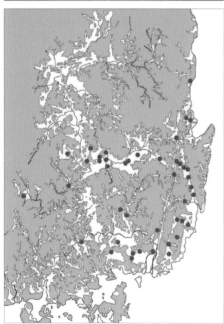

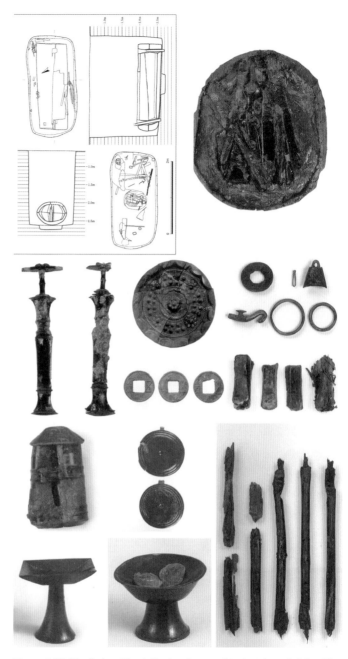

Figure 6.29 Most of the Wooden Coffin Burials of the early Proto-Three Kingdoms Period in the Gyeongsang Basin are found along the main and tributary channels of the Nakdong River. Their distribution should be closely related to the location of Jinhan and Gyeonhan polities. The burial shown above is known at Tap-dong in Gyeongju, signalling the rise of Saroguk, the predecessor of the kingdom of Silla. © National Research Institute of Cultural Heritage

Figure 6.30 The Daho-ri Tomb No. 1 and some of its burial goods (after The Korean Archaeological Society 2010, Figures 136, 144). Luxury items were put inside a basket laid within a hollow prepared beneath the coffin and at various spots inside and outside of the coffin.

zly practice of human sacrifice was not in practice yet, which was quite widespread during the Three Kingdoms Period in this area.

New Orders Emerging

During the Proto-Three Kingdoms Period, the southern Korean Peninsula was full of thriving farming communities collectively known as Samhan. People continued to live in the way established at the end of the Bronze Age. However, society in general had become much more complex. During the period, burials of elites in the inland region of central Korea are represented by stone mound burials while the western part of South Korea is characterized by pit-burial mounds. Such regional characteristics remained unchanged until the 3rd century CE for about 400 years. Southeastern Korea also demonstrates its own characteristics in mortuary practice. Differences in mortuary practice seems to match roughly the distribution of different groups of Samhan as recorded in history. It could be that agricultural productivity was behind the rise of these early polities. Long-distance trade of iron and other specialty products should have stimulated such development. As polities were more organized structurally, peaceful relationships between the polities began to be threatened as told by the record about the conflict between Baekje and Mokjiguk, the leading poity of Mahan, in the middle of the 3rd century and other similar examples. Although inter-group competition should have been inevitable as polities were growing, however, archaeological evidence of such conflicts is yet to be found. It seems that the wealth demonstrated by elite burials bodes ill that there would soon be powers to behold. In coming years, massive burial mounds were constructed for the rulers of the competing kingdoms.

CHAPTER 7

THREE KINGDOMS PERIOD AND AFTER

Korean History - A Quick Overview

The beginning of the Three Kingdoms Period in South Korea is best indicated by the impressive mound burials in Gyeongju (**Figure 7.1**) and other centers of ancient states. If historical accounts until this time are somewhat blurry and obscure with elements of mythology and legend, they become clearer in their description with more facts than tales. In many ancient centers such as Gyeongju, archaeological research will never end just like any other historical city around the world. Here, known as the thousand-year capital of Silla, there are all kinds of archaeological remains waiting to be excavated. For example, excavation at the ruin of the Hwang-nyongsa temple and its vicinities [**Figure 7.2**] began in 1972 and will continue for several more decades to come.

During the Three Kingdoms Period, Goguryeo, Baekje and Silla had maintained complex military and political relationships with each other as well as China and Japan. As mentioned, Silla started as the minor Jinhan polity of Saroguk. For a long time, it had been subject to frequent intimidations by others until the 5th century. However, it annexed the Gaya federation in the 6th century, and ultimately defeated Baekje in 660 and Goguryeo in 668 in alliance with Tang China. It took another eight years for Silla to mop up the remnant Baekje forces and their Japanese allies while getting rid of the expeditionary forces of Tang who attempted to take over Silla. Thus, final unification was achieved in 676 and the Unified Silla Period began.

Meanwhile, written accounts may not always be accurate in delivering information of the past, and it tends to be more so as we go further back in time. This is also the case for Korea. For example, there is no record about some political entities that once existed during the Three Kingdoms Period, and their presence is revealed only by recent archaeological research. Particularly, in the southwestern provinces of Jeolla-do, excavation since the 1990s has resulted in new and surprising discoveries. It turned out that large mound burials dotting the area predate Baekje's domination there in the 6th century. However, there is no available record about

Figure 7.1 Silla mound burials in the Daeneungwon archaeological park in Gyeongju. Large residential area to its east has been cleared for excavation, revealing a number of early Silla burials since the early 2000s. © Cultural Heritage Administration

their makers whatsoever. Archaeological research suggests that they represent the remnant groups of the Mahan federation or, simply, the Late Mahan.

While Silla had won the whole territory of Baekje, it got only a small portion of Goguryeo so that its northern limit barely reached its capital, Pyeongyang, which fell in the hands of Chinese forces. Nevertheless, it seems that most of Goguryeo's territory had been left free as Tang was interested in maintaining their presence only at some key places. In the year of 698, thirty years after the fall of Goguryeo, the kingdom of Balhae emerged and reclaimed most of Goguryeo's territory. The border between Silla and Balhae had been set roughly along the line connecting Pyeongyang and Wonsan in central North Korea. Balhae collapsed in 926 by the nomadic people of Kidan, who later humiliated the Song dynasty of China and occupied its northern half as the empire of Liao. With the collapse of Balhae, the Korean Culture Sphere had been confined to the Korean Peninsula for good. Silla's demise came in 935 when the last king gave himself up to the rising Goryeo.

It seems that Balhae was a multi-ethnic nation and its constituents included non-Korean groups such as Mohe. Therefore, researchers of different countries tend to show differences in their opinion about the nature of Balhae society and culture, often reflecting nationalistic inclinations. As Balhae is known to be established by a former Goguryeo general and the majority of the population were former Goguryeo subjects, it is treated as another Korean state in South Korea. As a corollary, the term of North-South State Period was suggested as an alternative to the Unified Silla Period so that both terms are now in use.

Considering the territorial size of Balhae, archaeological information is poorly known. Since the 1950s, excavation began at some burial and temple sites scattered across China, Russia and North Korea, and some excavations are known to be quite large in scale. However, the available information is still limited. In comparison, much has been studied for Silla after unification. One interesting aspect of Silla archaeology is that those luxurious mound burials of the Three Kingdoms Period

Figure 7.2 A scaled model of the main complex of the Hwangnyongsa temple on display at the Gyeongju National Museum. Historical records indicate that the wooden pagoda shown in the middle was 90m tall.

disappeared after unification and cremation had spread due to the influence of Buddhism.

Prosperity of the post-unification Silla is well recorded, which is confirmed by archaeological evidence. But corruption and dissipation had destroyed the social stability in the 9th century and induced peasant rebellions. In the final years of the century, the new dynasty of Hubaekje(892-935) was born, its name literally meaning Late Baekje. Soon, another dynasty of Taebong(901-918) also appeared but it was taken by the founder of Goryeo(918-1392). After Goryeo defeated Hubaekje in 935, Silla surrendered to Goryeo the same year. The Late Three Kingdoms Period indicates these several decades of the late 9th and the early 10th century during which Hubaekje, and Taebong, and later Goryeo, were competing with Silla for dominance.

During the Goryeo Period, the most significant incident was the Mongol invasion. Starting from 1231, Mongols invaded Goryeo six times. In 1232, Goryeo elites escaped to Ganghwado, an island off the mouth of Han River, and resisted for many decades. But their endurance was paid off by severe and rampant sacking and destruction. In Gyeongju, for example, Hwangnyongsa temple with its nine-storied wooden pagoda was burnt down in 1238. The pagoda was the architectural gem of Silla originally built in the mid-7th century. In 1270, Goryeo gave up and got incorporated into the empire of Yuan (1271-1368), the Mongol dynasty of China, as a son-in-law country. Successive Goryeo kings married to Mongol princesses for over a century and a number of Goryeo people were accepted in the Yuan court and the government. One of them even became the empress to be the mother of the last Yuan emperor. The close cultural relationship between Goryeo and the Mongols during the period is well demonstrated by the fact that traces of Mongol customs and language are still around. For example, in a traditional wedding ceremony the bride puts a pink dot on each cheek as the final touch of makeup, which is known as a remnant Mongol custom.

In the late 14th century, Yuan China was in chaos with peasant rebellions. Goryeo also had to deal with invasions by the Chinese rebels as well as massed Japanese pirates. Their subjugation required a military hero, who ultimately overthrew Goryeo and started the new dynasty of Joseon in 1392. Until it was annexed by Japan in 1910, Joseon was ruled by 27 kings. History of the first two hundred years of Joseon was relatively quiet and peaceful. Then, its fate was almost doomed with the Japanese invasion of 1592. The bitter war lasted a full six years and utterly devastated the country. Treasures and relics were destroyed and pillaged, and some of the looted items are now national treasures of Japan. Joseon experienced another disaster in 1636 with the invasion by Qing, the last dynasty of China built by the ethnic Manchus, who wanted to pacify its rear before initiating the invasion of China. Following these two disasters, the 18th and the 19th century were full of drought, famine, peasant rebellions, political purges and religious persecutions. The weakened Joseon had to give up its policy of isolation and opened its gate to the outside world in 1876. In a few years, archaeological observation of Korea was made for the first time by the visitors as mentioned in the introductory chapter.

Review of the archaeology for all these historical periods will begin with Goguryeo and Balhae. Although the main body of the territory of Goguryeo had been across North Korea and northeastern China, its southern boundary had fluctuated, sometimes expanding as far south as central South Korea so that there are known fortresses and burials. Balhae's territory never stretched that far south.

Goguryeo

As Goguryeo had appeared many years before the other two of the Three Kingdoms, its archaeological remains are found from as early as c. 300 BCE, if not earlier. Its first capital was in today's Huanren county in Liaoning province in China and was relocated to Zhian on the Amnok River in 3 CE and remained there until 427. Ruined walls of the capital can be seen in the town of Zhian. Nearby there are impressive burials and monuments. The capital was relocated again to Pyeongyang in 427 during the reign of King Jangsu(394-491) as he pursued the policy of southwardly expansion.

As the territory of Goguryeo was vast, naturally its remains are found at many places in Korea and northeast China as burials, fortresses, city walls, architectural foundations, etc. Early burials were constructed as stone mounds and found mainly along the Hun River, a tributary of Amnok on the China side, and around Zhian.

Figure 7.3 Janggunchong and the stele of Gwanggaeto the Great (after The Korean Archaeological Society 2010, Figures 157, 147)

Figure 7.4 Goguryeo pottery excavated in the Seoul area. Compared to the dark greyish surface of Silla, Gaya and Baekje pottery, they generally appear buff in color. These are utensils of daily use like the steamer sitting on top of an iron kettle found at a hilltop fortress in Seoul. © Seoul National University Museum

Among them, the most famous is Janggunchong. Measuring 34 by 34m at its base with a height of 13m, this stepped pyramid is regarded as the tomb of Gwanggaeto the Great(374-412). Nearby the tomb, there stands a monument of 6.39m tall whose four sides are covered with inscriptions depicting his great achievements [**Figure 7.3**]. Close to them are many ruins of fortresses occupying strategic locations.

Among various artifacts, ceramics demonstrate unique features of Goguryeo both in terms of their shape and style as well as texture and color. They had remained unchanged [**Figure 7.4**]. While various artifacts from many sites have been retrieved, personal ornaments made of precious metals are relatively few. If found, unlike Silla and Baekje, they are usually made of gilt bronze, not gold and

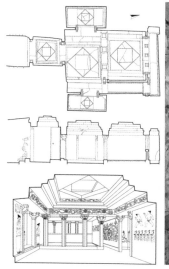

Figure 7.5 Stone chamber burial known as Tomb No. 3 of Anank (after The Korean Archaeological Society 2010, Figures 158, 159). Goguryeo burials had changed from simple stone mound to complex stone chamber burials with mural paintings. Inscription written next to the painting indicates this tomb was built in 357.

Figure 7.6 Goguryeo mural paintings with mythological figures and symbols drawn on the wall and the ceiling (after The Korean Archaeological Society 2010, Figure 161). These three are all in the vicinity of Pyeongyang.

Figure 7.7 Ruins of Hongnyeonbong Fortress No. 2 on the foothill of Achasan and Achasan Fortress No. 4 (lower right). A number of Goguryeo fortresses were constructed in this strategic area in Seoul at the locations indicated by arrows in the top left photo. In the next one, the location of Pungnap and MongchonToseong is indicated by <B> and <C> (cf. Figure 7.9). <A> indicates Achasanseong, a fortress built later by Silla. <D> indicates another Goguryeo fortress. © Institute of Archaeology and Environment, Korea University (Hongnyeonbong)

silver.

By the time King Jangsu moved the capital to Pyeongyang, stone chamber burials with mural paintings were being made. Themes of the early paintings include scenes of warfare, hunting, parades and portraits [**Figure 7.5**], which were gradually replaced by religious symbols and mythological themes [**Figure 7.6**]. Some 80 of them are known, about two thirds in North Korea, mostly around Pyeongyang. These burials with mural paintings are designated as UNESCO World Cultural Heritage. Also, in North Korea, palace ruins and Buddhist temples were excavated. In Pyeongyang, the ruin of Anhakgung palace had been excavated partially along with the fortress protecting the palace.

Goguryeo fortresses known in South Korea are relatively small. They were first discovered as late as 1977 on a hilltop on the northern shore of the Han River. Later, more of them were located along the nearby mountain ridges and other strategically important places [**Figure 7.7**]. Ruins of fortresses, walls and fences are also found along the Imjin and the Hantan River to the north and as far south as the Daejeon area. These military facilities had been built and abandoned as the frontline fluctuated. Reflecting the nature of the sites, various weapons, personal armors, and utensils have been found. Structural remains include ruins of barracks, storage pits and articulated stone walls. In some cases, a scene of a surprise attack by an enemy can be inferred from the state and distribution of the remains, such as burnt stockpiles of grains and hastily abandoned personal armor.

Goguryeo burials found in South Korea are not comparable to those grand ones built at Pyeongyang and other centers, and only a few small stone chamber burials are known. When found by archaeologists, they were already devoid of any artifacts inside. Nevertheless, their ceilings demonstrate typical structural features of Goguryeo stone chamber tombs, namely, the intersecting triangular ceiling as shown in **Figure 7.6**.

Balhae

For Balhae, sites consist of ruins of palaces and administrative buildings, fortresses, burials and Buddhist temples. While there should be many of such sites, only a few have been reported. Also, excavation has been small-scale at most of the sites except some burials. From the limited information, stylistic elements in material culture seem to demonstrate the multi-cultural and multi-ethnic nature of Balhae society.

The first archaeological study of Balhae was made in the 1930s at a palace ruin about 200km north of the northern tip of the Korean Peninsula. It was the most important center among the so-called Five Capitals of Balhae. Ruins of a palace and temple buildings were tested, and traces of city and palace walls, roads and gates were noticed. Collected artifacts for the most part consist of ceramics, roof tiles and other building materials as well as Buddhist figurines [**Figure 7.8**]. They were divided and sent to three Japanese imperial universities at that time. As a result, they are now kept separately in Seoul National University in Korea, the Uni-

Figure 7.8 Roof end-tiles and a clay figurine of Buddha collected in the 1930s and on display at the Seoul National University Museum. © Seoul National University Museum (figurine)

versity of Tokyo in Japan and National Taiwan University in Taiwan. From the 1990s, South Korean researchers have participated in excavation at Balhae sites in the Russian Far East. Among them, the fortress site in the township of Kraskino is regarded as one of the provincial centers.

For burials, sites are reported scattered across its territory so that burials are found in China, northeastern Korea and the Russian Maritime Region. Among them, the best known ones are the royal tombs of the 8th century. In 1949, the tomb of Princess Jeonghye (Zhenhui in Chinese) was found about 120km southwest of the Upper Capital. Nearby, in 1980 a votive pagoda and the tomb of Princess Jeonghyo (Zhenxiao in Chinese), a younger sister of Jeonghye, was found. From the 1990s, large-scale excavations have been carried out at several burial sites, revealing hundreds of brick and stone chamber burials. Balhae burials excavated in Russia turn out to be of similar design.

As Buddhism was the official religion, Buddhist temples were built in major centers. Temple sites are also known in Russia and North Korea, like the one known at Omae-ri in Sinpo, Hamgyeongnam-do. Interestingly, a guilt bronze sutra panel found here was reported as a product from the Goguryeo period.

Other than these highly visible remains, there is little information which may tell us about the everyday life of people. If any, it is limited to a few dwelling structures found at the residential quarters within the ruins of fortresses such as the ones known at Kraskino. They look little different from those of the Early Iron Age pit-houses equipped with primitive *Ondol* [cf. **Figure 6.12**]. There is little evidence indicating the importance of agriculture in terms of subsistence. Given the climate of its territory, it is not surprising that people relied on hunting, fishing and animal husbandry rather than agriculture.

Baekje

Began as a minor Mahan polity, Baekje gradually became strong enough to attack even Lelang and Goguryeo. In 371, Baekje attacked Goguryeo and killed the king. Goguryeo began a series of retaliatory campaigns, and, finally in 475, the Baekje capital Hanseong was sacked and the captured king was humiliated and beheaded. Frightened, Baekje relocated the capital far south to Ungjin on the Geum River, hoping that the rugged landscape would provide protection. It regained its strength only after the second relocation of the capital to Sabi in 536. Baekje met its demise in 660 due to a mass invasion by the allied forces of Silla and Tang China.

The history of Baekje is often divided into three periods according to the location of the capital. Thus, the period until 475 is called the Hanseong Period, followed by the Ungjin and the Sabi Period. Archaeological research has traditionally focused on these three capitals so that much work has been done in and around Seoul, Gongju and Buyeo where they had been located. Of course, many more archaeological sites are known throughout its territory. As is the case for Goguryeo and the others, most of the works are about burials, architectural ruins and fortresses. In recent years, other types of sites are also actively investigated, such as common settlements, production facilities, agricultural fields, roads as well as ritual and cer-

Figure 7.9 Pungnap and MongchonToseong. Being located next to the Han River, the northeastern part of PungnapToseong and its adjoining areas had long been destroyed by flooding. Also, uncontrolled urban expansion had filled its inner area with residential buildings, inflicting a lot of damage to archaeological deposits. The surviving part of the earthen wall of Pungnap Toseong is indicated by a smooth white line running across the 11m-tall section exhibited in the lobby of the Seoul Baekje Museum (top right). Around MongchonToseong are athletic facilities constructed for the 1988 Seoul Olympic Games (bottom). After the sack of the Baekje capital, Goguryeo had kept a series of fortresses at high points on the opposite side of the Han River (cf. Figure 7.7). © National Research Institte of Cultural Heritage (aerial view of Pungnap Toseong); Seoul Baekje Museum (MongchonToseong)

emonial sites.

The capital of the Hanseong Period is represented by two neighboring earthen walls of Pungnap and Mongchon Toseong [**Figures 6.22, 7.9**] as well as mound burials at Seokchon-dong [**Figure 7.10**]. They are within walking distance from each other. It is generally believed that Pungnap was built only after it had become strong enough to compete with its powerful neighbors in the 4th century. It was originally 3.5km long in total, protecting an area of about 840,000m² inside. The width of its base was about 40m with a height of 11m. The surviving wall measures about 2.1km long and 9m high at the highest point. Within the wall, the Proto-Three Kingdoms Period settlements are overlaid by the remains of the Three Kingdoms Period. Many of the structures and features of Baekje appear to be related to administrative and religious activities.

In comparison, Mongchon Earthen Wall was less heavily occupied. It seems that the place had become important only late in time. Excavation revealed that the army of Goguryeo was once stationed here, befitting the story of the sack of Hanseong in 475. The area in and around the wall was turned into a well-groomed sports park as a result of the Seoul Olympic Games of 1988 [**Figure 7.9**].

Two kilometers away from here lies the royal burial ground of Seokchon-dong, where Baekje royalty of the Hanseong Period were buried [**Figure 7.10**]. The earliest burials here are not the stone mounds as we see today but unassuming pit burials

Figure 7.10 Mound burials of Seokchon-dong and Burial No. 3. A survey map of the 1930s indicates that there were a lot of stone and earthen mounds in this area. Most of them had been destroyed by 1970 before systematic archaeological research was possible. Burial No. 3 is the largest, whose base measures 55 by 55m, thus, even larger than Janggunchong. However, its original height cannot be estimated. Smaller ones lying to its south are Burial No. 4 and 2. Excavation of the empty space between the mounds began in 2017 to reveal many infrastructures of the destroyed burials. © Seoul Baekje Museum (aerial view)

and earthen mound burials of the late 3rd century. The latter is sometimes regarded as a continuation of the mound burials of the Proto-Three Kingdoms Period. It is believed that the stone mound burials were built in the 4th century until the abandonment of the capital.

Today, a mere half a dozen or so mounds can be seen here. However, at least 290 stone and earthen mounds once existed scattered over a larger area. Before the first excavation conducted in 1974, a tin can village had occupied the area following the Korean War. The largest mound, Tomb No. 3, was destroyed and covered by a number of ramshackle residential units. The surviving part of the mound is only 4.3m tall but it would have been quite an impressive structure as its base measures

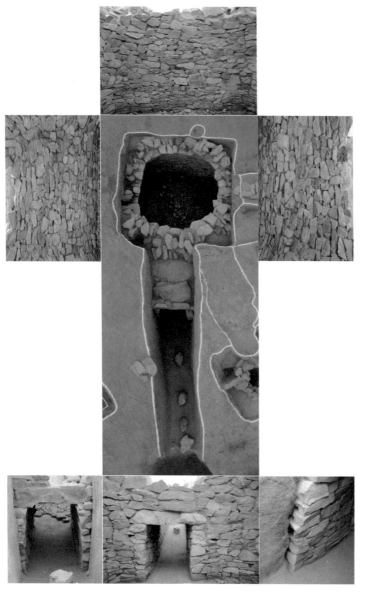

21m longer than Janggunchong on four sides [**Figure 7.3**].

Including Seokchon-dong, the most common remains of Baekje are burials. Stone Chamber Burials of the ruling class began to appear from the late 4th century in the vicinities of the capital and at key locations mixed with other simpler burials. By the time the capital was moved to Gongju, stone chamber burials of the capital area had been spread to the provinces [**Figure 7.11**]. More importantly, various types of burials were in use by the late 5th century. They are regarded as somehow reflecting the social status of the buried. Also, distribution of different burials and mortuary goods is considered as evidence demonstrating that Baekje had completely prevailed over the remnant Mahan polities by this time and that provinces were governed by the officials dispatched from the central government.

Outside of the capital area, the Low Mound Tomb of the Proto-Three Kingdoms Period had not been abandoned but made continuously with local modifications. Thus, along the west coast, they continued to demonstrate the features of the previous period and occasionally mounds had become very large and complex with multiple burials. In some cases, burials were added later so that multiple burials may be found within a single mound. In comparison, those of the inland area began to lose those shallow ditches dug around the mound [cf. **Figure 6.8**] in the late 5th century. Also, sometimes the pit in which the coffin was laid had its walls made of gravels or split rocks.

Figure 7.11 Tomb No. 16 of Songwon-ri in Yeon-gi (after The Korean Archaeological Society 2010, Figure 192).

For the Ungjin Period, the most famous discovery is of course the Tomb of King Muryeong [**Figure 7.12**]. Born in 462 on an island off the coast of northern Kyushu, Japan, he was the 25th king of Baekje who reigned from 501 until his death in 523. He was later joined by his wife in 529. She was buried next to him in the same chamber made of bricks in the style of contemporary south China. With all the mortuary goods including two pieces of stone epitaph with inscriptions detailing the life of the king, it was one of the most spectacular archaeological discoveries of

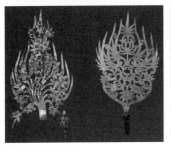

Figure 7.12 Tomb of King Muryeong. Parts of gold headgear, Queen's bronze mortuary shoes and a silver cup on bronze saucer are shown (after The Korean Archaeological Society 2010, Figures 194, 202, 204 and 210).

the 20th century in Korea.

In 538, King Seong, the son of Muryeong, moved the capital to Sabi which is a short distance away from Ungjin down the Geum River, thus, began the Sabi Period. Baekje flourished there for 122 years. However, at the time of its fall, the capital was turned to ashes. Desperate circumstances at the time of the sack are suggested by another spectacular discovery. In 1993, excavation conducted at the ruin of a shrine in front of the royal burials at Neungsan-ri in the outskirts of the Buyeo town retrieved a guilt bronze incense burner [**Figure 7.13**]. With all the delicate and exquisite decorations, this magnificent burner should have served for some ancestor-related royal ceremony. It was found with other valuables hurriedly tucked together in a wooden box which was thrown into a well.

In addition to the burials, ruins of Buddhist temples are also important for the archaeology of Baekje. Buddhism was known to Baekje in 384 and the first temple was built in the following year at the capital. However, virtually all of the known ruins of Baekje temples are from the Sabi Period. Among them, there is one particularly important site, which is the ruin of the temple of Mireuksa. Lying about 30km south of Buyeo, the temple was constructed during the 7th century as one of the biggest Buddhist temples ever built in Korea with its precinct covering almost 1,400 hectares. Close to the temple lies another vast ruin of a Bakeje

Figure 7.13 The Incense Burner of Baekje on display at Buyeo National Museum.

palace. Together, they are taken as evidence telling that the secondary capital of Baekje was here. The temple had originally three stone pagodas but only the so-called West Pagoda has endured the test of the time and retained much of its original shape [**Figure 7.14**]. Now, visitors can appreciate what the stone pagodas were like in the 7th century from the reconstructed East Pagoda which was revealed to the public in 2018 after 20 years of research and stone work.

With so many temple ruins, various figurines of Buddha and Bodhisattva as well as other religious crafts are of course frequently found. Baekje is said to have been a nation with superb artisans, and many treasures of Silla and Wa were made by them. Some of the finest examples are now in Japan, at such temples as Horyuji and Koryuji in Nara, the ancient capital of the Aska Period. Here, masterpieces such as the so-called Standing Statue of the Baekje Bodhisattva of Mercy have survived. In fact, so many other exquisite relics from Korea are kept in many places throughout Japan, reflecting the close but often turbulent history between the two.

Yeongsan River Basin before Baekje

As Baekje gradually attained control of the southwestern parts of Korea by annexing and absorbing others, it took a while for Baekje to exert its power over the southernmost parts of the country. It is believed that its territory had not reached the south coast before the mid-6th century. Until this time, archaeological evidence suggests that there existed an independent power or powers in the southwestern corner of Korea, about which not a single word among the written records has been found. It could be that the unique culture here had grown out of the local Mahan culture.

Here, the presence of large earthen mounds has been noticed from the early days of archaeological research. Testing carried out in the 1910s and 1930s revealed jar

Figure 7.14 The West and the East Pagoda of the Mireuksa Temple. The East Pagoda had been in the state of almost complete collapse before reconstruction.

coffins underneath the mounds. They are quite large and thick, capable of laying inside a whole body stretched with various glittering ornaments and other status items, thus, completely different from Baekje burials. These mortuary jars were produced at special kilns devoted to their manufacture [**Figure 7.15**].

Since the late 1980s, active inquiries began to be made about these burials distributed along the drainages of the Yeongsan River and in the adjoining coastal region. It was revealed that, from around 300 CE, large, conspicuous burial mounds with specially manufactured jar coffins were being built.

Among them, the most interesting one is Tomb No. 3 excavated at Bokam-ri in Naju [**Figure 7.16**], within whose mound were found virtually every kind of burial so far known in the basin. That is, a total of 41 burials of 7 different types forming layers of burials were found within the square mound measuring 43 by 41m on the base and 6m high. The lowermost 21 jar coffin burials are dated to the 4th century. They are overlaid by stone chamber burials of the 5th and the 6th century. A single chamber may contain up to four jar or wooden coffins. Some of the artifacts came from Japan and so is the timber for some coffins. On top of all these burials were built the Baekje-style stone chamber burials, seemingly signifying the dominance of Baekje over the indigenous power.

In the Yeongsan Basin, other surprising discoveries have been found. The most unexpected one was the so-called key-hole shaped mound resembling those of the contemporary Kofun Period of Japan [**Figure 7.17**]. Not only the overall shape of

Figure 7.15 Sinchon-ri Tomb No. 9 in Naju. Black and white photos were taken in 1918 at the time of excavation. Jar coffins found here contained a number of luxurious mortuary items including a gilt bronze crown. The mound and its surroundings were re-excavated in 1999 to obtain information about its construction. © National Museum of Korea; National Research Institute of Cultural Heritage (aerial view)

the mound is similar but also evidence of funerary practice shows unmistakable Japanese affinities, such as aligning the Haniwa mortuary figurines in front of the mound. The identity of the group who left these key-hole shaped mounds is a matter for debate. Popular opinion is that they were for the elites of the relic Mahan group(s) who had maintained a close relationship with Wa and who might have ruled the region independently or survived as a surrogate of Baekje. In any case, all of these interesting burials had disappeared suddenly and were replaced by Baekje-style burials in the mid-6th century.

Regardless of the nature of the political entity, construction of these burials would not have been possible without a fairly large population. A number of large farming villages have been excavated which continued from the Proto-Three Kingdoms Period. At Taemok-ri [cf. **Figure 6.19**], for example, more than 300 dwelling units of the period were revealed from the excavated area in addition to hundreds of those of an earlier period. Villages of such scale would have formed in quite a lot of places in this region of rich soil suitable for agriculture. If pit-houses were for common people, residences of the elites were built above the ground among the

Figure 7.16 Tomb No. 3 of Bokam-ri. Within the mound are found many burials of diverse kinds. Some stone chambers are found with multiple jar coffins. © National Research Institute of Cultural Heritage

pit-houses or close to them. Sometimes these structures are arranged orderly and/ or surrounded by a trench.

Artifacts of the region also demonstrate their unique and independent characteristics. Especially, ceramics share both indigenous and foreign elements so that there can be detected some characteristics of the Baekje pottery of the Hanseong Period, Gaya pottery, especially those of Sogaya, and the Sueki pottery of the Japanese Kofun Period [**Figure 7.18**]. Along with the burials, these were replaced by Baekje potteries in the mid-6th century.

Figure 7.17 Key-hole shaped mound burials known at Wolgye-dong, Gwangju, and the stone chamber inside Mound No. 1 (after The Korean Archaeological Society 2010, Figure 228).

Figure 7.18 Pottery from a burial at Ssangam-dong and Tomb No. 1 of Wolgye-dong, Gwangju. They demonstrate similarities with those of Gaya and Japan (after The Korean Archaeological Society 2010, Figure 232).

Gaya

While there is no record telling who left the mound burials in the Yeongsan Basin, the history of Gaya is better known. Moreover, a lot of records were made in Japan because Gaya and Wa had maintained a close relationship. What the historical sources say is that independent state-like entities had grown out of the Byeonhan polities, thanks to the iron trade mentioned earlier and they together had formed a political federation. The distribution of Gaya polities was roughly bounded by the Sobaek Mountains to the north and the Nakdong River to the east although not fixed by these natural barriers. Among many polities, there were four major forces: Geumguangaya, Aragaya, Sogaya and Daegaya. Their centers were in today's Gimhae, Haman, Goseong and Goryeong, respectively, where impressive burial mounds welcome visitors.

Figure 7.19 Burial ground of Geumgwangaya in Daeseong-dong in Gimhae, and its burials. Early Gaya burials tend to have main and auxiliary receptacles prepared separately. Human sacrifice is fairly common in these and other Gaya burials. © National Research Institute of Cultural Heritage

It is believed that, led by Geumguangaya, the federation was cemented by the late 3rd century when each member polity shared the suffix of Gaya in its name. The strength of Gaya waxed and waned. Sometimes they were strong enough to threaten Silla, and to cross the Sobaek range to penetrate into Baekje's territory. At other times, they were utterly defeated. Especially, in the year 400, Goguryeo dealt Gaya a devastating blow when it sent an army to fend off the Wa forces who crossed the sea to invade Silla. Goguryeo followed the defeated Wa force into Gaya territory and crushed the Gaya allies. Badly shaken, Geumguangaya could not hold the leadership of the federation anymore and Daegaya became the new leader. In the following years, Daegaya had become strong enough to be a worthy competitor with Baekje and Silla and expanded its territory as far north as the Geum River across the Sobaek Mountains. Nevertheless, smaller Gaya polities were absorbed by Silla one by one, and the fate of the federation was sealed in 562 as Daegaya surrendered to Silla.

Figure 7.20 The Jisan-dong Tomb No. 44 in Goryeong. © National Research Institute of Cultural Heritage

Figure 7.21 Stone chamber burials of Sogaya at Songhak-dong, Goseong. © National Research Institute of Cultural Heritage

Archaeological remains of Gaya are mainly found as burials. Early ones are represented by the Wooden Receptacle Burials at Daeseong-dong in Gimhae and Bokcheon-dong in Busan. They were made in the late 4th century for the rulers of Geumgwangaya. While they demonstrate the continuation of the burial customs of the Proto-Three Kingdoms Period, the receptacles had become much larger to accommodate more mortuary goods. Many are found with auxiliary receptacles which were usually prepared in a separate pit aligned with the main burial [**Figure 7.19**]. Contemporary Wooden Receptacle Burials in the Gyeongju area are also found with auxiliary receptacles but both receptacles were prepared within the same pit.

Figure 7.22 Regional types of Gaya Pottery. Top: Aragaya style pottery in Haman area; Middle: Sogaya style pottery in the Jinju-Goseong area; Bottom: Daegaya style pottery in the Goryeong area (after The Korean Archaeological Society 2010, Figure 299)

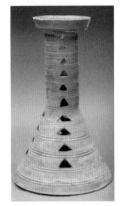

More importantly, human sacrifices began to be found within the burials from this time on. Historical records mention that the custom was popular in Buyeo and Goguryeo. However, direct evidence is known only from the burials of Gaya and Silla. Samguksagi says that five males and five females were sacrificed for a king's burial in Silla, which was banned in 502. Nevertheless, archaeological evidence suggests that it was not abolished either in Silla or in Gaya. It seems that human sacrifice had been more prevalent and persistent in Gaya. Many Gaya burials are usually found with three to five human sacrifices, and those of the highest tier have

Figure 7.23 Comparison of Silla (left) and Gaya Pottery (right). © National Museum of Korea (top); Gyeongju National Museum (bottom)

twenty or more of them. In the case of Tomb Number 44 at Jisan-dong in Goryeong, a 5th century royal burial of Daegaya, at least 32 and as many as 45 individuals of both sexes were sacrificed. Their ages range between about 8 to 40, and the bodies were put into stone cists surrounding the main burial [**Figure 7.20**].

While Wooden Receptacle Burials continued to be made as late as the late 5th century at some places, there began to appear Stone Receptacle Burials in the late 4th century. By the late 5th century, all of the Gaya burials had become Stone Receptacle Burials covered by a large earthen mound. Including Jisan-dong, at every place where the center of a Gaya polity was once located, there can be seen a number of burial mounds of substantial size. As each polity constructed the burials in their

Figure 7.24 Gilt bronze crown from Tomb No. 32 in Jisan-dong, Goryeong. © National Heritage Administration

Figure 7.25 Gaya elite burials are often found with helmets and body armor which were made by riveting iron plates. Stylistic variations can be seen between the polities. The one shown here is of Daegaya style and recovered together with the crown above. © National Museum of Korea

own style, Gaya burials demonstrate a lot of structural diversity. Such differences are also seen in various artifacts found in them as if testifying that Gaya was not completely unified culturally as well as politically [e.g., **Figure 7.22**].

Changes in the burials are accompanied with changes in pottery-making. In the late 3ʳᵈ century, pottery began to be fired under much higher temperatures in the Gyeongsang Basin. As a result, Wajil Togi was replaced by more hardened products showing occasional and accidental vitrification of the surface. Their manufacture marks the beginning of the production of Gaya and Silla Pottery. Although some

Figure 7.26 Bonghwang Toseong in Gimhae now sits in the middle of bustling town. Testings have revealed complex overlapping of structures. © National Research Institute of Cultural Heritage

minor local traits can be seen, both types throughout the whole basin looked similar at the time of their appearance. However, in the late 4th century, a major regional divergence had occurred so that Gaya and Silla Pottery demonstrate differences in style [**Figure 7.23**]. Their border was the Nakdong River but with a couple of bulging penetrations. In the 5th century, Gaya Pottery evolved, showing three major regional styles developed in the areas roughly corresponding to the territories of Aragaya, Sogaya and Daegaya [**Figure 7.22**]. Similar stylistic diversification is seen in personal ornaments and armaments.

Along with tons of pottery, personal ornaments of gold and guilt bronze are found [**Figure 7.24**]. Also, Gaya burials are rich with iron ingots, armor for warriors and horses, horse fittings and various weaponry as if demonstrating that they were producers of iron [**Figure 7.25**]. Heightened inter-group tension and conflict are suggested by various military gadgets found in the burials and many ruins of fortresses and defensive walls. The latter are relatively small ones, and many were built from the 5th century along the western shore of the Nakdong River facing Silla.

Compared to burials, there are relatively few settlements and other kinds of sites which provide information about everyday life. Residences of elites are known at a couple of Gaya centers. For example, the royal residence of Geumgwangaya was surrounded by the earthen wall of Bonghwang Toseong in Gimhae. A limited excavation made here found evidence of shrines, workshops and a marketplace [**Figure 7.26**]. Meanwhile, settlement sites of the common rural villages of Gaya states changed little from the previous period. Thus, individual dwellings are generally small and round in shape and equipped with primitive *Ondol*. Excavations of settlement sites suggest some sort of functional differentiation among them. For example, a settlement site may be found with facilities for smelting iron ore, which might have been a village of ironsmiths. For other sites, remains of roads are found suggesting the presence of a transportation network. Discovery of the remnants of a pier and related architectural remains suggests the importance of waterways.

Silla before Unification

According to legend, the first king of Silla was born out of a gourd-shaped egg in 69 BCE which was found at a place called Najeong by the elders of six "villages" of Saroguk who happened to have a meeting there [**Figure 7.27**]. In 57 BCE, he was crowned as the king to lead the country for 60 years.

Counting from the legendary birth of the first king, Gyeongju had been the capital of Silla for almost a millennium. Thus, archaeological remains are found literally at any and every corner of this small basin. Unlike the situation for early Baekje remains in Seoul, burial mounds had somewhat worked as a barrier against indiscriminate urban expansion. As mentioned in the introductory chapter, a full set of gold crown with other dazzling ornaments were found in 1921 from the ruin of a forgotten burial. Four more sets have been found in 1924, 1925, 1973 and 1974, all dated to the 5th and the 6th century [**Figure 7.28**]. As is the case for Gaya, because of their high visibility and rich burial goods, the archaeology of Silla has been dominated by research of these burials.

However, people have been living on the very ruins of Silla in Gyeongju for centuries, making it impossible to conduct systematic study at many important sites. From the 1970s, the government began to purchase privately-owned parcels of land to preserve and protect important ruins such as the Hwangnyongsa temple. The project has been expanded ever since so that archaeological excavation has been carried out at many places [cf. **Figure 7.27**].

The mound burials in Gyeongju had appeared in the late 4th century. They were preceded by the Silla-style Wooden Receptacle Burial. It is different from the contemporary Gaya burials in that the main and the auxiliary receptacles were made in the same pit as mentioned. By the time that mound burials were built in Gyeongju,

Figure 7.27 Core area of the Silla capital with Wolseong at its center. Excavations are going on at many places, whose locations are suggested by blue protective coverings. Government buildings of Silla once filled the area between Wolseong and the burial ground. A patch of woods close to Wolseong to its northwest is Najeong, the legendary birthplace of the first Silla king. The royal villa of Donggung is to the right of Wolseong across the road running diagonally in the photo. The ruin of Hwang-nyongsa covers the large area abutting the villa. The white dome shown in the upper left side is the open-air museum where the public can observe an on-going excavation of a mid-sized mound burial. © NAVER/SPOT/National Geographic Information Institute

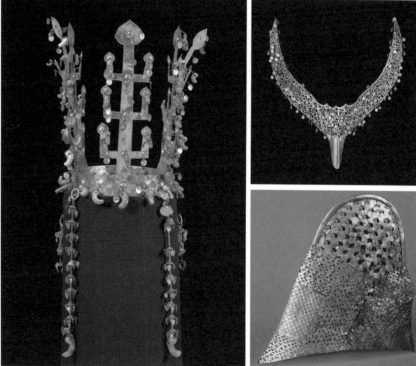

Figure 7.28 Golden crown and its inner cap and outer decoration from Cheonma-chong. © National Museum of Korea

Silla-style burials and Silla Pottery began to spread quickly across the Gyeongsang Basin and well north into Gangwon-do along the east coast.

Beneath the large earthen mounds in Gyeongju, wooden receptacles are found covered with layer upon layer of boulder-sized gravels and chunks of rocks [**Figures**

Figure 7.29 Early Silla burials in Gyeongju are protected by layers of rock piled on top of the wooden receptacle. The size of the mound varies a lot. © National Research Institute of Cultural Heritage

7.29, 7.30]. Compared to these Silla burials, Gaya burials tend to be found severely destroyed as they lack these protective layers. The beginning of the construction of these burials in Gyeongju coincided with the bestowment of a new title of Maripgan(마립간) to the ruler, thus, this period of mound building is also known as the Maripgan Period.

Figure 7.30 shows one of the largest burials in Gyeongju, Hwangnamdaechong, also known as Tomb Number 98. Measuring 120 by 80m at the base with a height of about 25m, this huge mound is made of two connected burials built probably for a royal pair. Excavation conducted in the 1970s revealed quite a lot of dazzling artifacts of various kinds. For archaeologists, however, the most interesting items are the iron implements and ingots as well as large and small pottery vessels with remains of foodstuff inside. Next to Hwanggamdaechong lies Cheonmachong, the Heavenly Horse Tomb. This relatively small mound was excavated in 1973 as a pilot test to make preparations for the main excavation of the former. Here, in addition to the glittering golden artifacts [**Figure 7.28**], mudguards made of birch bark and bamboo amid various horse fittings were found. They were painted with celestial horses, which gave the name to the tomb [**Figure 7.31**].

In the early 6th century, Silla reorganized its social system and legal codes and accepted Buddhism as the religion of the state. With the adoption of Buddhism, large and small temples began to be constructed in Gyeongju and many other places. At this time, cremation began to spread and construction of the traditional mound burial had ended effectively so that only the ruling class of the highest rank were buried under mounds. However, instead of wooden receptacles with tons of burial goods and layers of gravels, stone chambers were built inside, thus, much more prone to looting and destruction. With entrances, these chambers could be opened whenever needed, thus, used for a whole family or related persons for many years. By this time, evidence of human sacrifice is seldom found in the capi-

Figure 7.30 Hwangnam-daechong in the early 1970s before excavation began in 1973 (top). Scene of excavation shown here was taken at the South Tomb in 1975. Among thousands of mortuary goods are included Roman glasswares. Most probably, they were produced in the Pontic or the Caspian region. © National Research Institute of Cultural Heritage (tomb); National Museum of Korea (glasses)

tal area but the custom continued in the provinces. In Silla archaeology, this change in mortuary practice is important in defining the early and the late phase for the period before unification. Silla in the 6th century had expanded its territory a lot. As a result, burials, military fortifications, buildings and various artifacts of Silla are found in the Han and the Imjin River basin. They are also distributed along the east coast as far north as Hamgyeongnam-do and across the former territory of the Gaya federation [**Figure 7.32**].

Compared to those highly visible burials and other ruins, evidence for everyday life of common people is relatively poorly studied. In Gyeongju, evidence of settlement did not survive well due to the urban planning conducted after unification. Such discoveries are only known at a small corner of the town so far, and the excavated quarter appears to be a special settlement for the families of ironsmiths.

Outside of Gyeongju, rural settlements made of 50 to 200 pit-houses have been excavated. Cultivation fields and articulated water management facilities for rice paddies are also found. Villages were well organized in their use of space, and residential units, production facilities and burials were separately distributed. For some large settlements, fortifications were built on the high ground behind to prepare for emergency. Also, communal wells and roads with imprints of wheel marks

Figure 7.31 Painting of a celestial horse drawn on a mudguard from Cheonma-chong. © Cultural Heritage Administration

Figure 7.32 The hilltop fortress Samnyeonsanseong in Bo-eun (after The Korean Archaeological Society 2010, Figure 235). It was built around 500 to defend the territory obtained on the other side of the Sobaek Mountains.

and footprints are frequently found.

The shape of individual pit-houses had become squarish during the Three Kingdoms Period but round ones were continuously made. They are also usually small in size with large ones of about 50m². The hearth was prepared above the floor nearby a wall to serve both for cooking and heating. Now, most of the dwellings are found with some form of *Ondol*. Foundation stones or postholes suggest there also were dwellings built above the ground.

Other important sites include those related to the production of iron and various earthen wares. Iron production had been conducted in a highly specialized and organized way in the 4th century. If different stages of production had been processed at one place previously, usually close to the mine, now ores were transported to a smelting facility to make ingots, which were forged into tools at different locations. Increased demand for iron required more production of fuel, the so-called white charcoal, so that charcoal kilns are found at many places. For pottery and tiles, kilns and workshops of different kinds may be found together to form a cluster. Given their number and distribution, it seems that pottery production had been conducted almost at an industrial scale.

As mentioned, Silla Pottery emerged in the 4th century when unique burials appeared in Gyeongju. Compared to contemporary Gaya Pottery, it demonstrates far less amount of variation in its style across the whole territory. The most characteristic aspect of Silla Pottery is the surface treatment, and many are incised with simple geometric designs. Also, they are often attached with small figurines of various kinds, including human and animal shapes. Even the whole pottery was made in various forms with interesting details, providing a glimpse of everyday life of Silla people [**Figures 7.23, 7.33**]. In time, such decoration had become less popular so that the surface of the pottery was often left blank. Then, a major change in style had occurred in the 6th century so that the new stone chamber burials are found with pottery which looks shorter and decorated by stamping instead of incising. Their production continued after the unification.

Figure 7.33 Examples of Silla Pottery. © National Museum of Korea

From the earliest days of Silla, its royal palace had been Wolseong. It sits on a hill about 20m above the surrounding plain lying to the south of the mound burials of the Maripgan Period. The total length of the stone wall protecting the palace is 2,340m, surrounding an area of about 112,500m² which is about 900m long and 200m wide. Its outline is sometimes said to resemble the shape of an elongated crescent, which gave the place its name [**Figure 7.27**]. The space between the palace and the royal cemetery to the north had been filled with government buildings. In this space was also erected Cheomseongdae, a 9.5m tall stone structure known as an observatory built in the mid-7th century. To the east of the palace was built the royal villa of Donggung [**Figure 7.34**]. Geophysical survey at Wolseong showed layers of older building foundations below the post-unification layer which was revealed by excavation [**Figure 7.35**]. Surrounding this center and beyond, many temples were built as well. These buildings had been continuously used after the unification so that much of the layers were later destroyed or overlain by the new ones.

Figure 7.34 The royal villa of Donggung. The pond is known to imitate the outline of the Silla territory after unification. Excavation revealed an elaborate flush toilet system as seen below. © National Research Institute of Cultural Heritage

Although there must be some exaggeration in the statement, a record says that Gyeongju had boasted 800,000 households, and people could go whichever direction without worrying about getting wet in the rain because they could walk continuously under the protruding eaves of the tiled roofs. It is further said that no smoke was seen in the sky at dawn and dusk as every household was cooking and heating with charcoal. Excavation has revealed that residents of the Silla capital lived in standardized housing units built within residential blocks. Each house was provided with its own well, kitchen and latrine, and drainage channels were built for sewage.

For post-unification Silla archaeology, especially the topic of the urban setting of Gyeongju is attracting a lot of attention as the capital had been systematically reorganized with a well-thought plan. Outside of the core area for the royals and governmental functions, the capital was divided into grids defined by roads crisscrossing the city. The size of these spatial units for urban planning turns out to vary.

Figure 7.35 Building foundations revealed in the uppermost layer of Wolseong. In the photo, ruins of 17 buildings are seen overlapped. © National Research Institute of Cultural Heritage

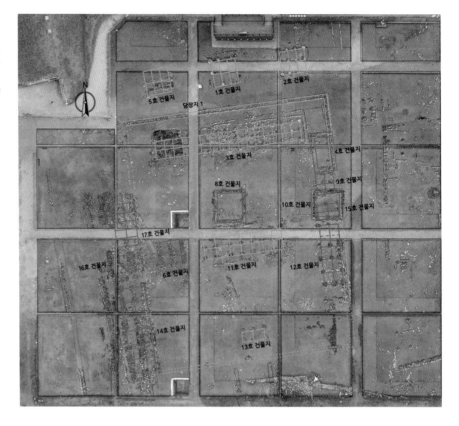

One such unit revealed by excavation measures 172.5m in E-W and 167.5m in N-S. The square is surrounded by wall on four sides within which were built a total of 19 houses and other buildings. Roads surrounding the grid were of three tiers, their width about 15, 10 and 5m, respectively. The surface of the road was treated with layers of gravels, silt and clay. Buildings were rebuilt and renovated. Tiles for their floor, roof and wall are sculpted with splendid and fanciful motifs. Likewise, temples and pagodas were covered with sculpted and glazed bricks [**Figure 7.36**].

As Silla had become a devoted Buddhist country, many temples were built in close proximity to the palace. So far, more than 180 temple ruins have been counted in Gyeongju alone, excluding those small, chapel-like ones and hermitages dotting the granite hill of Namsan to the south of the palace. About two dozen temple sites have been excavated. It turns out that buildings for worship and lecture, pagodas and other structures were arranged following the so-called one-worship-hall-with-two-pagodas pattern. Of course, a number of religious sculptures, bells and various paraphernalia have been found [e.g., **Figure 7.37**].

Although Buddhism was the national religion, it seems that indigenous beliefs were kept strong among the populace. Thus, a number of shrine-like sites with devotions such as ceramics and miniature iron horses have been found. Among them, an interesting one is known at Ssangcheong-ri in Cheongwon in central South Korea where a ritual site surrounded by seven parallel circles of trenches was

Figure 7.36 Examples of roof tiles found in Gyeongju (after The Korean Archaeological Society 2010, Figures 327, 328).

Figure 7.37 Sarira reliquary retrieved from the East Pagoda at the ruin of the Gameunsa temple. The inner case (left) containing sarira was found inside the outer case © Cultural Heritage Administration

found. In the innermost area were found roof tiles with inscriptions, and perhaps a ritual was presided over here by persons of high esteem [**Figure 7.38**].

For archaeological exploration at provincial centers of Silla, there are few examples. One such place is the mountain-top basin surrounded by the fortress of Namhansanseong. Stone walls of this famous fortress south of Seoul were built in the early 17ᵗʰ century, but the place had been already important during the Three Kingdoms Period, and Silla built a defensive wall in 672 in their struggle to get rid of the Tang forces. Later, it had been used as the provincial center. Here, below the Joseon layer where the 17ᵗʰ century temporary palace was built, the ruin of a large Silla building measuring 53.5 by 17.5m was revealed. Its roof was covered by

Figure 7.38 A ritual site encircled with multiple trenches. Perhaps the religious tradition inferred from the encirclements of the Bronze and the Early Iron Age had been kept for a long time (cf. Figures 4.28, 5.8). © National Research Institute of Cultural Heritage

Figure 7.39 Ruin of a Silla building and its roof tiles found at the Namhansanseong. Roof tiles used for this building (left) are ten times heavier than those used for the 17th century building built above the Silla ruin (right). © National Research Institute of Cultural Heritage

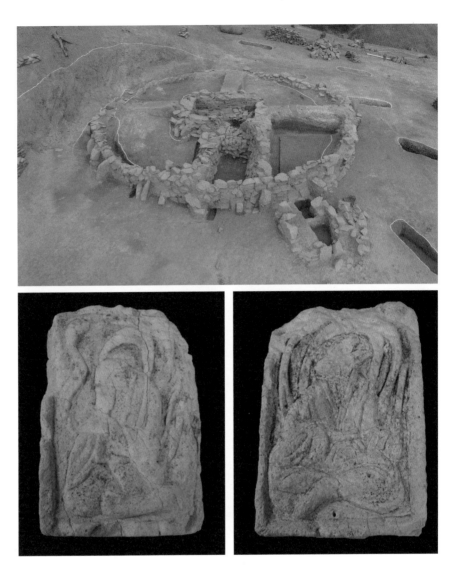

Figure 7.40 A post-unification Silla stone chamber burial excavated at Sohyeon-ri in Gyeongju. Sculpted zodiac figurines were found at the base of the stone circle. Figurines shown here represent horse (left) and lamb (right). © National Research Institute of Cultural Heritage

oversized tiles, each weighing 19kg in average, many times heavier than the usual ones [**Figure 7.39**].

As Buddhism exerted more influence after unification, cremation had become all the more popular but cremation burials are hard to find. For cremation vessels, most commonly used were pottery of everyday use but imported ceramics and metallic and stone utensils are found occasionally. Nevertheless, elites residing in Gyeongju continued to build stone chamber burials covered by earthen mounds of a smaller size. Sometimes human and zodiac figurines were buried within the chamber or distributed around the mound, indicating the introduction of contemporary Chinese mortuary customs [**Figure 7.40**]. None of the royal tombs scattered in the Gyeongju basin has been excavated but they are believed to be stone chamber burials. They are usually protected by stone sculptures of zodiac animals either surrounding the mound or buried underneath. Sometimes human and animal statues are lined in the foreground befitting the royal burial.

After unification, pottery-making appeared little changed but the scale of production had increased a lot. Kilns are found forming clusters. Judging from a short phrase written on the surface of a vessel found in a kiln site in south Seoul, it appears that craftsmen were living in a village of their own, apart from the populace.

Although technology of ceramic production had not changed much, there can be seen changes in the style of pottery. In general, they had become more suitable for practical use. For example, mounted cups [cf. **Figure 7.23**] disappeared to be replaced by simple ones with flat bottoms. Bowls of diverse sizes and shapes with or without tops were made and bottles began to have long necks. Also, the elongated

Figure 7.41 Ceramics of the terminal Silla in the late 9th and the early 10th century. (after The Korean Archaeological Society 2010, Figure 325).

and round-bottomed steaming pot had become large-mouthed and flat-bottomed like today. Surface decoration by stamping continued and specially prepared cremation vessels were decorated with a number of complex motifs. But surface decoration in general began to disappear in the 9th century. At that time, various forms of bottles were made, and vessels were fired under higher temperature to make them stronger and glossier [**Figure 7.41**]. By this time, Chinese porcelains were imported for the elites, which might have something to do with the spread of tea drinking following the popularization of Zen Buddhism. In a few years, trial production of porcelain began, which ultimately led to the appearance of those famous Goryeo Cheongja, the Goryeo Celadon.

After Silla – Goryeo and Joseon

The glory and prosperity of Gyeongju after unification was a short-lived one, and Silla began to fall into disarray in the middle of the 8th century. Then, as the 9th century was ending, she was in great turmoil. Local powers were emerging while new religious cults swept the country. The whole society was upended with rebellions. Soon, there began the short-lived Late Three Kingdoms Period as self-claimed states emerged. While society and culture of this transitional period are believed to be unique, however, there is little known archaeological data which may tell us so. For example, attempts to determine the location of the capital of Hubaekje failed to obtain meaningful information. At the same time, research at the capital of Taebong, although preserved well, cannot be made as it is located in the middle of the DMZ.

The founder of Goryeo located his capital in Gaeseong, just north of the DMZ today but below the 38th parallel. The main Goryeo palace of Manwoldae was burnt down in 1361 by Chinese peasant rebels who had invaded Goryeo. Its ruins had been excavated in the 1970s [**Figure 7.42**]. In the 2000s, it was investigated for a few seasons by a joint South-North Korean research team, and excavations were conducted at several parts of the ruined complex. At the same time, some royal tombs and other sites in the Gaeseong area were also tested but with little results.

In South Korea, quite a few Goryeo sites have been investigated. Goryeo burials and settlements are frequently found whenever a large-scale salvage excavation is conducted, which is also the case for the Joseon period. Also, many ruins of temples, manors or government buildings have been investigated, sometimes taking many years to complete [**Figure 7.43**].

For archaeological research of Goryeo, Ganghwado is a special place because Goryeo elites took refuge in this island against the invading Mongols in the 13th century. Ruins of temporary palace and stone chamber burials have been excavated which sometimes are adorned with paintings on the walls. Commoners were buried in plain pit burials or in Lime Mortar Burials. The name of the latter indicates that the coffin was covered with a thick layer of slaked lime. It had become popular during the Joseon period.

During the Goryeo period, due to frequent invasions both from the north and the south, military facilities were newly built at many places, and they are also an

Figure 7.42 Ruin of Manwol-dae. As the rare example of cooperation between South and North Korea, this palace site had been tested on and off by archaeologists from both sides between 2007 and 2015. The photo shows a group of building foundations in northwest side of the ruin excavated in 2007 and 2008. Discoveries include a ceramic dragon head used to decorate the rafter of the building. © National Research Institute of Cultural Heritage

important target for archaeological research. **Figure 7.44** shows one such facility, a beacon mound on the south coast.

Another important field for Goryeo archaeology is the study of porcelain kilns [**Figure 7.45**], a subject which is also important for the Joseon Period as well. At first, they were made of bricks and located in close proximity to the capital. The famous Goryeo Celadon was not produced from the beginning. The earliest products were white and green colored ones. Soon kilns were built where high-quality kaolinite was available, many of them in southwestern Korea. There, Goryeo Celadon of the highest quality was produced in the new clay-walled kilns.

As porcelains produced here and other tributes were sent to the capital by ship, maritime accidents were bound to occur. As a result, quite a few shipwrecks off the west coast have been found. At the same time, vessels of international trade busily moving between ports of China, Korea and Japan occasionally had sunk to be buried in the muddy bottom of the Yellow Sea. They provide unusual opportunities for underwater archaeology, which in Korea began in 1976 with the accidental

Figure 7.43 Foundations for a large lecture hall revealed at the ruin of Yeongguksa in northern Seoul (top), and an entrance gate of Hoeamsa in Yangju (middle). Bronze paraphernalia shown at the bottom were excavated from the ruin of Ingaksa in Gunwi. © National Research Institute of Cultural Heritage

Figure 7.44 A signal fire station on a mountain top in Busan. © National Research Institute of Cultural Heritage

Figure 7.45 A Goryeo kiln and porcelain fragments excavated at Dotong-ri in Jinan. © National Research Institute of Cultural Heritage

Figure 7.46 Sinan Shipwreck on display at the National Research Institute of Maritime Cultural Heritage with a scaled model of the ship and a scene from the video display demonstrating the parts recovered. Discovered in 1976, thousands of artifacts were hauled off from the bottom of the 20m deep seabed over 11 years. Originally, the ship would have been 30.1m long and 10.7m wide and 10m high from the bottom to the deck. The international trade ship left the port of Ningbo in southerm China full of valuables most probably in the summer of 1323. After crossing the Yellow Sea, the unfortunate ship was on its way to Hakada in western Japan along the coastal route of Korea when it sank.

discovery of a shipwreck of Chinese origin, the Sinan Shipwreck [**Figure 7.46**]. The unfortunate ship was full of fine Chinese porcelains and other valuables and on its way to Japan. Now, two research centers established on the west coast are actively investigating shipwrecks of the Yellow Sea.

Much of what has been said about Goryeo can be applied to Joseon. During the period, Seoul was known as Hanyang, meaning the city north of the Han River. As a pre-planned city reflecting both Confucian ideology and Fengshui philosophy, it was built at the beginning of the 15th century in a closed basin drained by a E-W running channel in the middle. Along the channel, the basin is about 3.5km wide from city wall to city wall. Its N-S axis at its longest is about 4.5km. The city wall ran about 18km in total with 8 gates and other installations.

Within the wall, the space was divided into various zones with palaces and royal shrines located on the foot of the ridges in the north to face south, and government offices, military facilities, markets and residential areas were arranged accordingly. Later, new palaces and other buildings were continuously added to the existing ones. However, the look of old Hanyang is almost completely lost and hard to remember in modern Seoul. During the last decade of the 20th century, the government initiated a project to reconstruct the severely damaged main palace of Gyeongbokgung, and excavation had revealed the foundations of the lost buildings and provided information about the original construction [**Figure 7.47**].

Nowadays, archaeological research is casually conducted in the very center of Seoul. Foundations of long forgotten buildings, structures, roads, embankments,

Figure 7.47 Scenes of excavation at the ruin of the royal kitchen in Gyeongbokgung and the palace wall. © National Research Institute of Cultural Heritage

Figure 7.48 City wall and the water gate under excavation nearby the East Gate in Seoul. Ceramics as utensils of everyday use are frequently found. © National Research Institute of Cultural Heritage

bridges, city walls, etc. are discovered, and various ceremonial offerings and other artifacts are retrieved [**Figures 7.47-7.49**]. In the summer of 2021, one such excavation retrieved actual samples of the world's oldest metal movable types [**Figure 7.50**]. Also, many salvage excavations carried out at provincial centers are revealing architectural foundations of buildings and town walls, among others. Interestingly, some earthen walls presumed to be town walls or fortresses turned out to be fences of stock farms.

As Joseon was built on Confucian idealism and disdained the Buddhism of Goryeo as greedy and corrupt, many Buddhist temples had been left to rot and dilapidated, and some were deliberately burnt down. The most famous incident occurred in 1565 when the temple of Hoeamsa was completely destroyed by the

Figure 7.49 Urban archaeology in action. Excavation revealed stone sewage structures and building foundations of the 15th century below the 20th century layers in the very center of Seoul. The large building behind the excavation area is the Sejong Center for the Performing Arts. Photo taken on April 25, 2021.

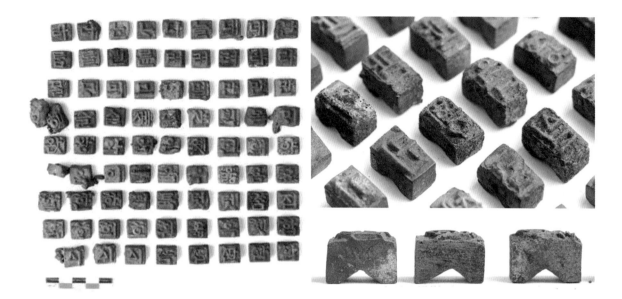

Figure 7.50 Metal movable types of the Korean alphabets of the 15ᵗʰ century. They were found with movable types of Chinese characters and parts of a clock. © Cultural Heritage Administration

hands of fanatic Confucian students. It was a national temple for the Goryeo dynasty once serving as many as 3,000 monks. Excavation revealed that the temple was thriving until its sudden destruction by arson and many rare artifacts of the late Goryeo and early Joseon period were found [**Figure 7.51**]. While Buddhist temples were neglected, Seowon, the private Confucian institutions of higher learning with government sponsorship, were constructed. First appearing in 1540, there were as many as 650 of them in the 19ᵗʰ century, causing so many economic problems. As a result, most of them were abolished in 1870 and only 47 of them were saved, thus, providing a target for archaeological investigation.

In relation to everyday life of common people, what is today called the *Hanok* (한옥), the traditional roof-tiled house, was as expensive to build and maintain as today, thus, not affordable for the majority of people. As such, pit-houses continued to be used throughout the Joseon Period. Quite a few of them are encountered when large-scale salvage excavations are conducted. When found, they are usually equipped with rather sophisticated *Ondol* inside.

For burials, the stone chamber burials of the Goryeo period with mural painting were continuously made in the 15ᵗʰ century but disappeared in the 16ᵗʰ century and replaced by the Lime Mortar Burial. In northwestern Seoul, a large burial ground was excavated before the construction of new residential blocks and some 5,000 burials of the ruling class were found. Most of them are Lime Mortar Burials [**Figure 7.52**]. As it had become popular, production of slake lime was in high demand, thus, special kilns are found for its production, a unique phenomenon observed only for Joseon.

Finally, porcelains of Joseon are represented by white-colored porcelains with or without decoration. This Joseon Baekja had undergone changes in its style and decoration. Thus, neither the so-called Pure White Porcelain nor the White Porcelain with Blue Paintings, which are widely regarded as representing the Joseon Period, appeared from the beginning. Among many kilns which produced the var-

Figure 7.51 Aerial view of the main part of the ruins of Hoeamsa. The area under excavation shown is about 250m long and 170m wide. The entrance gate shown in Figure 7.43 is about 360m to the right. © National Research Institute of Cultural Heritage

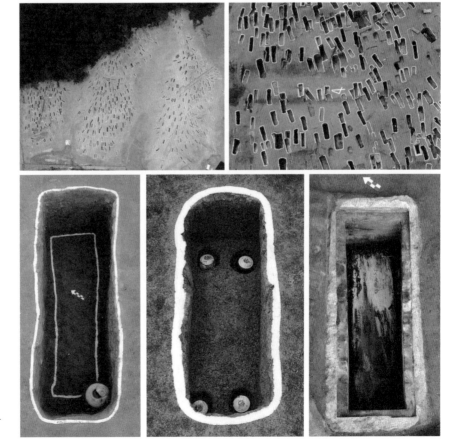

Figure 7.52 A Joseon cemetery excavated in the Eunpyeong New Town district in northwestern Seoul (after The Korean Archaeological Society 2010, Figure 363). Most of the burials are the Lime Mortar Burials (lower right).

Figure 7.53 Workshop area of a Joseon porcelain kiln revealed at Hapan-ri in Gapyeong and some discarded specimens excavated from the rubbish deposit. © National Research Institute of Cultural Heritage

ious ceramics, the finest ones were fired at the governmental kilns of Gwangju Bunwon, which is about 50km upstream on the Han river from Seoul. Study of these and other porcelain kilns are of course important for the Joseon period along with those numerous kilns where pottery of lesser quality and tiles were produced [**Figure 7.53**].

SUMMARY AND PROSPECTS

Archaeological research in South Korea since the 1960s has succeeded in revealing some aspects of its prehistoric past. Although there are a lot of questions and many details that need to be clarified, it is evident that early hominins had entered the peninsula at least by the late Middle Pleistocene. Given the geographical proximity to many Lower and Middle Pleistocene localities in China, there is no reason not to believe that *Homo erectus* or others similar had reached this eastern edge of the Eurasian continent even earlier.

One of the most interesting aspects of the earliest evidence is that the archaic-looking stone tools made of quartz and quartzite cobbles had been manufactured continuously well into the late Upper Pleistocene. It may be taken as an indication that archaic hominins might have survived in this sanctuary for a long time despite the arrival of anatomically modern humans. Stone tools seem to tell us that *Homo sapiens* had arrived Korea as early as 45,000 BP or slightly later as indicated by the sudden appearance of totally different stone tools made by a new technology, exploiting completely new raw materials. Later, the distribution of obsidian artifacts suggests interaction across southern parts of northeastern provinces of China and Korea on one hand, and northern Kyushu and Korea on the other. Such interaction had continued into the Holocene, and the occurrence of similar technology and artifacts implies that similar mode of adaptation had been shared across a wide area surrounding the East Sea towards the end of the Pleistocene.

If we can define the beginning of the Neolithic with the appearance of pottery, it now seems that there is little gap between the Palaeolithic and the Neolithic, which is expected to be filled soon. The earliest pottery found in the island of Jeju demonstrates similarities to those known at some pre-Holocene localities in the Russian Maritime Region. But it is not clear yet what had been going on in the mainland at the beginning of the Holocene.

The earliest Holocene evidence in the mainland is related to the so-called Appliqué Pottery, not the Comb-Patterned Pottery. Now, the latter cannot represent the Korean Neolithic as once believed. For early pottery, many diverse forms are known. Such diversity may have something to do with the limited population size and the lack of interaction between small and relatively mobile groups who relied on foraging for subsistence. While cultivation of millet was introduced perhaps by 6,000 BP at least, its impact had been limited and natural resources had remained important.

Similarities in assemblage composition along the east coast and the spread of the Comb-Patterned Pottery around 6,000 BP may mean population had somewhat increased by this time, which may be corroborated by the appearance of sites with more than 50 pit-houses on the west coast and nearby inland localities in central western Korea. These sites might have been occupied year-round or perhaps represent a place for gathering of small bands who for the most of the time were scattered over a large area. Such social fusion and fission are implied by the very small number of dwelling structures found at most of the so-called 'settlement' sites.

By the beginning of the second millennium BCE, it seems that the stability of the Neolithic society was disrupted as the archaeological evidence is seldom found. Soon, around 1500 BCE or slightly later, new kinds of sites appeared which are made of larger and more durable pit-houses. Their appearance may be the result of the influx of a population that practiced agriculture and made new ceramic wares collectively known as Mumun Pottery. Thus, began the Bronze Age.

However, bronze is rarely found for the whole Bronze Age. Their total number does not exceed a couple of hundred including fragments. It might be that early bronze artifacts were manufactured outside of Korea, and their production began in earnest long after the appearance of the earliest Mumun Pottery at least in the southern parts of the peninsula. As the representative bronze artifact of the period, there is the Bipa-shaped Bronze Dagger. Along with this dagger of unique shape, dolmens, Mumun Pottery and ground stone tools represent the Bronze Age of Korea. They are important cultural traits for defining the boundary of the Korean Culture Sphere of the period, which includes Korea and much of northeastern China. In general, Bronze Age society, especially during the latter part, is regarded as relying on cultivation. As time went on, with markedly increased population, social complexity had advanced a lot as suggested by the seemingly hierarchical organization of settlement sites.

At the beginning of the 4th century BCE, the stability of Korean Culture Sphere had been threatened with the expansion of Yan, one of the Seven Warring States of China. Around this time, the name of the first Korean nation, Gojoseon, was recorded in history. It is generally believed that its center had been somewhere to the north of the current Sino-Korean border. The introduction of iron to Korea may slightly predate the Yan invasion of Gojoseon, and the name of the Early Iron Age was given to the period between 400 and 100 BCE. What is interesting, however, is that the evidence from this Early Iron Age is limited to elite burials and a handful of 'settlements'. If the current chronology is correct, this means that all those successful farming villages of the late Bronze Age had vanished overnight. It is more puzzling because villages reappeared in larger and more complex forms as soon as the period had ended. Such an anomaly demonstrates well a weak point of Korean archaeology, namely, the blind adherence by many to the belief that the construction of culture history based on ceramic typology is the ultimate goal for archaeological research.

By this time, Buyeo and Goguryeo states were gradually rising to the north and east of Gojoseon. Some three hundred years later, the Han empire of China destroyed Gojoseon, and its commandery Lelang had existed until around 300 CE as a somewhat independent political entity. It was absorbed by Goguryeo, one of the three main players of the Three Kingdoms Period in Korean history. Like the previous invasion by Yan, the Han invasion should have shocked the indigenous societies down south where many small polities had formed. In archaeology, the period between 100 BCE and 300 CE is named the Proto-Three Kingdoms Period in recognition of the burgeoning states of Baekje and Silla, the other two main players of the Three Kingdoms Period. As meaningful and detailed description of culture and society began to be made from this time, we may be allowed to say that the boundary between prehistory and history, although blurry, can be drawn at the beginning of the Proto-Three Kingdoms Period in the archaeological sequence. While the early state of Gojoseon was established before or during the first millennium BCE, there hardly exists any written account of its society and culture, which is also the case for Buyeo as well as Goguryeo in its early years. Archaeological evidence demonstrates marked inter-regional differences in the composition of material culture during the Proto-Three Kingdoms Period. Regional characteristics had become increasingly stronger in time, leaving diverse and interesting archaeological remains as briefly mentioned in Chapters 6 and 7. Research of the historical periods has overwhelmed prehistoric archaeology in South Korea simply because there are so many remains.

For the future of Koran archaeology, there is one critical factor which hinders its development, especially for prehistoric archaeology. It is the North Korea problem. We simply do not know what is there. This North Korea dilemma is a matter which cannot be resolved in the foreseeable future. In the meantime, there is a plenty of room for improvement for archaeological research in South Korea. More than anything else, what is urgent is upgrading the research methodology and incorporating new perspectives in interpreting the archaeological data. Adherence to culture history as the goal of archaeology is partially due to the historical background that archaeology had begun and grown with the excavation of the Three-Kingdoms Period burials. In doing so, archaeologists had focused upon establishing the age of the given burials by typological analysis of pottery and other artifacts in the fashion of an art historian trying to determine the age and the identity of the painter of a previously unknown drawing.

Many of the retired or retiring third generation archaeologists including myself had been taught to follow the lead and accept such a viewpoint. The number of its adherents has never decreased but rather increased alarmingly as huge demand for rescue excavation could have been met only by hastily awarding academic degrees. One of the results of mass production of poorly educated archaeologists is the repetition of old arguments. Thus, for example, there have been proposed so many meaningless pottery types and the excavation reports are filled with page after page of line drawings of artifacts in expectation of finding the 'best' typology for building the 'perfect' chronology. Unfortunately, many other important aspects are ignored so often in field research and in academic discussions, degrading archaeology to a stupefying and boring discipline. But, of course, one can be sure that the situation will improve. No doubt, we will have a much better understanding of the archaeological past of Korea. Starting from nothing, archaeologists in South Korea have achieved a lot, and there certainly is more to achieve. Let us wait and see what can be learned in the coming years.

SUGGESTED READINGS

For more information about the archaeological past of Korea, readers may refer to the writings listed below. The list is by no means meant to be comprehensive or exhaustive. Rather, it is a mere sample of recent publications which are relevant to the period dealt with in each chapter. They were chosen in consideration of their introductory nature and/or comprehensive treatment of the subject, thus, journal articles and short papers were included only when absolutely necessary. References listed in each publication may provide a guide for further inquiry into the subject.

For the Goryeo and the Joseon Period, because of the sheer amount of data and publications, readers are advised to refer to the website of <http://smgogo.sookmyung.ac.kr/view/main.asp> for information about new discoveries. Maintained by the Middle Age Archaeology Group of Sookmyung Women's University, it is an important source for archaeological data from around the 9th century on. Also, the homepage of the Society of Middle Age Archaeology in Korea provides information about academic activities and publications at <http://www.kmaas.or.kr>.

CHAPTER 1

Bartz, Patricia. 1972. *South Korea*. Clarendon Press, Oxford.

Han, Changgyun. 2020. *A Study of North Korean Archaeology*. Hyean, Seoul. [한창균. 2020. 북한 고고학 연구. 혜안. 서울]

Kim, Won-yong. 1986. *Introduction to Korean Archaeology (Third Edition)*. Iljisa, Seoul. [김원용. 1986. 한국고고학개설(제3판). 일지사. 서울]

The Korean Archaeological Society. 2010. *Lectures in Korean Archaeology (revised edition)*. Sahoe Pyeongron, Seoul. [한국고고학회. 2010. 한국고고학강의 (개정 신판). 사회평론. 서울]

Yi, Seonbok. 1991. A critical examination on the theory of population replacement between the Neolithic and the Bronze Age in Korea. In *Essays on the Ancient History of Korea*, vol. 1. Edited by the Hanguk Godaesahoe Yeonguso. pp.41-65. Garakguk Sajeok Gaebal Yeonguwon, Seoul. [이선복. 1991. 신석기-청동기시대 주민교체설에 대한 비판적 검토. 한국고대사론집 1. 한국고대사회연구소 편. pp.41-65. 가락국사적개발연구원. 서울]

_____. 2001. On the Thunder Axe. *Journal of The Korean Archaeological Society* 44:151-188. [2001. 뇌부고. 한국고고학보 44:151-188]

————. 2003. On the records of the Thunder Axe and King Sejong's 'gonorrhea'. *Journal of the Historical Society of Korea* 178:59-81 [2003a. 뇌부와 세종의 임질에 대하여. 역사학보 178:59-81]

————. 2003. *The Thunder Axe and the Stone Axe – A Study of the Traditional Perceptions about the Archaeological remains*. Seoul National University Press, Soeul. [2003. 벼락도끼와 돌도끼 - 고고자료에 대한 전통적 인식 연구. 서울대학교출판부. 서울].

————. 2017. Dangun's Tomb, Daedong-gang Civilization and Prehistory Archaeology in North Korea. In *Ancient History of Korea for Our Times, Vol. 1*. Edited by The Korean Society of Ancient History. pp. 150-164. Juryuseong, Seoul. [2017. 단군릉, 대동강문명론과 북한의 선사고고학. 우리 시대의 한국고대사 1. 한국고대사학회 편. pp.150-164. 주류성. 서울]

CHAPTER 2

Seong, Chuntaek. 2008. Tanged points and late Paleolithic hunting in Korea. *Antiquity* 82:871-883.

————. 2011. Evaluating radiocarbon dates and late Paleolithic chronology in Korea. *Arctic Anthropology* 8(1):56-67.

————. 2018. Ending of the Palaeolithic – A reconsideration of the "Light Brown Layer" in the uppermost part of the palaeolithic deposits. Proceedings of the Annual Conference of the Korean Palaeolithic Society, 2018. pp.47-64. [성춘택. 2018. 구석기시기대의 종말 - 구석기 퇴적층 최상부 "명갈색층" 재고. 2018년도 한국구석기학회 발표논문집. pp.47-64].

Yi, Gigil. 2018. *The Study of Palaeolithic Culture in Southwestern Korea*. Hyean. Seoul. [이기길. 2018. 호남 구석기문화의 탐구. 혜안. 서울]

Yi, Seonbok. 1989. *A Study of Northeast Asian Palaeolithic*. Seoul National University Press. Seoul. [이선복. 1989. 동북아시아 구석기 연구. 서울대학교출판부. 서울]

Yi, Seonbok (ed). 2011. *Handaxes in the Imjin Basin*. Seoul National University Press. Seoul.

Yi, Seonbok, and Jwa, Yongju. 2015. On the provenance of prehistoric obsidian artifacts in Korea. *Journal of the Korean Palaeolithic Society* 31:156-180. [이선복 · 좌용주. 2015. 흑요석 산지 추정 연구의 재검토. 한국구석기학보 31:156-180].

Yoo, Yongwook. 2019. Examination of the chrono-technological features of the handaxes from the Imjin-Hantan River Area in Korea. *Quaternary International* 503: 97-104.

CHAPTER 3

Ahn, Sungmo. 2016. *A Study of the Neolithic Period in Korea*. Seogyeongmunhwasa, Seoul. [안승모. 2016. 한국 신석기시대 연구. 서경문화사. 서울]

Central Institute of Cultural Heritage (ed.). 2011. *Introduction to the Neolithic Culture of Korea*. Seogyeongmunhwasa, Seoul. [중앙문화재연구원 (편). 2011. 한국 신석기문화 개론. 서경문화사. 서울]

————. 2012. *Aspects and course of the Neolithic Culture of Korea*. Seogyeongmunhwasa, Seoul. [중앙문화재연구원 (편). 2012. 한국신석기문화의 양상과 전개. 서경문화사. 서울]

————. 2017. *History of Neolithic Research in Korea*. Jininjin, Gwacheon. [중앙문화재연구원 (편). 2017. 한국 신석기시대 고고학사. 진인진. 과천]

Ha, Insu. 2017. *Neolithic Implements*. Jininjin, Gwacheon. [하인수. 2017. 신석기시대 도구론. 진인진. 과천]

Jeju Cultural Heritage Institute. 2014. *Gosan-ri Site, Jeju*. Jeju Cultural Heritage Institute, Jeju. [제주문화유산연구원. 2014. 제주 고산리유적. 제주문화유산연구원. 제주]

The National Museum of Korea. 2015. *Neolithic people: A New Life and A New Climate*. The National Museum of Korea, Seoul. [국립중앙박물관. 2015. 신석기인, 새로운 환경에 적응하다. 국립중앙박물관. 서울]

Ulsan Museum. 2019. *2019 Ulsan Museum Special Exhibiion - Sinamri, Take Stage in the Sea*. Ulsan Museum, Ulsan. [울산박물관. 2019. 2019년 울산박물관 특별기획전 - 신암리 바다를 무대로 삼다. 울산박물관. 울산]

CHAPTER 4

Bae, Jinseong. 2007. *Formation of the Plain Coarse Ware Culture and the Stratified Society*. Seogyeongmunhwasa, Seoul. [배진성. 2007. 무문토기문화의 성립과 계층사회. 서경문화사. 서울]

Central Institute of Cultural Heritage (ed.). 2011. *Introduction to the Bronze Age Culture of Korea*. Jininjin, Gwacheon. [중앙문화재연구원 (편). 2011. 한국 청동기문화 개론. 진인진. 과천]

Cheongju National Museum (ed.). 2020. *Re-encounter the Korean Bronze Culture in 2020*. Cheongju National Museum, Cheongju. [국립청주박물관 2020. 국립청주박물관 특별전 - 한국의 청동기문화. 국립청주박물관. 청주]

Gwangju National Museum. 2016. *Goindol - Dolmens in Korea*. Gwangju National Museum, Gwangju. [국립광주박물관. 2016. 세계유산 고인돌 – 큰 돌로 무덤을 만들다. 국립광주박물관, 광주]

Lee, Yeongmun. *A Study of the Korean Dolmen Society*. Hakyeonmunhwasa, Seoul. [이영문 2002. 한국 지석묘사회 연구. 학연문화사. 서울]

National Museum of Korea. 2010. *Agrarian Society and the Leader*. National Museum of Korea, Seoul. [국립중앙박물관 2010. 청동기시대 마을 풍경. 국립중앙박물관, 서울]

Oh, Gangwon. 2006. *The Bipa-shaped Bronze Dagger Culture and the Bronze Culture of Liaoning Region*. Cheonggye, Seongnam. [오강원. 2006. 비파형동검문화와 요령 지역의 청동기문화. 청계. 성남]

Son, Junho. 2006. *A Study of the Ground Stone Tools of the Bronze Age*. Seogyeongmunhwasa, Seoul. [손준호. 2006. 청동기시대 마제석기 연구. 서경문화사. 서울]

Yi, Hyeongwon. 2009. *Structure of the Bronze Age Settlements and Social Organization*. Seogyeongmunhwasa, Seoul. [이형원. 2009. 청동기시대 취락구조와 사회조직. 서경문화사. 서울]

CHAPTER 5

Jo, Jinseon. 2005. *A Study of the Sehyeong Donggeom Culture*. Hakyeonmunhwasa, Seoul. [조진선. 2005. 세형동검문화의 연구. 학연문화사. 서울]

Mun, Changro, *et al.* 2020. *Religious Beliefs and Rituals of Samhan*. Gimhae National Museum, Gimhae. [문창로 외. 2020. 삼한의 신앙과 의례. 국립김해박물관. 김해]

Oh, Gangwon, Yi, Seongju, Park, Jinil and Kim Ilgyu. 2019. *Potteries of the Iron Age and Their Change*. The Academy of Korean Studies Press, Seongnam. [오강원·이성주·박진일·김일규. 2019, 철기시대 토기와 토기문화의 변동. 한국학중앙연구원 출판부. 성남]

Oh, Gangwon, Kim, Ilgyu, Park, Jinil and Yi, Seongju. 2019. *Dispersal and Acceptance of the Pottery Manufacturing Technology during the Iron Age*. The Academy of Korean Studies Press, Seongnam. [오강원·김일규·박진일·이성주. 2019, 철기시대 토기 제작기술의 확산과 수용. 한국학중앙연구원 출판부. 성남]

Song, Giho. 2019. *History of Korean Ondol*. Seoul National University Press, Seoul. [송기호. 2019. 한국 온돌의 역사. 서울대학교출판문화원. 서울]

CHAPTER 6

Central Institute of Cultural Heritage (ed.). 2014. *Introduction to the Archaeology of Lelang*. Jininjin, Gwacheon. [중앙문화재연구원 (편). 2014. 낙랑고고학 개론. 진인진. 과천]

_____. 2018. *Introduction to the Archaeology of Mahan*. Jininjin, Gwacheon. [중앙문화재연구원 (편). 2018. 마한고고학 개론. 진인진. 과천]

Choe, Jonggyu. 1995. *Archaeology of Samhan*. Seokyeongmunhwasa, Seoul. [최종규. 1995. 삼한고고학연구. 서경문화사. 서울]

Kang, Inwook. 2020. *Okjeo and Eumnu*. Northeast Asian History Foundation, Seoul. [강인욱. 2020. 옥저와 읍루. 동북아역사재단. 서울]

Kang, Inwook, Kim, Jaeyun, Klyuev, N. A., Subotina, A. L. 2008. *New Perspectives on the Okcho (Wuju) People Based on Newly Found Archaeological Materials from Maritime Region of Russia and Neighboring Regions*. Northeast Asian History Foundation, Seoul. [강인욱·김재윤·N.A.클류에프·A.L.수보티나. 2008. 고고학으로 본 옥저문화. 동북아역사재단. 서울]

National Museum of Korea. 2008. *Special Exhibition of Daho-ri*. National Museum of Korea, Seoul [국립중앙박물관. 2008. 갈대밭 속의 나라, 다호리 – 그 발굴과 기록. 국립중앙박물관, 서울]

Oh, Yeongchan. 2006. *A Study of Lelang*. Sagyejeol, Seoul. [오영찬 2006. 낙랑군 연구. 사계절. 서울]

The Yeongnam Archaeological Society. 2015. *The Archaeology of Yeongnam Region*. Sahoepyeongron, Seoul.

[영남고고학회. 2015. 영남의 고고학. 사회평론. 서울]

Yi, Hyeonhye. 1998. *Production and Trade in Ancient Korea*. Iljogak, Seoul. [이현혜. 1998. 한국고대의 생산과 교역. 일조각. 서울]

CHAPTER 7

Central Institute of Cultural Heritage (ed.). 2013. *Data of the Middle Age Archaeology of Korea – from Unified Silla to Joseon Period*. Jininjin, Gwacheon. [중앙문화재연구원 (편). 2013. 한국 중세고고학 자료집성 – 통일신라시대~조선시대. 진인진. 과천]

————. 2016. *Introduction to the Archaeology of Gaya*. Jininjin, Gwacheon. [중앙문화재연구원 (편). 2016. 통일신라고고학 개론. 진인진. 과천]

————. 2017. *Burials of Goguryeo and Balhae*. Jininjin, Gwacheon. [중앙문화재연구원 (편). 2017. 고구려 발해의 고분 문화. 진인진. 과천]

————. 2017. *Introduction to the Archaeology of Silla (Vol. 1 and 2)*. Jininjin, Gwacheon. [중앙문화재연구원 (편). 2019. 신라고고학개론 (상, 하). 진인진. 과천]

————. 2019. *Introduction to the Archaeology of Unified Silla*. Jininjin, Gwacheon. [중앙문화재연구원 (편). 2019. 통일신라고고학 개론. 진인진. 과천]

————. 2020. *Archaeology of Goguryeo*. Jininjin, Gwacheon. [중앙문화재연구원 (편). 2020. 고구려고고학. 진인진. 과천]

Yeongnam Archaeological Society. 2015. *The Archaeology of Yeongnam Region*. Sahoepyeongron, Seoul. [영남고고학회. 2015. 영남의 고고학. 사회평론아카데미. 서울]

Kim, Ilgyu. 2015. *A Chronological Study of Baekje Archaeology*. Hakyeonmunhwasa, Seoul. [김일규. 2015. 백제고고학 편년 연구. 학연문화사. 서울]

Kim, Seogho, *et al*. 2020. *Horse Armors of the Ancient Korea*. Gimhae National Museum, Gimhae. [김성호 외. 2020. 한국 고대의 말갑옷. 국립김해박물관. 김해]

Korean Association for Ancient Studies. 2018. *Ancient History of Korea and Archaeology of Baekje*. Seogeong-munhwasa, Seoul. [한국고대학회 (편). 2018. 한국고대사와 백제고고학. 서경문화사. 서울]

Kwon, Ohyeong. 2005. *Muryeongwangneung – Splendor in the History of Cultural Exchange in the Ancient East Asia*. Dolbegae, Seoul. [권오영. 2005. 무령왕릉 – 고대 동아시아 문명 교류사의 빛. 돌베개. 서울]

Park, Cheonsu, *et al*. 2003. *Archaeological Sites and Artifacts of Gaya*. Hakyeonmunhwasa, Seoul. [박천수 외. 2003. 가야의 유적과 유물. 학연문화사. 서울]

Park, Sunbal. 2001. *Birth of the Hanseong Baekje*. Seogyeong, Seoul. [박순발. 2001. 한성백제의 탄생. 서경. 서울]

Song, Giho. 2020. *Research History of Balhae*. Seoul National University Press. [송기호. 2020. 발해 사학사 연구. 서울대학교출판부. 서울]

The Korean Archaeological Society (ed.) 2008. *Archaeology of State Formation*. Sahoepyeongron, Seoul. [한국고고학회 (편). 2008. 국가 형성의 고고학. 사회평론. 서울]

FIGURE SOURCES

It is the policy of the government of the Republic of Korea to provide the public free access to information about cultural heritage. Thus, the majority of the photographs used in the book can be obtained on the internet. As open sources, there are the National Museum of Korea (http://www.emuseum.go.kr/main), the Cultural Heritage Administration (http://www.cha.go.kr) and the National Research Institute of Cultural Heritage (https://www.nrich.go.kr). The e-museum website of the National Museum of Korea is an image bank of registered artifacts kept at major public and private museums across the country. One may obtain images by filling out the questionnaire provided. A lot more may be found at the websites of the other two institutions which maintain the National Cultural Heritage Portal and Cultural Heritage Research Information Portal. At these two excellent sources, readers can learn a lot of information about individual sites and discoveries and download photographs. In addition, the Cultural Heritage Administration provides up-to-date information about archaeological fieldwork and high quality pdf copies of excavation reports freely. As of April 2021, there are listed 4,914 items, which except five were all published since 2014. Each item may be of a single volume or dozens of volumes with thousands of pages. For reports published prior to 2014, most of them can be found at the website of the Korea History and Culture Research Database (http://www.excavation.co.kr). If necessary, readers may contact institutions responsible for the reports and request more data including visual images. In addition to the images obtained from these open sources, some figures in the text can be found in the publications listed below. Photos without copyright declaration are the author's own.

Bartz, Patricia. 1972. *South Korea*. Clarendon Press, Oxford.

Cheongju National Musuem (ed). 2020. *Re-encounter the Korean Bronze Culture in 2020*. Cheongju National Museum, Cheongju. [국립청주박물관 2020. 국립청주박물관 특별선 - 한국의 칭동기문회. 국립청주바물관. 청주]

Chuncheon National Museum. 2017. *Chuncheon National Museum – History and Culture of Gangwon*. Chuncheon National Museum, Chuncheon. [춘천박물관. 2017. 춘천박물관 – 강원의 역사와 문화. 춘천박물관,

춘천]

Gyeonggi Ceramic Museum. 2017. *The Excavation Report of Daeneung-ri Site in Paju, Gyeonggi-do*. Gwangju, Gyeonggi Ceramic Museum.[경기도자박물관. 2017. 파주 대능리 유적. 경기도자박물관, 광주]

Gyeonggi Cultural Foundation. 2009. *The Sin-gi Site, Manjeong-ri, Anseong – Excavation Report of the Anseong Gongdo Housing Development Area.* [경기문화재단 경기문화재연구원. 2009. 안성 만정리 신기유적 – 안성 공도 택지개발 사업지구 시발굴조사 보고서. 경기문화재단, 수원]

Gwangju National Museum. 2016. *Goindol - Dolmens in Korea*. Gwangju National Museum, Gwangju. [국립광주박물관. 2016. 세계유산 고인돌 – 큰 돌로 무덤을 만들다. 국립광주박물관, 광주]

Honam Cultural Propery Research Center. 2014. *Shinpung Site, Wanju. Vol. I.* Honam Cultural Property Research Center, Damyang. [호남문화재연구원. 2014. 완주 신풍유적 I. 호남문화재연구원, 담양]

Jeju National Museum. 2917. *Jeju National Musuem*. Jeju National Musuem, Jeju. [국립제주박물관. 2017. 국립제주박물관. 국립제주박물관, 제주]

Joint Excavation Research Team of Jungdo-dong Site, Chuncheon. 2020. *The Integrated Excavation Report of Jundo-dong Site, Chuncheon. Vol. 1-IV.* Joint Excavation Research Team of Jundo-dong Site, Chuncheon. [춘천 중도동유적 연합발굴조사단. 2020. 춘천 중도동유적 I-IV. 춘천 중도동유적 연합발굴조사단, 춘천]

Kim, Bum Cheol. 2005. Settlement pattern in the middle and lower Geum River basin during the Middle Bronze Age. *Journal of the Korean Archaeological Society* 57:99-124. [김범철. 2005. 금강 중하류역 청동기시대 중기 취락분포유형 연구. 한국고고학보 57:99-124]

Lee, Jungeun. 2010. Reduction strategies of handaxes from Imjin-Hantan river area. An Unpublished MA thesis. Department of Archaeology and Art History, Seoul National University. [이정은. 2010. 3차원 스캔을 이용한 주먹도끼 제작 패턴 연구. 서울대학교 고고미술사학과 석사학위 논문]

National Museum of Korea. 2010. *Agrarian Society and the Leader*. National Museum of Korea, Seoul. [국립중앙박물관. 2010. 청동기시대 마을 풍경. 국립중앙박물관, 서울]

_____. 2015. *Neolithic People: A New Life and A New Climate*. National Museum of Korea, Seoul. [국립중앙박물관. 2015. 신석기인, 새로운 환경에 적응하다. 국립중앙박물관. 서울]

Oh, Gangwon. 2020. The origin and the formation of the Korean-style Bronze Dagger Culture (the Attached-rim Pottery Culture). In *Re-encounter the Korean Bronze Culture in 2020*. Edited by the Cheongju National Musuem, pp.234-249. Cheongju National Museum, Cheongju. [오강원. 2020. 한국식동검문화(점토대토기문화)의 기원과 형성 과정. 국립청주박물관 특별전 - 한국의 청동기문화. pp.234-249. 국립청주박물관. 청주]

Park, Y., *et al.* 2006. *Quaternary Environment of Korea*. Seoul National University Press, Seoul. [박용안 외. 2006. 한국의 제4기 환경. 서울대학교출판부. 서울]

Seong, Chuntaek. 2018. Ending of the Palaeolithic – A reconsideration of the "Light Brown Layer" in the uppermost part of the palaeolithic deposits. *Proceedings of the Annual Conference of the Korean Palaeolithic Society,* 2018. pp.47-64. [성춘택. 2018. 구석기시기대의 종말 - 구석기 퇴적층 최상부 "명갈색층" 재고. 2018년도 한국구석기학회 발표논문집. pp.47-64].

The Korean Archaeological Society. 2010. *Lectures in Korean Archaeology (revised edition)*. Sahoe Pyeongron, Seoul. [한국고고학회. 2010. 한국고고학강의 (개정 신판). 사회평론. 서울]

Yi, Gigil. 2018. *The Study of Palaeolithic Culture in Southwestern Korea*. Hyean. Seoul. [이기길. 2018. 호남 구석기문화의 탐구. 혜안. 서울]

Yi, Sangheon. 2011. Holocene vegetation responses to East Asian Monsoonal changes in South Korea. In *Climate change - geophysical foundations and ecological effects*. Edited by J. Blanco and H. Kheradmand. DOI: 10.5772/23920. IntechOpen

Yi, Seonbok. 1989. *A Study of Northeast Asian Palaeolithic*. Seoul National University Press, Seoul. [이선복. 1989. 동북아시아 구석기 연구. 서울대학교출판부. 서울]

Yi, Seonbok, *et al.* 2004. *Jangsan-ri - A Lower Palaeolithic Site in Paju, Korea*. Seoul National University Museum. Seoul. [이선복 외. 2004. 파주 장산리 구석기유적 시굴조사 보고서. 서울대학교박물관. 서울]

_____. 2006. *Excavation report at Jeongok ACF site and its vicinity*. Seoul National University Museum, Seoul. [이선복 외. 2006. 연천 전곡 농협 신축부지 일대 발굴조사 보고서. 서울대학교박물관. 서울]